# The Employer's and Personnel Manager's Handbook of Draft Letters of Employment Law

including: Employment Protection, Appointment, Dismissal, Discrimination and Health and Safety at Work

EWAN MITCHELL

# The Employer's and Personnel Manager's Handbook of Draft Letters of Employment Law

including: Employment Protection, Appointment, Dismissal, Discrimination and Health and Safety at Work

*Illustrations by Tobi*

*First published 1977*
*Second impression 1977*

© GREVILLE JANNER, 1977

ISBN 0 220 66323 8

*This book has been set 10 and 11 on 12 point Press Roman.*
*Printed in Great Britain by*
*Thomson Litho Ltd., East Kilbride, Scotland.*
*for the publishers, Business Books Limited,*
*24 Highbury Crescent, London N5*

*For*
Mrs Pat Garner
*with my thanks for*
*all her help and kindness*

# OTHER BOOKS BY EWAN MITCHELL

The Employer's Guide to the Law on Employment Protection and Sex and Race Discrimination

The Employer's Guide to the Law on Health, Safety and Welfare at Work

The Director's and Company Secretary's Handbook of Draft Legal Letters

The Director's and Company Secretary's Handbook of Draft Contract Letters

The Business and Professional Man's Lawyer

The Caterer's Lawyer and Hotelier's and Restaurateur's Legal Guide

The Retailer's Lawyer

The Sales Executive's Lawyer and Businessman's Guide to the Laws of Buying and Selling

The Merchandiser's Lawyer

The Lawyer and His World

Farming and the Law

You and the Law

All You Need to Know About the Law

Your Property and the Law and Investor's Legal Guide

The Businessman's Guide to Speech-making and to the Laws and Conduct of Meetings

The Director's Lawyer and Company Secretary's Legal Guide

Coping with Crime—the businessman's guide to dealing with stealing, spying, fraud, false trade descriptions and other common commercial crimes

The Businessman's Guide to Letter-writing and to the Law on Letters

The Businessman's Legal Lexicon

The Business and Professional Man's Lawyer

The Employer's Lawyer

The Businessman's Guide to Travel

Businessman's Guide to Commercial Conduct and the Law

The Transport Manager's Lawyer and Transport Operator's Legal Guide

# Contents

**Part two   DISMISSAL**

**Part five   HEALTH AND SAFETY AT WORK**

# Introduction

Every modern employer and personnel manager must write letters. Thnaks to the Trade Union and Labour Relations Act, the Health and Safety at Work Act and the Employment Protection Act, these letters have become increasingly complicated. This book provides nearly five-hundred drafts of the sort of letter that must be written with care and precision, for the sake of the company or firm — and also for the satisfaction of the writer himself.

Take 'unfair dismissal'. Failure to follow the correct procedures and to put them into writing may now cost employers up to £11,760 for each mistake. The burden of proving that a dismissal is 'fair' rests on them. Conversely, the executive who is dismissed 'unfairly' may win a small and probably tax-free fortune from the law. The better his documentation, the greater his prospects of success before the Industrial Tribunal.

There are (literally) masses of letters of appointment and dismissal which the employer or personnel manager may have to write — many of which, in the past, were better left unwritten. Today, if you wish to protect the company's position or your own (as employer's representative or as employee) writing the correct letter at the right time may prove crucial. This book starts with a wide selection of the right letters.

Or consider the new rules introduced by the Employment Protection Act, providing for maternity rights and benefits, redundancy consultations and warnings, insolvency rights, guarantee payments, the disclosure of information to trade unions and written reasons for dismissal. The employer or personnel manager who can produce the correct letter will do justice to his company or firm — and to himself. But the executive who makes a mess of his documents will destroy his own case or that of the business, long before it gets to the court or tribunal.

Above all, letters of appointment and written particulars of contracts of employment must be accurate; must follow all the statutory rules; and must contain all necessary terms. Restraint clauses; search clauses; requirements that a mother states *in writing* any intention to return; the duty of employees to follow the health and safety rules, on pain of possible dismissal . . . . This book explains them all, and provides sample clauses.

Then there are collective bargains . . . closed shop agreements . . .

negotiations over disputes, actual or threatened . . . . You may, of course, concoct your own series of letters dealing with these and other employment problems. But precedents, carefully prepared and adapted to your own use, should provide you with an invaluable guide, saving you time and anxiety — and your company's money.

Still, just as no two employees — or legal cases, for that matter — are identical, so it is unlikely that you will be able to use a precedent letter without translating it to your needs. By all means help yourself to letters in this book and use them as standard documents. But mind how you adapt.

In order to explain the use of letters, you have to understand why they are drafted in the particular form used. So I have included explanatory notes with each part and chapter and with most individual letters. These of themselves amount to unique 'potted' versions of labour law and of the rules on dismissals, employee protection, and health, safety and welfare at work.

This book is entirely concerned with employment law. You will find more general letters in my companion volumes: legal letters in *The Director's and Company Secretary's Handbook of Draft Legal Letters,* and contract letters in *The Director's and Company Secretary's Handbook of Draft Contract Letters.* This new book replaces *Letters of Industrial Law: An Executive's Practical Guide to the Industrial Relations Act* which died, along with that unlamented legislation.

Finally, *The Health and Safety at Work etc. Act, 1974* — which is a permanent and very powerful addition to the statute book — has created new perils for employers and managers at every level. Any executive or manager who breaks the rules through his 'consent', 'connivance' or 'neglect' may (at worst) be sentenced to up to two years imprisonment and/or to an unlimited fine. In broad terms, the whole of the civil law on industrial safety has been codified and transferred to the realm of crime.

Once again, to keep out of trouble you need the right letters. These include not only letters to employees, inspectors, the Health and Safety Commission and Executive and to visitors or neighbours affected by your work. But they also involve letters to employees who do not make use of the safety procedures or protective clothing or guards which you provide for their safety. You must not only 'persuade' and 'propagandise' your workers to induce them to take care — you must also, if necessary, be able to prove that you did so. Under the 1974 Act, if you maintain that you took 'reasonably practicable' steps to comply with the rules, then the burden of proving that allegation rests on you.

The Part devoted to letters of health and safety should do as much to keep you out of the criminal courts as those dealing with unfair dismissal should ensure that you dismiss 'fairly' — and provably so. Equally, they should protect your own position as an employee — however mighty.

Finally, some notes on the use of this book. While every care has been taken in the preparation of these precedents and of the chapters and notes which accompany them, the author and publishers wish to emphasise the following:

1    The precedents are guides, to be used or adapted to suit particular circumstances; care must be taken by the writer in so doing.

2    The law (both as laid down by Parliament and as interpreted by the Courts) is subject to change — not least in the interpretation of words. It is confidently expected that judicious use of this book will save many unnecessary visits to lawyers — and, indeed, that the precedents may prove useful to solicitors themselves. But in the event of legal disputes arising or coming into prospect for the non-lawyer there is no substitute for the advice and assistance of an experienced solicitor, in possession of all the facts and knowing the new interpretations placed by courts on the statutes — and knowing also of any changes which may have been made by Parliament or the Courts in the rules themselves.

3    You may find that certain precedents in the book are of particular use and you wish to use or adapt them on a regular basis. In that case, it may be advisable to invite your solicitor to cast a careful eye over your revised draft.

4    Because of the foregoing — and as a further encouragement to care in the use of these drafts — it must be emphasised that **no legal responsibility can be accepted by the author or by the publishers in respect thereof, or arising in any way whatsoever from the use or adaptation thereof, in whole or in part, in any circumstances whatsoever.** (The above statement is known, in law, as a 'disclaimer' — and is a form of 'contracting out' — a subject fully dealt with in the book. The use of disclaimers is particularly important in connection with references — Chapter 17.)

5    In order that each chapter may be as comprehensive as possible, some repetition of the more important points and Sections of the Act is inevitable.

So here — fully annotated — are hundreds of precedents, which I hope will save you time, effort, worry and expense. With them, and with extracts from the relevant Acts of Parliament as Appendices, I wish you good luck!

\*      \*      \*

I am very grateful indeed to His Honour, Judge Brian Clapham, to Mr Desmond Sturman, to Mr Howard Gaventa and to my wife for their encouragement, help and guidance, and to Paul Tobias (Tobi) for his brilliant illustrations.

| | |
|---|---|
| *The Temple* | GREVILLE JANNER |
| *London EC4* | MA(Cantab), QC, MP, FIPM |
| *December 1976* | (Ewan Mitchell) |

# Note on topping and tailing

In previous, companion precedent volumes (*The Director's and Company Secretary's Handbook of Draft Legal Letters* and *The Director's and Company Secretary's Handbook of Draft Contract Letters*), each letter has started: 'Dear Mr Jones' (or as the case may be), and has ended 'Yours sincerely' or 'Yours faithfully'. To save space – and to avoid creating mythical Mr Jones's or Mrs Smiths' – the tops and the tails of letters in this volume have been omitted, with most of the 'with best wishes'.

'Topping' creates few difficulties. Sometimes there may be doubt as to whether to address the recipient by his Christian (or fore) name. Otherwise, you have the choice between 'Dear' and (for very good friends) 'My dear'. 'Dear Sir' or 'Sirs' are (of course) reserved for formalities or strangers.

The choice for 'tailing' lies between 'Yours sincerely' for people whom you know and (in general) like. Otherwise use 'Yours faithfully'.

# Scotland, Wales and Northern Ireland

All the employment law explained and illustrated in this book applies to England and to Wales; and all the relevant statutes (including the Trade Union and Labour Relations Act, the Employment Protection Act, the Health and Safety at Work Act, the Equal Pay Act, the Sex Discrimination Act and the Race Relations Act) also apply to Scotland. Scottish readers should check terminology and contents of precedents with local lawyers, if in doubt.

In the main, Northern Ireland employment laws are the same as those applied in the rest of the United Kingdom — supplemented by *The Fair Employment (Northern Ireland) Act, 1976* (which covers religious discrimination). The Labour Relations Agency has similar functions to ACAS. The unfair dismissal rules are the same although protection for more part-timers (16 hours normal working or 8 hours after 5 years' continuous service) is not — as we go to press — announced.

The rules of redundancy consultation are the same. Additional claims from the Redundancy Fund on insolvency apply, e.g. wages and holiday pay, but not the new priority rules. Equal pay and sex discrimination provisions are the same. It is unlawful to discriminate in employment on grounds of religion and the Fair Employment Agency enforces the rules. Details (once again) from local lawyers.

Like the laws themselves, the precedents in this book will serve employers and their representatives throughout the United Kingdom — with rare and usually minor exceptions which can easily be checked and adapted with the help of Scots or Northern Ireland lawyers (as the case may be).

*Part One*

# APPOINTMENT
# AND HIRING

# Chapter 1

# Contracts of Employment — written particulars

A contract of employment is merely an agreement between employer and employee under which the employee agrees to give service to the employer and the employer to engage the employee. Like most contracts (with the exception of hire purchase, insurance, share transfer, transfer of interests in land and contracts of guarantee), contracts of employment are just as binding if made orally as if every term is set out in writing. I repeat: There is no law which requires a contract of employment to be in writing in order to have binding legal effect.

However, *The Contracts of Employment Act, 1972*, as amended by *The Employment Protection Act, 1975*, requires the main terms of a contract of employment to be put into writing. The employee is entitled to receive his written particulars within 13 weeks of the start of the employment — and if there is any variation in the terms, then the employer must put these into writing and deliver them to the employee within 4 weeks.

Failure to provide written particulars will not lead to a prosecution or to a civil action. Theoretically, the employee who has not received his particulars may bring a complaint before an Industrial Tribunal. In practice, when a case involving the employee reaches the tribunal the particulars are asked for and if they are not available the employer starts off on the wrong legal foot.

Anyway, particulars should be provided. Like all useful documentation, they avoid disputes. They enable the employee to know his rights and to prove them. Also, the employer is less likely to act in breach of the employee's rights if they are set out on paper.

At best, written particulars are supplied at the start of the employment — often, in the case of managers or executives, in letters of appointment. Particulars supplied later are not to be used as an excuse for introducing terms which were never agreed. They are intended to confirm and to provide a written record of an agreement.

By all means say to an employee who is not to get his written particulars for a few weeks: 'You will be subject to our works' rules and to our normal terms of service'. Why not let the prospective employee read a copy of your standard terms and works' rules, at the time when you are taking him on?

Parliament has regulated by Statute the *minimum* information to be set out for the employee in writing. There are many other vital terms which *should* be included – ranging, in appropriate cases, from the requirement that a woman who intends to return to work after child-birth should say so in writing to a restraint clause or one entitling the employer to search employees for stolen goods.

The three new terms required by the Employment Protection Act and introduced into the contract of employment, as from 1 June 1976 are: job title; whether the current employment is or is not continuous with any previous employment and, if so, when the previous employment began; and the employer's disciplinary rules or where to find them.

Employees who normally work 16 hours or more a week (or 8 hours after 5 years' continuous service) are entitled to written particulars – although you should certainly consider providing written particulars to all employees, however part-time. The threshold for part-timers' rights for this purpose as well as for redundancy payments and unfair dismissal protection is reduced from 21 hours normal weekly working, as from 1 February 1977.

**Details for inclusion in written particulars of contracts of employment or in letters of appointment**

*Part 1 – Requirements of law*

1    Name of employer. In the case of associated companies, be careful to insert correct employing company.
2    Employee's job title – his function or position. (Employment Protection Act. You are only bound to set out the name of the job so that the employee may know what job he is employed to do. It is often better to be more detailed – although allowing leeway. Thus: 'You will be employed as a driver and to do all other work normally incidental thereto'.
3    Date of start of employment. (Vital for assessing periods of continuous employment e.g. for purposes of assessment of period of notice; of continuous employment for unfair dismissal protection; and for redundancy claims – also potentially for pension rights and sick pay.)
4    Whether or not current employment is continuous with any (and if so what) previous employment, and if so, when it began.
5    Remuneration. (Salary or wage, commission or bonus.)
6    Fringe benefits. (For example, use of company car; share options; subsidised canteen facilities; protective or other clothing allowance.)

7    Hours of work. (If you may wish to change the employee's shift, then obtain his agreement at the start of his employment. If you wish hours to be flexible, say so. Also, state whether overtime is guaranteed or compulsory and on what terms.)

8    Holidays and holiday pay. (Remember to include the manner in which holiday entitlement is calculated — especially when employment comes to an end. Is employee entitled, for instance, to a pro rata payment if he leaves during the middle of a year? Will he lose his holiday entitlement if he does not give his agreed notice?)

9    Place of work. (If you may need to shift employee from place to place, so provide. Otherwise, a shift may amount to a dismissal.)

10   Sick pay. (If any. Also, if private health insurance provided, say so.)

11   Pension rights. (If any.)

12   Grievance procedure. (To whom should the employee go if he considers himself unfairly treated?)

13   Disciplinary rules. (Reference may be made to an 'easily accessible' document containing the rules not only in respect of grievance procedures — see above — but the particulars themselves must state to whom the employee can apply 'if he is disatissfied with any disciplinary decision relating to him' — and how the application must be made.)

14   Notice. (How much is the employee entitled to receive — and how much must he give?)

*Part 2 — Suggested additional items*

15   In the case of all women of childbearing age; request that any intention to return after leaving on ground of pregnancy or confinement be stated to personnel manager (or other named person) in writing.

16   Restraint clause (restriction on employee's right to compete after leaving employer's service — lawyers' help needed in drafting because only if clause is 'reasonable' will it be enforceable).

17   Employee to devote full time to employer's business and/or not to engage in other paid employment without employer's consent. (Is 'moonlighting' a problem in your business? How do part-timers cope?)

18   Employee's inventions to be property of employer. (This is automatically implied by law — but positive statement avoids potential misunderstandings. Of course, alternative variation must also be stated.)

19    Accommodation provided (if any). (Take care: If employee is not to become a 'tenant', and hence protected by the Rent Acts, he must be 'required' to occupy the premises 'for the better performance of his duties'. Again: Professional drafting vital.)

20    Right to search. (The employee agrees to the searching of his personal property at the request of the management. Consent at the time of the search is necessary, even if this clause is inserted — but in those businesses where the inspection of employee's person or property is normal and necessary often includes search clause.)

21    Employer's secrets. (Do you need a special clause regarding confidential or secret information or documents? Should specific items or processes be referred to? Once again, this is to make implicit what is otherwise only implied into the contract.)

22    Accounts. (Is the employee to keep or render special accounts — perhaps for expenses claims?)

23    Employee to disclose other business interests.

24    Health and safety at work — employee should agree to follow safety procedures. (Implied term made explicit — perhaps with warning that failure to comply may — or, in the case of a specially dangerous process, system or operation referred to, 'will' lead to dismissal.)

25    Requirement that employee submit to medical examination at employer's request.

26    Any special terms applicable to the particular employee or employment.

*    *    *

## 1   Written particulars

I am happy to confirm your appointment, upon the following terms:

(a)   Employment by: The . . . Company Limited.

(b)   Employment to begin on the . . . , 19. . . . This employment is continuous with your previous employment by . . . which commenced on . . ./This employment is not continuous with any previous employment.

(c)   Your job title to be . . . .

(d)   Your scale or rate of remuneration and the method of calculating remuneration (including bonus and/or commission — if appropriate), to be. . . .

(e)   Payment to be made every . . . , i.e. weekly/monthly on the. . . .

(f)  Your normal working hours to be as follows. . . .
(g)  Overtime. . . .
(h)  You will be entitled to usual public holidays. Your holidays and holiday pay to be calculated as follows:. . . . Your entitlement to accrued holiday pay on the termination of your employment will be . . . .
(i)  In the event of your being absent from work due to sickness or injury, you will receive sick pay as follows . . . .
(j)  We operate the following pension scheme arrangements/ there will be no pension arrangements made by the company and applicable to you . . . .
(k)  You will be entitled to receive the following periods of notice . . . .
(l)  You will be obliged to give the following notice if you wish to leave the company's employment . . . .
(m)  In the event of your having any grievance relating to your employment, kindly see your supervisor/foreman/ personnel manager/shop steward. Details of grievance procedures are available, if required, from . . ./are in the collective agreement which applies to you and which is available from . . . .
(n)  Disciplinary procedures are as follows . . . . If you are dissatisfied with a disciplinary decision, you should inform Mr/Mrs/Miss/. . ./me.

If you have any questions concerning the above, please do not hesitate to contact me – or Mr . . . , your . . . , who will normally be found in . . . , from . . . a.m. to . . . p.m.

Please sign and return the enclosed copy of this letter to show your agreement to the above terms.

Hoping that this will be the start of a long and happy association between the company and yourself and with my best wishes.

## 2  Draft contract (alternative)

I confirm that your terms of service are as follows:

1  *Date of employment*  Your employment commenced on . . . , 19 . . and is/is not continuous with other employment by . . . which commenced on . . . , 19 . .
2  *Job title*  You are employed as a . . . .
3  *Place of work*  You will work at . . . and/or at such other of the company's places of business as the manage-

ment may from time to time require. (In the event of your being required to move, your reasonable removal and/or relocation costs will be paid by the company.)

4   *Remuneration*   Your remuneration will be calculated as follows:

(a)  . . .

(b)  . . .

(c)  . . .

The company pays the net salary of all monthly paid employees directly into their bank account, one month in arrear, at the end of each month. Weekly and hourly paid employees are paid one week in arrear on the . . . of each week.

5   *Hours of work*   Your normal hours of work will be:

(a)  . . .

(b)  . . .

(c)  . . .

6   *Shift working*   The company does not implement shift working, but if it becomes necessary to do so in the future, it reserves the right to require you to work shifts.

7   *Overtime*   Overtime is not guaranteed. Employees above the level of supervisor or equivalent are not paid for overtime. In other cases, overtime is paid at the following rates:

(a)  . . .

(b)  . . .

(c)  . . .

8   *Holidays*   You will be entitled to the following periods of holidays:

(a)   All public holidays;

(b)   . . . days/weeks per year after . . . service;

(c)   . . .

(d)   . . .

The holiday year is from . . . to . . . and no payment will be made (except on termination of employment) for days no taken. Holiday entitlement may not be carried forward from one year to another. Any five consecutive working days constitute one holiday week.

Your entitlement up to the end of the current holiday year will be . . . days.

Holiday pay is calculated at your basic hourly/weekly/ monthly rate on a pro rata basis.

9   *Holiday entitlement on leaving*   If the company termin-

ates your employment due to misconduct, holiday pay may be forfeited at the management's discretion. In all other cases, payment will be made for all holiday entitlement accrued in the current holiday year but not taken at the time of the termination of the employment. In the event of holidays being taken but not earned, appropriate holiday payment will be deducted by the company from money owed on termination.

10  *Retirement*   The company's normal retirement age is 65 for men, 60 for women.

11  *Pension rights*   All eligible employees will be invited to join the company's contributory pension scheme which operates for full time, permanent employees, subject to the eligibility rules of that scheme and to the discretion of the trustees.

12  *Absence from work*   If you are absent from work for any reason, you must inform your departmental manager whenever reasonably practicable by . . . a.m. on the first day of absence. Where possible, you should obtain permission for absence from your departmental supervisor or manager; such permission is in any event required in respect of absence for any reason other than sickness or accident. If the period of absence exceeds two days, then you must forward a medical certificate without delay to your departmental manager; further certificates must be forwarded when previous certificates expire; and a final certificate must be produced before commencing work. If you are admitted to hospital, then you must submit a medical certificate of both entry and discharge.

   If you are entitled to claim sickness benefit otherwise than from the company you must do so and the amount equal to the basic sickness benefit will be deducted from sums payable by the company. No deductions will be made while half salary is being paid. The company will pay sick pay on the following scale, according to length of service:

(a)   Up to four weeks' service – nil;
(b)   Four weeks to three months – two weeks' full pay;
(c)   One to two years – three weeks' full pay;
(d)   Three to four years – four weeks' full pay;
(e)   Five to six years – eight weeks' full pay;
(f)   Seven to ten years – twelve weeks' full pay;

(g)   Eleven to fifteen years — eighteen weeks' full pay;

(h)   Over fifteen years — twenty-six weeks' full pay.

In each case, these periods will be followed by similar periods of half pay. (Any day from Monday to Friday counts as one day and one week equals five working days).

The above allowances will apply to each tax year April through March but unused allowances may not be transferred from one year to the next.

13   *Medical examinations*   The company reserves the right to require employees to submit to medical examination by the company doctor or by an independent medical advisor. If you are medically examined and wish a copy of the report to be sent to your own doctor, in addition to being supplied to the management, then the company agrees so to do.

14   *Notice*   Your employment will be subject to the statutory minimum periods of notice or to such additional periods as may be given by the management at its discretion. You will be required to give like periods of notice to the company if you wish to terminate your employment. Notice should be given in writing to the departmental manager.

15   *Confidential information*   You will not divulge to any individual, firm or company, any confidential information acquired by you in the course of or for the purposes of your employment. Breach of this duty will normally lead to instant dismissal.

16   *Other work*   You will not engage in any other form of paid activity, whether during or outside working hours, without having obtained the prior written consent of the company.

17   *Restraint*   You will not engage in any branch of the . . . trade/industry within a radius of . . . miles/within the area within which you have been working for a period of . . . months/years after leaving the company's service, without having obtained the prior written consent of the company.

18   *Search*   The company reserves the right to search employees or their property while they are at work for the company.

19   *Disciplinary procedures*   In the event of disciplinary action being necessary, the normal disciplinary procedure

is as follows:
(a)  Verbal warning;
(b)  Verbal warning, in presence of employee's represen-
     tative or shop steward;
(c)  Written warning;
(d)  Final written warning;
(e)  Suspension or dismissal.
In the case of serious misconduct, it may not be possible
to follow this procedure and the company reserves the
right to suspend on full pay at any time for the purpose
of carrying out investigations.

   If you are dissatisfied with a disciplinary decision, you
should appeal in the first place to the supervisor at the
level above the person who took the disciplinary action.
Alternatively, you may appeal to the personnel manager.

20   *Grievances*   Any grievance relating to your employment should be discussed with your immediate superior.
If you are not satisfied with the result of such discussion,
then you may appeal to your departmental manager or,
in the event of still further dissatisfaction, to the personnel manager or to your director. The person appealed
to will give careful consideration to the grievance and
notify you of his decision.

21   *Inventions and suggestions*   Any inventions made by
you in the course of your employment will belong to
the company. However, the company normally makes
substantial *ex gratia* payments to employees who produce inventions or suggestions which contribute to the
company's productivity or which lower costs of production.

22   *Health and safety at work*   You are required to comply
with the company's health and safety rules, and with all
rules laid down by the Health and Safety at Work Act,
The Factories Act, the Offices, Shops and Railways
Premises Act and all regulations made under them or
under any other industrial safety statute. Failure to
comply with such rules may lead to dismissal.

   The company places paramount importance on the
health, safety and welfare of employees at work and a
copy of the company's written statement of its health
and safety policy, organisation and arrangements is
supplied herewith.

   Every employee is further required to take such steps

as are reasonably practicable to ensure the health and safety of himself and of others affected by his work; he must make use of all protective clothing and equipment; and he must co-operate with the management in all respects for the full implementation of the health and safety policy.

23   *Fire alarm*   If the fire alarm bell sounds, all employees must walk to the nearest fire exit door and assemble at their allocated area. You must familiarise yourself with your fire drill.

24   *Accidents*   If you are in any way involved in any accident, however minor, you must report this to your departmental manager as soon as possible thereafter. You should also report to your supervisor any accident involving any other employee.

25   *Company property including purchases by staff*   Employees may purchase company products from the company's shop, which is normally open on working days from . . . to . . . . The receipt for payment must be retained by the employee and shown at the gate when the products are taken from the company's premises. All such purchases must be taken off the company's premises within 24 hours.

I have read and understood the above terms of service and I accept them.

Signed . . . . . . . . . . . . . . .
Date . . . . . . . . . . . . . . . .

## 3   Staff appointment

I am happy to confirm your terms of appointment as follows:

1   This offer is made subject to the obtaining of satisfactory references. Where an employee commences work before references have been obtained and approved, the management reserves the right to terminate the employment by the giving of minimum statutory notice or equivalent pay in lieu, notwithstanding periods of notice which would otherwise apply.

2   Staff are appointed on an initial trial period of sixteen

weeks. On satisfactory completion of that period, an employee will (if eligible) be offered the opportunity of inclusion in the staff pension scheme, subject to proof of age, medical examination and such other documents as may be required by the rules of the pension scheme. Particulars of the scheme are available on request.

3  Medical examination. Medical examination will be required for all those eligible employees who wish to join the pension scheme. Other employees may be required to undergo medical examination by the company doctor at any time.

4  You will be employed by . . . Ltd and will normally work at its premises at . . . . The company reserves the right to require members of staff to move to branches within the UK. The company will meet all reasonable removal expenses; the company's decision on what expense is reasonable in the particular circumstances shall be final.

5  Your employment will begin on the . . . , 19. . This employment is not continuous with any previous employment/ is continuous with your employment by . . . , which commenced on the . . . .

6  Your normal working hours will be from 9 a.m. to 5.30 p.m., Mondays to Fridays inclusive, but you may be required to work overtime if the exigencies of the business render this necessary. You will then be paid time and a half during the week or double time at weekends.

7  You will be entitled to . . . weeks holiday per annum. The company's holiday year is from the 1st April until the following 31 March and completed years of service are counted at the 31 March preceding the holiday year concerned. In the event of your leaving the company's service, you will be entitled to pro rata holiday pay, unless you are dismissed for misconduct in which case any accumulated holiday pay will be forfeited.

8  You will be employed as a . . . . , and do all work reasonably incidental thereto.

9  Your rate of pay will be as follows . . . .

10   In addition, you will be entitled to the following benefits:

(i)   Christmas bonus of . . . per cent up to a maximum of £ . . . . This bonus qualifies for pension payments and is also subject to tax. It will be paid pro rata to staff joining in the current year but for those joining after 30 September, it will be added to the bonus for the following year. Staff who leave for whatever reason before payment or who are at that time under notice, given or received, are not entitled to this bonus.

(ii)   Free canteen lunches provided at headquarters/canteen lunches are subsidised.

11   Any employee who is absent through illness is required to notify (or to ensure the notification of) his immediate supervisor by telephone before noon on the first day of such absence. The management reserves the right not to pay sick pay in respect of any period during which notification of absence has not been given.

12   If an employee is absent due to illness for more than three days, then he must obtain a certificate of absence for this period and for any subsequent week of absence. Subject to the foregoing, you will be entitled to sick pay on the following basis . . . .

13   Unless the company is entitled to dismiss summarily, notice will be given upon the following basis:
After one week's service, 7 days;
After six months service, four weeks;
After five years service, five weeks;
Thereafter, an additional week's notice for each year of service up to twelve years.

14   Any employee who wishes to seek redress of any grievance relating to his employment should discuss the matter with his immediate superior; if the matter is not satisfactorily resolved, then he should explain the grievance in writing and both the employee and the supervisor concerned must together and as soon as possible submit the grievance for a ruling at an interview with their departmental or branch manager. The manager concerned may refer the matter further in writing to the general manager and will supply both

employee and supervisor with copies of his report within two working days of the interview.

15   If the cause for the complaint is not resolved satisfactorily, the employee may appeal to the chief general manager.

16   Details of the company's disciplinary procedures are contained in the head office rules, a copy of which is supplied herewith. Note: An employee may at any time be suspended on full pay during investigation of any alleged breach of the disciplinary rules. The employee will always have a right of appeal against a disciplinary decision to his department or branch manager and in the event of a dismissal to the chief general manager.

## 4   Representative, traveller or agent

We are pleased to confirm your appointment as (sole) representative for the above Company within the area of . . . , with effect from . . . . This employment is not continuous with any previous employment.

It is agreed that you will be paid a salary of £ . . . per annum. You will be provided with a car, to the extent that it is used for the purpose of the Company's business. The running and maintenance expenses will be paid by the company. All expenses claimed must be supported by receipts and dockets. (Alternatively: The company will pay £ . . . per week towards your car expenses.)

In addition, you are to be paid a commission of . . . per cent on the value of goods delivered and invoiced in your area, such value to be calculated after deduction of the average cash discount of . . . per cent. Payment of such commission will be made to you during the month following delivery of such orders as are accepted by the Company.

Please note that any business connected with . . . will be excluded from your area and no commission will be paid in respect of orders taken therefrom.

After one calendar year's employment, you will be entitled to (. . . week's) holiday with pay. After two years' service your entitlement will rise to (. . . weeks). After three years, you will get (. . . weeks') paid holiday. This will be the maximum. In the event of your employment being terminated for whatever reason during the course of a calendar year, holiday pay will be reckoned pro rata.

While in the employment of the Company, it is specifically agreed that you shall not represent any other company, in respect of any goods or services whatsoever. You will devote yourself full time to the Company's affairs. In the event of this agreement being terminated by either party, you will not deal in any products in which the Company trades during your period of employment, within the area in respect of which this agency is given, for a period of twelve calendar months.

This agreement may be terminated by . . . weeks notice, in writing, on either side to be increased to . . . weeks after . . . years service. This may be given to you by the Company at your last known address or by you to the Company at its registered office or main place of business. After the termination of your employment, you will be entitled to commission in respect of orders introduced by you which are received and accepted (and delivered) by the Company during the period of your employment, but not thereafter.

In the event of any grievance or dissatisfaction with a disciplinary decision arising, please consult with me personally/with Mr . . . . Details of the Company's disciplinary procedures are attached.

Kindly sign the carbon copy sent with this letter and initial the first page thereof, to indicate that the above terms correctly represent the agreement come to between us, and that you are prepared to serve the Company upon that basis.

We hope that this will be the start of a long and happy association between the Company and yourself and wish you every success in your efforts.

NOTE:
*The above draft is for employed (and* not *self-employed) representatives etc.*


## 5  Appointing scientist, researcher or technician

I am pleased to inform you that you have been selected from many applicants, for the post of (research . . .). Full particulars of your terms of service are enclosed herewith. If any queries arise thereon, kindly inform me at once.

I confirm that you informed me that you have for some time been working on developments in . . . . We agreed that if this work produced results which would be of use to the Company, you would licence the Company to use the same, during your period of service or for fifteen years from the date when application is made for the appropriate patent, whichever is the longer. Save as above, the terms of the licence shall be as agreed or failing agreement, as settled by an arbitrator to be appointed by . . . .

No other licenses shall be issued by you to anyone else during this period, without the Company's prior written consent. It is further confirmed that the Company will not object to the patent being issued in your name.

Hoping that you will have a long and happy period of service with the Company, and looking forward to meeting you again.

NOTE:

*In the absence of some agreement to the contrary, employers own all inventions produced by employees, during the course of their employment or within its scope. It follows that the employee has no right to patent his invention – and his employers may demand that a patent be taken out in their name. Inventions outside the scope of the employment – in fields other than that for which the man was employed – do not come within this rule. The term may be varied by consent – as above and as in next letter.*

## 6 Employee retains rights

I confirm that if you are prepared to accept the appointment offered to you, the Company will not object to your retaining or obtaining *(as the case may be)* all patent rights in respect of your inventions, whenever and however made.

## 7 Employee writes

Thank you for your letter concerning my proposed appointment. Perhaps you would arrange for your solicitor to draw up the appropriate agreement as discussed, concerning rights to inventions – it would be as well, I think, to have the entire matter clarified before I finally agree to take up an appointment with the Company.

## 8   Reference to other document

I am delighted to confirm your appointment as . . . of the above Company. Full particulars of your terms of service are contained in the Company's standard contract of service, which is enclosed herewith, including our agreed arrangement as to your probationary period. This has, of course, been completed and amended so as to comply with the arrangement reached between us, when we discussed the matter yesterday morning. Kindly detach and sign the portion at the foot of the contract, to confirm that the same correctly sets out your terms of service.

On behalf of our board, I am delighted to welcome you into the Company's service, and look forward to a long and happy collaboration with you.

NOTES:
*1   Every large or medium sized employer should have standard contracts of service, prepared by solicitors. But you can prepare the sort of terms which you would like to include by using or adapting or consolidating precedents in this chapter. Equally, standard letters of appointment may be prepared for more senior employees, setting out main terms.*

*2   When checking your own terms of employment (actual or prospective), if you run swiftly through the notes of the letters which follow you will find pointers to the main traps to avoid.*

*In any event, do not regard a standard letter as immutable. Negotiating alterations (for yourself or for others) is an important art.*

*3   There is no legal necessity for the employee to confirm his agreement with the terms set out in the employer's letter – but once he has done so, he will have little joy if he later maintains that the terms of service are not set out correctly. Confirmation is particularly advisable where there is a restraint clause or some other term which may prove disadvantageous to the employee. And silence from the employee after receipt of the written particulars may be taken to imply consent.*

## 9 Company Secretary

I am pleased to confirm your appointment as Company Secretary of the above company, commencing on the first of next month. Your employment is not continuous with any previous employment. Your salary will be . . . payable on the . . . of each month by Banker's Order. Your office will be at the Company Head Office at the above address and you have agreed to devote yourself full-time to the business and not to engage in any other form of remunerative work, either on your own behalf or otherwise, without the company's prior consent.

You will be entitled to four weeks paid leave per annum, such entitlement to accrue at the completion of a year's service and thereafter in the event of your employment being terminated for any reason, you will be entitled to holiday remuneration pro rata.

Your employment will be terminable by three month's notice, on either side. Such notice must be in writing. Details of the Pension Scheme will be sent to you under separate cover. Senior staff such as yourself will be enrolled into the BUPA Scheme, at the company's expense.

In the event of illness, you will be entitled to your full remuneration, less National Insurance or other benefits to which you would be entitled on the basis that you have paid full contribution and subject to provision of a Medical Certificate.

You will be responsible directly to the Managing Director, to whom any grievance should be directed and who will take any necessary disciplinary action. Full details of our grievance and disciplinary procedure are available from our personnel manager.

If you have any queries regarding the foregoing, please inform me at your earliest convenience.

NOTE:
*If you wish to insert a restraint clause, see Chapter 2.*


## 10 Holidays and holiday pay — as amended

To avoid misunderstanding, I am happy to confirm that employees such as yourself who have been with us for over

. . . years are entitled to . . . weeks holiday in each calendar year – in addition, of course, to the usual public holidays. If your employment is terminated during the course of a year, then you will be entitled to accrued holiday pay on a pro rata basis – that is, the appropriate proportion having regard to the part of the year which you have actually been with us since the date of your last holiday.

## 11   No holidays until full year served

As appears from the written particulars of your contract of employment which we supplied to you in accordance with *The Contracts of Employment Act, 1972* (as amended) you are only entitled to a holiday or to the equivalent accrued holiday pay, after the completion of a full year's service with the company. Equally, on the termination of your employment, there is no pro rata entitlement – only those who leave at the end of a full year's service are entitled to their holiday money.

NOTE:
*The absence of a pro rata payment is lawful but undesirable*

## 12   Mobility clause

I have discussed your place of employment with the Board. They are agreeable to your being stationed at . . . for a minimum period of . . .years. But bearing in mind the nature of the company's business, it must be understood that you will if necessary accept transfer to any of our factories/shops/branches/offices in the . . . area, if given . . . weeks/months notice of such transfer. The company will pay all reasonable moving expenses.

I hope that the above suggestion will be acceptable to you. Please inform me at your earliest convenience.

## 13   Right to search

Please note that, as I explained to you when we met, all employees are required to agree to submit to their person or property being searched, while on the company's premises, at any time at the request of . . . . This is, of course, essential having regard to the nature of the company's business.

NOTE:

*To search an employee's person without his permission is an assault. To search his property without consent is a trespass. Permission may be obtained in advance – but should be confirmed at the time of the search. If you are satisfied that a theft has occurred and a suspect refuses to be searched, then the police should be called.*

## 14   Promotional prospect

Thank you for your letter, applying for the post of. . . . Those who serve the company in senior positions on a permanent basis work their way up through the ranks. We are, however, an expanding organisation and if you are prepared to start as . . . we hope that you would soon be promoted to . . . .

If you are interested in joining our company on the above conditions, we would be pleased to see you, and we could then go into the matter more fully. Would you please let us have two or three alternative dates and times when you could call here, and we would then make arrangements accordingly.

## 15   Food – requirement to inform of illness

As your job involves the handling of food, the company requires that immediately you (to your knowledge) contract any contagious or infectious disease, you will at once inform your immediate supervisor. You are also required to attend at our sick room if you have any cut or other accident to your hands, arms, neck or face, however minor. As hygiene is vital in your work, failure to comply with these rules may lead to instant dismissal.

## 16   Disagreement over written particulars

Thank you for your letter of today's date, enclosing purported written particulars of my terms of service, under *The*

*Contracts of Employment Act, 1972,* (as amended).

I regret that I cannot agree that the form of particulars sent to me correctly sets out the terms of my appointment. In particular, I have at no time even discussed with you or anyone else on the company's behalf the question of a restraint clause. I reread our detailed correspondence, prior to my taking up my appointment with the company and this confirms my recollection that there was no such clause to be included in my contract.

Apart from the foregoing, I agree that the written particulars are correct. Would you like me to strike out the clause in question, sign the slip and return the document? Or would you prefer to send me different particulars?

Incidentally, I would like to point out that I sincerely hope in any event that the question I raise will remain purely theoretical — you were good enough to indicate that the Board are satisfied with my services, and I am very happy in my position and look forward to a long period of service with the company.

NOTE:
*The contents of this letter may be put into an inter-office memorandum — and if you wish to make it appear informal, by all means write the letter by hand — but nevertheless, be careful to retain a copy.*


## 17   Approval of variation

Thank you for your letter, confirming that my salary is to be increased. I am much obliged — and in the circumstances I agree to my terms of service being varied by the inclusion of the proposed restraint clause.

NOTE:
*Employers who wish to insert restraint clauses or other new terms which will react to the employee's detriment should choose their time — the best being, of course, when the terms of service are being improved in other respects. The employee who is getting a rise should be in a very amenable frame of mind. But he should ensure that his employer does not attempt to insert new terms under the guise of giving written particulars — or of confirming terms previously agreed. Trade unions, professional associations and even individual employees are generally on to that one. See Chapter 5 for rules on varying contracts of service.*

## 18    Acceptance of agreed terms

Thank you for your letter. I confirm that it correctly sets out the terms upon which I have agreed to be employed by the company as its . . . . I look forward to starting work on the . . . .

## 19    Brief acceptance

I happily acknowledge receipt of your letter of . . . and confirm that I agree to serve the company on the terms set out therein/in memorandum attached thereto.

NOTE:
*One object of a swift and unequivocal reply is to prevent the offer from being withdrawn until you have had time to say 'yes'.*

## 20    Contract accepted – but terms queried

I am obliged to you for your letter of . . . . In general, I agree that it sets out very fairly the arrangements arrived at between us when I saw you last Thursday. However, I would like clarification of the following matters please:
1    . . . .
2    . . . .
I would be grateful if I could hear from you concerning the above, at your early convenience.

## 21    Record of reasons for non-appointment of applicant

Name . . . .
Address . . . .
Age . . . .
Job applied for . . . .
Reason/s for non-appointment:
1    Inadequate experience of job/trade/generally.
2    Lack of skill in job/generally.
3    Age.
4    Personality.
5    Sex (only where 'essential qualification for job').

6     Colour, national origin, nationality, race or ethnic origin (only where 'essential qualification for job').
7     Non-union member (where closed shop — and no religious objection).
8     Other.

NOTE:
*All those who appoint should be warned to beware of (5) and (6) above. If in doubt, then neither should* be *(nor, of course, be* shown as*) a reason for rejection. Omit (5) and (6) altogether if you have no jobs where sex, etc., is an 'essential qualification'.*

# Chapter 2

# In restraint of trade

Everyone is entitled to use his talents, knowledge, contacts and know-how to his own best advantage or as he sees fit. If an employee — however senior or junior — leaves your service, he may enter into competition with you, in your own immediate territory.

*Exception* — where there is a valid, binding restraint clause in the employee's contract of service. These clauses (by definition) restrain a person's freedom to earn his living as, where and when he sees fit. They are therefore *'prima facie* void' as 'contrary to public policy'. They will only be upheld by a court if they are 'reasonable' — in every respect.

A valid restraint clause must not be wider than is reasonably necessary for the protection of the employer's business. It must not place an unreasonable restraint on the employee's freedom to earn his living; and it must not be unreasonable from the public viewpoint. A clause that is too wide in time or space is normally a dead letter.

It is a grave error to draft your own restraint clauses. Only a lawyer who knows what clauses have been upheld by courts in similar cases, can hope to create an enforceable obligation. For that reason, the restraint clauses embedded in the letters which now follow are not precisely stated. To make a will; to convey property — or to draft restraint clauses — you need in each case the help of a lawyer.

Naturally, the converse applies. If you wish to compete with your present company when you leave its service, check your contract of service or the written particulars of your terms. If there is no restraint clause, worry not. You may compete to your heart's content. If there is a clause, do not panic — with any luck, it will not be enforceable. If in doubt, consult your solicitor.

\*　　\*　　\*

## 22　Standard restraint

I confirm that if you join this company, it must be a term of your employment that you will not engage in . . . for a period of . . . years after leaving the company's service, anywhere in . . ./within a radius of . . . from the company's works.

## 23   Representative's restraint

I confirm our conversation — that in consideration of the Company agreeing to employ no one else in the counties of . . . and . . . , you undertake as follows:

1   That within . . . years of leaving the Company's service, you will not engage directly or indirectly, whether for yourself or for others and where there is principal or agent in the sale of . . . , in the counties of . . . and . . . .

2   That you will not during the above period solicit orders from any person, firm or company who or which was a customer of the Company during the subsistence of your service/agency.

3   That you will not during the above period employ, directly or indirectly, whether for yourself or for others, any person who was in the Company's employment or employed by the Company as an agent, during the subsistence of your service/agency.

## 24   Breach of restraint — complaint

I have been informed that you are employed by the . . . Company at . . . , in the capacity of . . . . If this correct? If so, you are acting in direct contravention of the restraint clause contained in paragraph . . . of your terms of service/set out in our agreement contained in our exchange of letters dated . . . and . . . ; and if the breach continues, the Company will instruct its solicitors to commence proceedings against you and against your present company for an injunction and damages, without further warning.

I am sending copies of this letter to the Chairman of your company and also to my Company's solicitors, Messrs . . . of . . . .

NOTE:
*With luck, the threat of action will suffice — particularly as the current employers may be unwilling to keep on the man if it could lead to legal proceedings. They may also contend that they would not have taken him on, had he told them of the existence of the restraint clause.*

## 25  Denial of breach

I was sorry to receive your letter dated . . . , alleging breach of the restraint clause in my contract of service. I am advised that this clause is too wide to be enforceable. I was employed only in the . . . area/operated only from the . . . branch. The restraint covers the whole of the United Kingdom. In the circumstances, I respectfully suggest that you might care to consult your solicitors — who no doubt will give you the same advice about the restraint as have mine to me.

Any proceedings which you may see fit to institute will be vigorously defended.

NOTES:

*1  The danger of including a restraint clause in your contract of service is that you may have to 'put up or shut up'. You should not wield the sabre unless you are prepared to strike with it, if necessary. Better to have no restraint clause than one which you are not prepared to enforce.*

*2  On receipt of a letter such as the above, you are in a real dilemma. On the one hand, if you attempt to enforce the restraint and succeed, all is well — on the other, if your attempt fails, everyone will know that the clause is worthless. If you do not sue, then (equally) you will have revealed your weakness. Still, you could try the following:*

## 26  Without prejudice — suggested compromise

*Without Prejudice*

Thank you for your letter. I do not accept — and nor do the company's solicitors — that the restraint clause is unenforceable. However, without prejudice to the company's rights, I will be prepared to see you to discuss whether we can come to some reasonable arrangement which would result in the company's interests being moderately protected while you do not risk being thrown out of work. We are prepared to see whether it is possible to find some sensible common ground.

I look forward to hearing from you.

## 27   Personal assistant

I am happy to appoint you as my personal assistant at a
salary of £ . . . per annum, payable monthly. Your employment will be continuous with your previous employment by
the firm, which began on . . . .

You will work with me at the above address and your
normal hours will be from . . . a.m. to . . . p.m., Monday to
Friday, with one hour break for lunch. You will have three
weeks' paid holiday, your entitlement to arise after a full
twelve months of service. Your appointment shall be subject
to four weeks' notice on either side for the initial twelve
months and thereafter to three months' notice on either side.

In the event of your leaving our employment, for whatever
cause, you must not under any circumstances for a period of
six months — whether on your own behalf on or behalf of
others — solicit custom from any individual, firm or company who was a customer of ours during your period of employment, other than those on the list attached, who you are
now introducing to the firm. Nor must you for . . . months
after leaving, employ or seek to employ any person employed
by the firm during your period of employment.

If you are ill you will be paid full salary for a period not
exceeding three months in any calendar year, minus any sick
benefits receivable on the basis of full contributions paid. All
applications for sick pay must be accompanied by a doctor's
certificate. Remittances will be made to you with deductions
in respect of your National Insurance benefits received — so
that you will receive exactly the same pay while ill as when
you are well. Details of our grievance and disciplinary procedures are enclosed herewith.

With all best wishes.

NOTE:
*It is vital to confine any restraint against soliciting custom to customers*
*(or clients) who dealt with the employers during the employee's period*
*of service. Any attempt to prevent the soliciting of those who started*
*to deal with the employers after the employment ended will fail and*
*will probably invalidate the entire clause.*

## 28   Manager's restraint — alternative

I was pleased to meet you and to appoint you as manager of our . . . branch, upon the terms set out in your letter to me of the . . . . You did omit one clause — namely that you agreed that upon leaving our service you would not engage in . . . within a . . . mile radius of our branch, for a period of . . . years, either on your own account or as an employee of any other agency/business. As I explained to you, this restraint is one upon which we must insist, due to the high degree of trust which we place in our senior staff and the very considerable measure of responsibility and independence which we give to them in their work.

Please confirm your understanding of the above — and that you will commence work on . . . .

Looking forward to a long and happy period of co-operation with you and with kindest regards.

## 29   Restraint on executive — alternative

I am pleased to confirm your appointment as . . . , upon the terms attached hereto.

Kindly note that you are restrained from engaging in the . . . trade/industry for a period of . . . months/years after leaving the company's service, within a radius of . . . from the company's headquarters/works/office where you are employed.

You are also restrained from employing (whether for yourself or others) any persons who were employed by the company at the date when your employment ceases or within six months prior thereto — this restraint likewise to apply for a period of . . . months/years after leaving the company's service.

Please acknowledge receipt of this letter and your agreement to the terms offered. And kindly confirm that you will see Mr . . . in his office by not later than . . . on . . . .

With kind regards and wishing you every success in your new position.

## 30   Company Secretary — alternatives

The Board is pleased to accept your application for the post of Company Secretary of . . . Ltd, but this must be on the strict understanding that you will not accept employment in the field in which the Company is engaged, anywhere in . . . , for a period of . . . months/years after leaving the company's service.

The work you will be doing will be highly confidential and it is essential for the protection of the Company's business that this restraint should be acceptable to you. If you will be good enough to confirm that you agree thereto, I will then confirm in writing all details of your proposed contract. I would be most obliged for an immediate reply.

NOTE:
*The more responsible the post . . . the more confidential the information entrusted to the employee . . . the greater the area covered by the company's business — the wider the restraint which would be enforceable by law. Once again, I repeat — these precedents are skeletons which should be fleshed out by the lawyers. However, a recent High Court decision has emphasised that restraints accepted by vendors of businesses will be enforced far more readily than those imposed upon employees.*

## 31   Letter before action — to new employers

We understand that you are employing Mr . . . , who was previously employed by this company under a contract of service which contained a restraint clause, a copy of which is attached hereto. His current employment by you is in clear and blatant breach of his agreement with the company. I have instructed the company's solicitors, Messrs . . . of . . . , that unless we receive from you not later than . . . a clear assurance that the employment of Mr . . . by you has been terminated forthwith, legal proceedings are to be commenced against you forthwith. I trust that this will not be necessary.

NOTE:
*The proceedings would be for an injunction — an order, restraining the employer from employing the person concerned in breach of his agreement. A claim may also be made for damages — and (if appropriate) for the return of any of the company's documents, e.g. mailing lists.*

*Chapter 3*

# Trial periods

A trial or probationary period is fine — provided that you know what it means. If you simply give an employee a 'trial period' of (say) three months, believing that during that period you can dismiss him without notice if you are dissatisfied with his performance — forget it. All unknowing, you have given him three months security of tenure in his job — which he would certainly not have had in any other circumstances.

If, then, you wish to have a trial or probationary period during which you can terminate the employment, then say so. Subject to statutory minimum periods of notice, help yourself. Thus:

## 32   Trial period — no notice

I confirm that we shall be pleased to employ you as . . . , on the terms set out in the attached sheet. This appointment is, as discussed, subject to a four-week trial period, during which notice will not be required.

With best wishes,

NOTE:
*Compare Chapter 6, Trial Periods for Promotion.*

## 33   Probationary period — three months

I am pleased to confirm your appointment as . . . , on the terms set out at the foot of this letter — kindly sign the attached sheet to confirm that you are in agreement with the arrangements. I also confirm that this appointment will be subject to a three month probationary period, during which it will be subject to seven days' notice on either side.

I hope that this will be the start of a long and happy association between us and send you my best wishes.

## 34  Trial period — followed by reassessment

I enclose herewith, as promised, a statement of your terms
of service — and am pleased to confirm that you will start
work for the company on the . . . .
I also confirm that after a six-month trial period, we will
be pleased to reassess your term of service, with a view — all
being well — to arranging an increase in salary.

## 35  Trial period terminates

Your trial period of service with the Company being due
to expire on the . . . , I am now instructed to inform you that
the Board is very pleased indeed with your efforts on the
Company's behalf and I am to offer you service with the
Company on a long-term basis. The terms to this offer are
set out in detail upon the enclosed contract. Will you kindly
confirm at your earliest possible convenience that these terms
are acceptable to you.

NOTES:
*1   The wording of the final sentence is important. It presupposes that
the employee will accept the terms — and provides a positive approach,
much better than the alternative: 'If any of these terms are not satisfactory to you, please let us know'. By taking it for granted that the
terms will be satisfactory, you are creating a psychological atmosphere
in which the employee will find it harder to challenge them.*

*2   The same effect is achieved by referring to 'our usual terms'. Of
course, if you are at the receiving end of such a letter, beware — check
each term with great care to make certain that it really does suit your
purpose. If it does not, never mind the fact that it may be 'normal' or
'usual' — the time to challenge it is now — once you have signed up, it
will be too late.*

## 36  Confirmation — trial satisfactory (alternative)

We are pleased with the manner in which your trial period
has worked out. I am happy to confirm that we shall be
pleased to employ you on a more permanent footing, upon
the same basis as at present — but subject to four weeks'

notice on either side. Kindly confirm that this is satisfactory
to you.


## 37   Trial unsatisfactory

I am instructed to inform you that the Company will not
wish to retain your services when your trial period comes to
an end.

NOTES:
*1   Many companies prefer to pay the employee his full entitlement,
up to the end of his trial period, and tell him at the same time that they
will no longer require his services. An employee who knows that he is
on his way out is unlikely to be the company's star turn during his
remaining period of service.*

*2   But note: if the trial period is sufficiently long (four weeks or
over), at least seven days' notice will be required. So the above letter
must be sent in due time.*


## 38   With short notice

I confirm that the company will employ you in the capacity of . . . as from the . . . . For a trial period of . . . your
employment will be terminable by the giving of . . . week's
notice on either side. Thereafter, the period will be . . . .
I trust that the trial will prove satisfactory both for us and
for you and look forward to your employment being put on
a long-term basis thereafter. I hope that you will have a long
and happy period of service with the company.


## 39   Offer of trial period

I am pleased to confirm our conversation. The company
will employ you for an initial period of . . . at a salary of
£ . . . . At the end of that period, we will assess the situation.
If all goes well you will then be offered an appointment on a
long-term basis.
Kindly confirm that you will be prepared to serve the company upon this basis. I would like you to commence work on

the . . . .

Hoping that this will be the start of a long and happy association between us, and with my kindest regards,

NOTE:

*It is wrong to regard the trial period as one during which the employer can sack without notice, whenever he sees fit. The above letter confers a fixed term during which the employee is entitled (unless he has earned a summary dismissal) to be kept on. If you wish a trial period to have some other meaning, then use the previous form of letter.*

# Chapter 4

# Fixed-term contracts

A contract is for a fixed term if neither party can put an end to that contract before the term expires. The BBC once dismissed an employee called Ioannou, who had a series of contracts, each of which was for a set time but contained a term which allowed either party to terminate by the giving of six months' notice to the other. The Court of Appeal held that this was not 'a fixed-term contract' for the full period.

The Trade Union and Labour Relations Act provides that where an employee under a fixed-term contract is not re-engaged when that term comes to an end, he is 'dismissed'. However, if the fixed term is for two years or more, he may contract out of his right to claim unfair dismissal remedies.

It follows that a contracting-out clause will only be effective if there is a fixed term in a contract with neither party being entitled to terminate prior to the expiry of that term.

If you have no job for the employee when his fixed term expires, then he will be 'redundant'. The redundancy itself will probably be 'fair'.

## 40   Executive — fixed-term contract

Your contract of service expires on the . . . . I regret that I am unable to offer you further employment with the company, for the following reasons:
   1 . . .
   2 . . .
   3 . . .

NOTE:
*The employee whose term is not renewed or extended is in precisely the same position as any other employee who has been dismissed — with or without notice. His dismissal may or may not be 'fair'. He may claim compensation for 'unfair dismissal'. You should therefore consult Part 2, and adapt the appropriate letter to your needs.*

## 41   To apprentice — who has not contracted out

I write to remind you that you will have completed your apprenticeship with this company on the . . . . As you know, the journeyman principle applies in this industry and it is not normal for apprentices to stay on with the company with whom they served their apprenticeship. In the circumstances, it is presumed that you would wish to seek employment elsewhere. Please let us know if you have any difficulty in finding a place and we will do whatever we can to help you. (We would also be prepared to consider an application for further employment with the company.)

NOTES:
*1   This letter leaves the door open for the apprentice to ask for further employment. If you receive such a request, you turn it down at your risk.*

*2   On the other hand, if there is no other work, available for the apprentice, he (like any other employee) must 'mitigate his loss'. He must keep it to the minimum (see Part 2 for the principles on which compensation is assessed). So if other work is available, even if the dismissal is technically 'unfair', it will not give the apprentice any rights against you. Alternatively, you may be able to make the youngster redundant, 'fairly'.*

## 42   Offer of fixed term to executive — provided he contracts out

We appreciate that you would like a lengthy period of security, if you are to pull up your roots and to join the company in London. In the circumstances, we are prepared to offer you a two-year contract. But you will appreciate that any continuation of your service when that contract concludes would have to depend upon the current facts which cannot be anticipated at the present time. In the circumstances, will you please confirm that you are prepared to accept an engagement on the above basis, and in particular that you are agreeable that you will not exercise such right (if any) as you might otherwise have to claim compensation for unfair dismissal under the provisions of the Trade Union and Labour Relations Act.

## 43 Rights excluded

I would refer you to your contract of service in which it was agreed that as the company was prepared to grant you a fixed-term contract of two years or more, any rights to claim compensation for unfair dismissal would be excluded.

I wish to add that, in any event and without prejudice to the above, it is denied that your dismissal was 'unfair'. As you well know, circumstances were such that it was not possible to re-engage you.

## 44 Employee alleges not 'fixed period'

I am advised by my solicitors that as either the company or I had the right to terminate my contract within the two-year period by giving a minimum of . . . weeks'/months' notice, mine was not a 'fixed-term contract', within the meaning of the Trade Union and Labour Relations Act.

## 45 Offer of apprenticeship — term excluding unfair dismissal rights to be included

I have considered your application for an apprenticeship with our company, and am pleased to say that we are pre-pared to take you on. I enclose herewith the proposed in-denture. Would you please read it through very carefully; discuss it with your parents — and if there are any points you would like to raise with me, please do so. If you and your parents are satisfied with the proposed arrangement, would you and they please sign, where indicated.

As you know, this agreement will last for four/five years — and we hope that you will have a very happy time here. If at the end of your apprenticeship we have a place for you and you are satisfied in every way with your work, we shall be pleased to offer you further engagement. However, the con-tract contains our usual term excluding any claim in respect of rights which you might otherwise have, if it is decided not to offer you further employment after your apprenticeship terminates.

I look forward to hearing from you.

NOTES:

*1 It is sensible to draw the attention of the proposed apprentice to the 'contracting out' clause. It is also fair. The law would not require you to do so.*

*2 There is no law which says that parents must guarantee that an apprentice will carry out his duties — and, in practice, it is very rare that such an agreement is enforced against a parent. However, it is as well to let the parents feel that they do owe you some responsibility. They may well, in the circumstances, feel it right to induce their son to carry out his obligations under his agreement.*

## 46   Variation of executive's contract, subject to contracting-out clause

I am pleased to inform you that we are prepared to increase your pay from £ . . . , to £ . . . per week/month. However, this is conditional upon your agreeing that in the (I hope, unlikely) event of the company not wishing to renew your contract after the present term expires, your contract will contain a clause excluding any possible claim for compensation for 'unfair dismissal'.

I look forward to hearing from you.

NOTES:

*1 You cannot force any employee, of whatever status, to vary his contract of service so as to include a contracting-out clause — which, after all, is against his interest.*

*2 On the other hand, any contract of service may be varied, by agreement between the parties. You are fully entitled to invite your employee to accept a variation.*

*3 Employees are far more likely to agree willingly to variations, if you put the matter to them at the time when you are increasing their pay. Hence the above letter. You may even want to serve written particulars (see Chapter 1) — and to revamp many of the employee's terms (including, for example, restraint clauses). By all means do so in one go — which includes contracting out.*

*If the employee is not prepared to contract out, then you certainly have no right to dismiss him for that reason, however early or late in his 'fixed term' it may be.*

*If you are asked to contract out of a possible right to compensation for unfair dismissal, think carefully before you agree. You are giving up a potentially extremely important claim. Before you invite your employees to do so, you may well wish to refer them to their unions – or at least to include the arrangement as part of a package deal, which when looked at as a whole, will be to the employee's considerable benefit.*

## 47   Effort to obtain another job for apprentice

George Smith has been apprenticed to this Company for
. . . years, and on the . . . , his apprenticeship will come to an end. In this Company, we feel strongly that it is best for apprentices to move on and not to serve their entire time with the same outfit – and we understand that you agree. In the circumstances, I was wondering whether you would have a vacancy for George? He is an excellent young man – and I am sure would be useful to your Company.

For our own part, if there are apprentices whom you would recommend, we would be pleased to consider taking them on to our books, when their training by and with you terminates.

With best wishes.

NOTE:
*If you dismiss your apprentice by not re-employing him, then the dismissal (as we have seen) may be 'unfair'. But if he immediately obtains other work, he will have suffered no loss as a result of his dismissal and will therefore obtain no compensation under the Act. Hence it is now not only an act of kindness to your apprentice but also of good sense and even necessity from the company's viewpoint, to use your best endeavours to obtain other work for him. There are, however, occasions when you have to provide an unhappy reference, thus:*

## 48   Poor reference for ex-apprentice

I note that George Smith has applied for a post with your Company, upon the termination of his apprenticeship with us. You ask for a reference.

If you would care to speak to me by telephone, I will be pleased to discuss Mr Smith with you.

NOTES:

*1   You are not bound to give a reference. If you give a bad one, then it is defamatory. Put it into writing, and it is a libel. Say it orally and it is a slander.*

*2   Slanders are much more difficult to prove than libels — hence if you feel bound to give a poor reference, it is normally best to do so by telephone. But in practice you have little to worry about because the honest givers of even poor references are protected by law. Apart from 'justification' — the defence that the statement made was substantially true — you would plead that the occasion was one of 'qualified privilege'. You were under a moral obligation to give the reference and the recipient had a direct interest in its contents.*

*3   Note that no 'disclaimer' will avoid defamation perils. But in case you give a good reference to the wrong person — and this does happen — particularly in large outfits — you should in fact disclaim — as in the next letter. (See Chapter 17 for law and precedents.)*

## 49   Satisfactory reference for ex-apprentice

I am pleased to say that George Smith has proved a very good apprentice. He is reliable and hard working and I am sure would be a credit to your company.

While we are pleased to supply references for ex-employees, this is done on the basis that no legal responsibility therefore is accepted by the Company or any of the employees.

With best wishes.

NOTE:

*There are many other angles to references, which cannot be dealt with fully in this book. They will be found in my companion book,* Letters of the Law.

## 50   Redundant ex-apprentice

I accept that by not re-engaging you at the end of your term as an apprentice with the company, you were in law 'dismissed'. However, I regret that there is no job available for you and the reason for your dismissal was on the grounds of redundancy.

Unfortunately, you are not entitled to redundancy pay because you have not been with the company for two years or more since reaching the age of 18. (*Alternatively:* You will be receiving your appropriate redundancy pay because you have served the company for over two years since reaching the age of 18.)

# Chapter 5

# Varying a contract

Any contract may be changed — with the consent of the parties. You may agree to alter your own terms of service or you may change those of your employees — with consent. Your supplier or contractor may induce you to allow him to put up his rates, if only to keep his business alive and to enable him to complete the work. Or you may induce your customer to accept a variation, to help you — or possibly, to assist him by enabling you to do the work or supply the materials quicker or better.

However: you have no legal right to impose a variation, without consent. To do that is a breach of contract.

Examples: Reducing an employee's pay or status — perhaps because he is old or ill or because your business is being run down or 'rationalised' . . . introducing a restraint clause . . . a clause allowing you to make deductions . . . an agreement that the employee will submit to medical examination or to search, at the request of the management . . . .

Vary, by all means — but get consent first. Conversely, recognise that 'unilateral variation' is a breach of the contract concerned, and if you are faced with a change in your own terms and do not agree to it, protest — loud and clear.

\* \* \*

## 51 Changing employee's terms of service

I am happy to inform you that as from . . . , your salary/ wage will be increased to £ . . . per week/month/annum. We are taking this opportunity to revise the company's terms of service, as a result of various recent legislation, including the Employment Protection Act and the Health and Safety at Work Act. Please read the enclosed document; if you have any questions about it, by all means contact me; and please sign the duplicate and return it to me, to show that you have received, read, understood and accepted these revised particulars.

We are very pleased to be able to make such a substantial increase in your wage/salary — and thank you for the service which you have given and are giving to the company. With best wishes.

NOTES:

*1 Always try to tie changes which may not be to the employee's benefit to those which undoubtedly are — in particular, increases in pay.*

*2 Conversely, do not try to sneak in adverse changes, without giving the employee full notice of them.*

*3 As usual, a signature is not vital — but it is certainly advisable, so that the employee cannot afterwards say that he has not received, understood nor agreed to the new terms.*

## 52 Restraint clause — added

In view of . . . , it has been decided to request all employees to agree that they will not compete with the company for . . . months/years after leaving its employment, by engaging in the manufacture or sale of . . . , whether on their own behalf or on behalf of others, for months/years after leaving the company's service. Please indicate your acceptance that this restraint is reasonable and necessary in the company's interests and in the interests of all those who depend upon the company for their livelihood — by signing the duplicate and returning it to me.
With best wishes.

NOTE:

*The employee may refuse to sign. In the event of an unreasonable refusal, it is conceivable that it would be 'fair' to terminate his employment. Everything would depend upon all the circumstances of the particular case. See also, Chapter 2.*

## 53 Refusal to accept variation

Your letter represents an attempt to impose a unilateral variation of the contract upon me/this company. This is unreasonable and cannot be accepted. I am sure that on reflection you will understand that it would not be fair to expect me/my company to agree to such a potentially substantial deterioration in its terms of service/contractual terms.

## 54   Variation essential if contract is to survive

I am entirely in your hands. If you are prepared to increase my pay by £ . . . , I will gladly stay on. If, on the other hand, I am not to receive an increase in spite of my increased responsibilities, then I will have to leave your service. Please do give this matter your most serious consideration and let me know at your earliest possible convenience.

## 55   Denial of variation

The clause which requires you to comply with the health and safety requirements is not a variation of your contract of service. It is merely making express a term which would in any event have been implied by law.

NOTE:
*Every contract has express and implied terms. In a contract of service, for instance, express terms invariably include the employee's pay – implied terms include: 'You shall not steal from the company . . . give away its secrets . . . ' and 'You will not engage in dangerous practices'. Hence the above letter. That which appears to be a variation may not be one after all.*

*Chapter 6*

# Promotion and demotion

Few employees mind being promoted — trouble comes when they cannot cope with their new responsibilities. To return an employee to his old status and pay is almost always a dismissal. You are reducing the man's current and future earning ability — and that is a very serious breach of his contract of service.

Promotions must be undertaken with care, not only for the sake of the business (and, for that matter, for the sake of the employee promoted) but also so as to protect the promoter against a potentially successful claim for unfair dismissal remedies.

Equally, you may demote in law even if you do not intend to do so in fact. Any change of status which acts to the employee's detriment may amount to a demotion. A transfer to a job with less responsibility . . . a reduction in status . . . a lowering of total remuneration . . . . All these involve a major variation in the contract of service — as does, for that matter, the movement of an outdoor worker into an inside job or the shifting of a headmaster from a permanent to a relief position, constantly on the move.

It is, of course, always possible to vary a person's contract with his consent (see preceding chapter) or to arrange the change in the contract so as to give scope for reversal, if all does not go as well as the parties have intended. As these letters will show.

\*    \*    \*

## 56    Promotion — for trial period

I am delighted to confirm that my recommendation to the Board that you be promoted to . . . has been accepted. But as explained to you, we felt that this change ought to be for an initial trial period of . . . months, so as to ensure that you are successful in coping with the new responsibilities as both we and you hope.

For the trial period, your salary will be increased to £ . . . per annum, payable monthly as before. Remaining terms of your contract will remain unaffected.

It must be clearly understood that if for any reason the management considers that the trial has proved unsuccessful, you will revert to your former position with the company, at the same pay as previously. But, of course, we hope that this will not arise.

Wishing you good fortune — and with my renewed congratulations.

NOTES:

1 *The word 'trial period' is often misleading — see Chapter 3. It is essential to set out the terms during that period — even if these are to remain the same as before.*

2 *The above letter gives a fixed trial period, during which it will not be possible to reduce the employee's (increased) pay, even if he is totally incapable of coping with his new responsibilities. The alternative is to provide for a return to the status quo during the trial period — thus:*

## 57   Promotion for trial period — subject to immediate return

Many congratulations on the Board's decision to promote you to the position of . . . for a trial period of . . . months. As is normal custom in this company, this promotion is for an initial period of . . . months, during which time if either you or the management considers that it would be in the company's interests for you to revert to your former post, this may be effected by the giving of seven days' notice on either side.

Your new remuneration will be . . . .

In all other respects, you will serve on the same basis as before.

Wishing you the best of luck in your new and important post and with my very best wishes.

NOTE:

*Obviously, the provision of a line of retreat means that the promoted employee's position has to be held open for him, or at least covered by someone else who can be moved out again, during the trial period. The alternative is to promote and to hope for the best. What matters then is to ensure that you can if necessary prove that you — and the employee — entered into the revised arrangement after adequate thought, training and that the employee's failure to cope with his new burdens was not due to any lack of backing from his superiors. Thus:*

## 58   Full backing of Board with new responsibilities

I congratulate you on your promotion to . . . − which I am happy to confirm. Your remuneration will be £ . . . per week/month, as from . . . . You will be entitled to receive and expected to give not less than . . . weeks'/months' notice to terminate your employment. In other respects, your terms of employment will be as before. We have carefully discussed the implications of your added responsibilities/and after your period of special training at/in . . . . You will of course have my full support and that of the Board/the management/your colleagues concerned as you will be with . . . , in your new tasks − and I wish you the very best of luck with them.

## 59   Executive − accepts promotion − on terms

Thank you for your letter. I shall be pleased to serve the company in the position of . . . , but I confirm our discussion. You have agreed that in the event of my not finding the work as satisfactory and rewarding as we both hope, I shall be entitled to return to my former position at any time within . . . months, giving you of course sufficient notice (of not less than . . . weeks nor more than . . . weeks), to enable you to find a replacement.

I further confirm that I am agreeable to remuneration at the rate of £ . . . per month/year in my new post − I appreciate that if I return to my former post, it will be at the former rate of pay.

With all best wishes − and with my thanks to you and to the Board for your confidence in me.

## 60   Acceptance of promotion − no reservations

I am happy to confirm that I shall be most pleased to work for the company in the position of . . . at a salary of £ . . . .

I am concerned, however, at your suggestion that this should be on a trial period. This was not agreed − once I have taken the plunge and have moved to different work/and to a different works/office/town, I shall not be willing to go back to square one. I am sure that on reflection you will agree that it would not be reasonable or fair to ask me to do so. Nor was this suggestion agreed or even discussed when we came to terms over my new appointment.

I have now worked for the company for . . . months/years; you certainly know of my devotion to the company and I need not emphasise my determination to make a success of my new position; but equally, both I and those who are working under me must feel that I have your full confidence and backing and that the job is one which I am to have the opportunity to see through to its end.

NOTE:

*If you do not agree to the trial period — or, indeed, to any other term of your proposed service — it is crucial that you say so, in writing and at the earliest possible date. Otherwise no court is likely to believe you if you later maintain that the letter from your employers does not correctly set out the agreement between you.*

## 61   Rejection of promotion on suggested terms

I have given the most careful thought to your kind sugges-tion that I accept the position of . . . . As you know, I am very happily settled into my present post and I was most reluctant to move — even at the generously increased salary which you suggested.

I have, as you asked, carefully considered the position, and I have come, with some reluctance to the conclusion that I would not be justified in accepting your offer. I prefer to have the certainty of serving the company well and happily in my present post, rather than take the risk of failing to cope with the wider responsibilities which you have in mind.

In the circumstances, I was wondering whether you had given thought to the possibility of appointing John Smith to the new position? He is younger than I am; he has shown considerable initiative and perseverance; he is a thoroughly reliable manager — and I for one would be very pleased to work under him.

I hope this letter will not disappoint you. I can assure you that I have not turned down your offer without the most anxious thought — and I greatly appreciate the confidence which you have shown in me by inviting me to accept promotion.

With my best wishes.

NOTE:

*In refusing to accept wider responsibilities, it is crucial not to lose existing goodwill. Hence the need for a careful, reasoned turn down — and, if possible, the suggestion of an alternative.*

## 62   Persuasion to accept promotion

My colleagues and I were very sorry to receive your letter and to learn that you are still worried about taking on the added responsibilities which would be involved, were you to accept our invitation to serve the company as . . . at £ . . . .

It occurs to us that you may be worried about . . . . May I assure you that your anxiety on this score is totally unjustified for the following reasons:

  1 . . .
  2 . . .
  3 . . .

Above all, if you do change your mind — as we earnestly hope — you will not only have the full support of the Board but it has been decided to provide you with a further assistant/secretary/deputy, so as to make your task less burdensome and more congenial.

In the circumstances, I hope to hear from you that you will in fact be prepared to accept promotion — and if you have any further doubts, please telephone and we will arrange to meet.

With my warmest good wishes.

# Chapter 7

# Sickness and health

An employee is entitled to sick pay if there is some express or implied term in his contract of service, giving him that right. Written particulars of contracts of service should set out whether or not there is such a term – and if so, then details should be specified.

In the absence of any express (or rarely – implied) agreement, hourly paid workers generally get no sick pay. But it has been held in a High Court case that there is no such implied term in the contract of a salaried employee who, in the absence of agreement to the contrary, is entitled to his pay, in sickness as in health, unless and until his contract is terminated.

You can dismiss an employee when he is ill, in the same way as if he were well. Unless the illness is so serious that the employee is never going to be able to return to his job, he will be entitled to his proper notice or pay in lieu, which will be the same as if he were fully fit. If his sick pay entitlement has expired before his notice begins, his right to his normal remuneration will revive for the period of that notice.

In addition, an employee is entitled not to be dismissed 'unfairly'. The Trade Union and Labour Relations Act specifies 'health' as one of the reasons which may make a dismissal 'fair'.

Whether it is 'fair' to dismiss any particular employee because he has been absent through ill health (actual or alleged) will depend on all the circumstances of the case. The sort of questions which an industrial tribunal would ask are these:

1    How long has the employee worked for you?
2    How many times has the employee been away through ill health in the past?
3    What is the prospect of the employee returning to work – or not being absent through ill health in the future?
4    What is the employee's age . . . status . . . responsibility. . . ?

Ask yourself, then, would a decent employer in these circumstances dismiss an employee for this reason? If you are sure that the answer is, yes – then you should be all right. If you are certain that it is, no – then restrain yourself. If you are doubtful, then either give the employee the benefit of the doubt or take legal advice.

Assuming that the employee has been with you for at least six months and is neither a part timer (normally working up to 16 hours a week or 8 hours after five years' service) and that he is not a pensioner, then he is protected against unfair dismissal. This means not only (as we have seen) that you may have to show not only the reason for the dismissal but that you acted reasonably in treating that reason as sufficient to deprive the employee of his livelihood. You must also operate a fair system. The Code of Industrial Relations Practice requires, in particular, that you give at least one written warning of pending dismissal (where practicable). This rule (like the rest) applies to the ill man, just as it does to his fit colleague.

If, then, you intend to dismiss a sick employee, write to him and at least give him the chance of coming back to work.

If you operate a sick pay scheme and you believe that a particular employee is taking advantage of it, then tell him so. You may even be justified in giving him the choice of being removed from the scheme or accepting dismissal. However, if you want to vary his contract of service by removing his sick pay entitlement and he is not willing to agree to that change, you must appreciate that insistence on such removal will itself amount to a termination of the employment. You are refusing to employ the man on the agreed terms. This termination may be fair or unfair, depending on the circumstances. If in doubt, take advice.

Here is a selection of the letters which you may need to write if your employee is ill.

\* \* \*

## 63 Confirmation – sick pay entitlement

You have been with the company for six months and I am happy to confirm that your sick pay arrangements will in future be as follows:

1 . . .
2 . . .
3 . . .

## 64 No sick pay

I was extremely sorry to receive your letter and to learn that you are unable to attend for work because of illness. If you will kindly refer to your terms of service, you will see that we have no sick pay arrangements for employees until they have been with us for 12 months, and your employment has lasted only 8 months.

We wish you, however, a speedy recovery and hope that you will soon be fully recovered. Please let me know at your early convenience when you hope to be able to return to work.

## 65   Written warning to ill employee

I was very sorry to learn that you are still unwell. As you will appreciate, the firm cannot continue to keep your job open indefinitely and I must regretfully inform you that unless you return to work by . . . , we shall have to give you notice to terminate your employment. However, even if you cannot return by the above date, do please let me know if you wish to return to the company later on and I shall make every effort to find a position for you.

With best wishes.

## 66   Notice – while ill

I was very sorry to learn that your illness continues. However, I am afraid that it will not be possible for the company to retain you in its employment because your continued absence is causing/absences have caused considerable difficulty and disruption in the office. I must therefore give you notice to terminate your employment on the . . . . , in accordance with your terms of service. I shall arrange with our accounts department to send you your pay for that period.

With kind regards.

NOTE:
*Even if the employee is not entitled to sick pay or if his sick pay entitlement has expired, it revives during the period of notice. Hence, pay in lieu may be given, thus:*

## 67   Pay in lieu – while ill

You have now been off work for the following periods:
   1 . . .

2 . . .
3 . . .

I refer you to my letter of . . . in which I warned you that any further absence could not be tolerated by the company because of the difficulty and disruption which it would cause.

Kindly accept this letter, therefore, as terminating your employment as from today's date. I am asking our accounts department to send to you your pay in lieu of notice for the period of . . . weeks, in accordance with your contract of service.

NOTE:
*You will probably use this letter for an employee whose 'illness' is in doubt. Note, however, the need to give written warning of intended dismissal, thus:*

## 68 Warning of intended dismissal — illness

I have been greatly concerned at your frequent (and often unexplained) absence from work. I appreciate that on occasion you have presented medical certificates and that at present you are away as a result of illness. However, I must warn you that unless you are able to return to work by not later than . . . and unless you thereafter attend regularly and without any further absences, whether caused by illness or otherwise, I shall have no alternative other than to terminate your employment.

## 69 Demand for sick pay — implied term

I appreciate that there is no express term in my letter of appointment concerning sick pay. I am advised, however, that as I am a salaried employee, there is an implied term that I am entitled to payment while absent due to illness. In the circumstances — and especially bearing in mind the difficulties which are being created through the withholding of this money — I would be grateful if I could receive a cheque at your early convenience.

I am pleased to tell you that I am making steady progress towards recovery and I hope to be back at work within . . .

weeks/months/by about . . . .
  With kind regards and best wishes.

NOTE:
*You could, if you wished, say: 'I am entitled to be paid, in sickness or*
*in health, while my contract of service subsists' — but that is almost an*
*invitation to terminate the contract of service.*


## 70   Denial that sickness warrants dismissal

  I was saddened to receive your letter, which I certainly
would not have expected from the representative of a company which I have served so loyally and so well and for so
long — and which has in the past always prided itself on
standing by its employees when they were ill. I am, of course,
protected against unfair dismissal — and I would ask you
kindly to reconsider your decision to terminate my employment. I have received preliminary advice from my solicitors
that the dismissal in my case would be extremely unfair. I
have no wish whatever to bring a claim against the company
— on the contrary, I look forward to returning to the company's service as soon as I am fit to do so. I shall therefore be
glad to hear from you at your early convenience.
  With my personal regards to you.

# DISMISSAL

# Chapter 8

# Introduction

There are many ways in which a contract of employment may be terminated. Dismissal is a termination by the employer, without the employee's consent. In law, dismissals may be divided into three categories.

## 1 Actual dismissal

A dismissal may be 'actual' if the employee is sacked, fired, discharged ... if the employer puts an end to the contract of employment, whether with or without notice.

The employer is saying, in effect: 'I refuse to continue to employ you'. He may also say: 'I will not employ you in future on the same terms as in the past'. In that case, there is an actual dismissal, even if he is prepared to keep the employee on the books on different terms. For instance:

1    An employee is engaged to work on a particular shift; the employer seeks to change that shift, without his consent; the employee refuses to move — but the employer insists.
2    An employee is promoted but fails to perform as hoped. Without his agreement, the employer has no right to move him back to his old job. A demotion is a dismissal from the old job — even if a new one is offered at a lower level.
3    An employee's status is important, not merely in his current job but because it affects his employability by others. A reduction in status may well amount to a dismissal, even if the employee works at the same pay and at the same place.
4    An employee who is engaged to work at one place may not be shifted to another, merely because such a transfer suits the management. An attempt at a 'unilateral variation' will produce a dismissal — whether or not the employer is conscious of the legal result of his behaviour.

\*    \*    \*

There is no dismissal, of course, if the employee agrees to the change, however basic that change may be (see Chapter 6 for variations of contracts). You should always attempt to achieve change by agreement. If you fail and you force that change upon your employee, you must recognise that you are 'dismissing'.

## 2   Constructive dismissal

An employer dismisses 'constructively' if he forces the employee out of his job. The two most common examples:

1    An invitation to resign which the employee cannot refuse. 'If you resign, you will get your severance pay and your reference – if you do not, you will be dismissed.'
2    The 'wearing down' of an employee by his manager or supervisor. Many employees are forced out of their position by being given the dirty jobs; because the foreman picks on them; because they get no favours and many kicks; because they are treated in a way that they do not have to put up with.

The Trade Union and Labour Relations Act established that where an employee leaves his job when he is entitled to do so as a result of his employer's conduct, he is dismissed.

In practice, the dangers of constructive dismissal are huge and largely unrecognised. Failure to train lower levels of management and supervision in the dangers of constructive dismissal frequently lead to heavy legal penalties.

\*   \*   \*

An employee has to prove that he was 'dismissed' before the burden shifts on to the employer to show the reason for the dismissal and that he acted reasonably in treating that reason as sufficient to warrant taking away the employee's livelihood. It is simple to prove an actual dismissal and often difficult to prove a constructive dismissal. Nevertheless, many employees successfully obtain unfair dismissal remedies when their employers have failed to realise that there was a dismissal at all. Every manager and supervisor should be taught to avoid forcing dismissals – which by definition do not go through the normal procedures – including warnings and documentation.

## 3   Expiry of fixed-term contracts

When a fixed-term contract expires without being renewed, since 1971 this has been treated by law as a 'dismissal'. Details in Chapter 4.

\*   \*   \*

A dismissal is 'wrongful' if the employee does not get his proper notice. Proper notice means:

1    That period which has been agreed between employer and employee — for details, see written particulars.

2    In the absence of agreement, then 'reasonable' notice — the period which is reasonable will depend upon all the circumstances of the particular case, including the employee's length of service, his status, responsibility and the intervals at which he is paid.

3    In any event, the employee must be given not less than the statutory minimum period which is now: 7 days after 4 weeks and then a week a year from 2 years to 12 years. *Note:* it is incorrect and even fraudulent to include a term in the employee's contract to say that he is entitled to 'statutory notice'. There is no 'statutory notice' — only a statutory minimum.

*Chapter 9*

# Constructive dismissal

Constructive dismissal avoids disciplinary procedures altogether. Suddenly you find that a person whom you had thought you still employed was dismissed.

Where an employee leaves when he is entitled to do so because of the employer's conduct, then he is 'dismissed'. If he is forced out of his job, he is entitled to go.

Where one spouse walks out on the other without due cause, that is 'desertion'. Where one spouse pushes the other out of the home, that is normally 'constructive' desertion.

The following conversations should be used with care:

'You have the choice. You may either resign — in which case, you will get your severance pay and a reference; or I would have to dismiss you.'

'OK, so the personnel manager won't dismiss you. I have to put up with you. So you are going to do the dirty jobs . . . . No favours from me . . . . I'll decide whom you'll work with and you won't like it . . . . You don't like being called 'Taffy' — that's too bad . . . ?

To wear someone down or push him out or force him into resigning at any level is to 'dismiss' — and can lead to precisely the same consequences in law as any other dismissal.

## 71 Allegation of constructive dismissal

By your actions and those of Mr . . . , you have made it impossible for me to continue to serve the company. I am therefore forced to regard my contract of service as repudiated by the company.

I have worked loyally for the company for over . . . years. The following are the major matters which have driven me out of that service:

1   My . . . transfer to X Department, contrary to my express wishes.

2 The requirement that I must work under Mr Y, whom you know has frequently expressed hostility towards me.

3 The reduction of my staff and in particular the transfer of my secretary, Miss Z.

4 . . .

5 . . .

6 Continual and unnecessary interference with my work.

7 The frequent and totally unwarranted complaints concerning the operation of my department — which has been doing remarkably well, in spite of great difficulties.

I would finally refer you to my letters of . . . and . . . in which I made it plain that the situation was becoming impossible.

The following payments are outstanding to me as at the above date, when my employment terminated, and I shall be pleased to receive the company's cheque at the earliest convenient date.

1 Salary to . . . .

2 Commission to . . . .

3 Agreed bonus . . . .

4 Holiday pay to . . . .

In addition, in the event of my not obtaining other equivalent work without delay, I shall apply to the Industrial Tribunal for compensation for unfair dismissal.

I am indeed sorry that my association with the company should end in this unhappy manner.

NOTES:

*1 A previous letter, warning that you cannot carry on, is advisable but not vital. There is no legal requirement — but provable previous warnings are of great help in showing repudiation by the employer as they are when provided for the employee as previously recommended by the (still effective) Code of Industrial Relations Practice.*

*2 Reduction in status is a major change in the term of employment, and amounts to dismissal, even if pay remains the same.*

*3 If you have any doubt as to the proper framing of the matters relied upon as amounting to a repudiation, see your solicitor. If your funds are sufficiently low, you may get his initial advice and help, to the value of £25, at little or no fee if you are short of funds. Ask your solicitor for details. Otherwise, at least make absolutely sure that the reasons are*

*either set out accurately and as fully as possible — or omitted altogether.*
*4   Other letters from executives are collected in Chapter 16.*


## 72   Employer's denial of repudiation

I acknowledge receipt of your letter of . . . in which you
allege that you have been forced out of your employment
with the company and further that you have been constructively dismissed. These allegations are denied. You left the
company of your own volition and in no circumstances can
the company accept that you were dismissed, unfairly or at
all.

You will receive your pay to date and all other money due
to you, together with your P45, as soon as possible.


## 73   Alternative denial — with counter-allegations

Thank you for your letter of . . . , in which you informed
the company that you have left its service. You were certainly
not forced out of that service, as you allege or at all. The
answers to your allegations are as follows:
  1 . . .
  2 . . .
  3 . . .


## 74   Alternative denial — alleging repudiation by employee

I am instructed to thank you for your letter of . . . and to
inform you that the company denies that you were constructively dismissed, as alleged or at all. You yourself repudiated your contract of service by your actions, and in
particular as a result of the following:

1   You failed to comply with lawful instructions given to
you by . . . , in particular:
  *(a)* . . .
  *(b)* . . .
  *(c)* . . .

2   . . .

You will receive all money due to you, as soon as this can be arranged.

## 75   Warning by employee

Unfortunately, I am continually being harassed and hampered in the carrying on of my duties for the company. I am doing everything in my power to produce the best results in my department/office — but I am slowly being driven to the conclusion that a concerted effort is being made to force me to resign from my position.

It is right for me to point out that in the event of my being unable to carry on with my work, I shall regard this as a clear case of constructive dismissal. I am sorry to have to write in this way, but it is obviously both fair and proper for me to let you know the situation — in the hope that matters may be corrected before they get any worse.

My specific complaints are as follows:

  *(a)* . . .
  *(b)* . . .
  *(c)* . . .

I shall, of course, be pleased to call upon you to discuss the situation at any time convenient to you.

# Chapter 10

# Warnings of intended dismissal

The Code of Industrial Relations Practice (which was introduced under the Industrial Relations Act and remains in force unless and until replaced by a Code produced by the Advisory, Conciliation and Arbitration Service) has only one really vital section. This requires that — whenever reasonably practicable — an employee shall be given at least one written warning of intended dismissal before he is deprived of his livelihood.

Note:-

1   It is not sufficient merely to send a note or a memorandum of dissatisfaction or complaint. The employee must be warned that continued behaviour (or *mis*behaviour) of the kind referred to will (or may) lead to dismissal.

2   If the warning brings the desired result but the employee's behaviour reverts, the warning may have gone stale. The more important the misconduct and the more serious the warning, the longer it will remain effective. Whether and when a further warning is required is a question of fact and of degree. Usually, after six months or so, the procedure should be restarted.

3   These warnings apply at every level. Even a board member is entitled to a written threat. Conversely: Employees at and below board level should protect their own position by replying to such warnings — in writing and keeping copies.

4   If you give proper written warnings, ensuing dismissal will probably be 'fair'. At least the procedure is likely to be so. However, there are circumstances in which it is not reasonably practicable to give a warning — as where the conduct complained of is immediate, serious and such that would make a reasonable employer refuse to keep the employee on his books or to give him another chance.

5   If the written warnings are properly and carefully drafted, then if the employee asks for written reasons for his dismissal (from 1 June 1976), the employer should merely refer the employee to the warnings.

6   Because the written warnings have a double effect — both to make the dismissal potentially fair (in compliance with the Code of Industrial Relations Practice), and to provide the basis of written reasons for dismissal (which inevitably are sought by an employee who has litigation in mind), these warnings should be most carefully drafted. They should, in general, specify with precision the conduct complained of. The employee will know then what is required of him if he is to retain his job; and the employer will have documentary evidence of the type, nature and date of the complaint.

\*   \*   \*

## 76   Warning — misconduct

I must warn you that if you persist in . . . we shall have no alternative other than to give you your notice. I do hope that this will not become necessary.

## 77   Alternative warning

We have now warned you on many occasions that we are dissatisfied with . . . . Unless the situation improves, we will have no alternative other than to dismiss you. Please take this warning seriously.

NOTES:

*1   A warning — or many warnings — may not justify dismissal, either summarily or with notice. The warnings themselves may be unreasonable or insufficient. Everything depends upon the facts of the particular case. However, the more warnings that are given, and the stronger the terms, the more likely it is that the Tribunal would regard the employer's behaviour as 'fair', if he eventually does have to dismiss.*

*2   As with agreements, so with warnings — there is no law which says that they have to be in writing. But a written warning is not only admissible in evidence but essential, where possible.*

## 78   First warning

Your foreman has now spoken to you several times about . . . . The management take these breaches of the works' rules extremely seriously and I must warn you that if there is any repetition, your employment may be terminated.

Please do not behave in the same way again/again give us cause for complaint in this regard.


## 79   Second warning

I refer to my letter of . . . , in which I complained to you about your misconduct in respect of . . . .

I regret that I have received a further complaint of the same kind. Bearing in mind that your conduct improved for several months/over six months (*or as the case may be*), it has been decided not to take further disciplinary action on this occasion/not to discharge you from the company's service on this occasion, as we would have been entitled to do.

I understand from your foreman/from the personnel manager that you have promised that there will be no further repetition of the conduct complained of. I hope that this is correct because although we have been lenient on this occasion, it is most unlikely that the company would be willing to tolerate any further repetition of this conduct.


## 80   Stale warning – renewed

I appreciate that since my letter to you of . . . , you have desisted from . . ./not again offended against the company's rules by . . . .

I was therefore most sorry to learn from Mr . . ./your personnel manager that he had once again found it necessary to complain that you have . . . .

After careful consideration, I have decided not to terminate your employment on this occasion, but I must once again warn you that any repetition is likely to lead to the end of your service with this company.


## 81   Reply to warning

I was most surprised to receive your letter dated . . . , containing a threat of dismissal.

As I explained to Mr . . . when he saw me, I deny that I

have been guilty of the alleged or any breach of the works'
rules. The situation is as follows:-
    1 ...
    2 ...
    3 ...
I wish to place on record my dismay that you should have
seen fit to write to me in the manner concerned, without
even having discussed the matter with me. I regard this as
most unfair.
I shall be glad to discuss this matter with you, if you wish.
We have always had a most happy relationship in the past
and I can assure you that I shall not allow this apparent
misunderstanding to interfere with my determination to continue to give loyal and vigorous service to the company.

NOTE:
*A warning should be answered, in kind and in writing.*


## 82   Record of warnings

I regret to inform you that I have had to warn Mr ... on
a number of occasions regarding his behaviour, and the time
has now come for the disciplinary procedure to be put into
action. Details of warnings are as follows:
    1 ...
    2 ...
    3 ...


## 83   Warning of dismissal after refusing alternative job for age or health

I was very sorry that you have so far turned down the offer
of a job as .... I appreciate that the pay is lower than demanded by your present position — but unfortunately, as you
know, your health/age is such that I do not feel that you are
able to cope with your present job. The alternative offer is
made because we want to be as helpful as possible and to
avoid the necessity of having to terminate your services.
I must ask you, though, to reconsider your refusal. Failure
to accept the alternative position will leave me with no alternative other than to give you your notice — a step which I

would greatly regret.

Please do call to see me, whenever you wish, so that we can discuss the position.

With best wishes.

## 84    Technical changes — warning: demotion or dismissal

Unfortunately, you have not been able to cope with the results of our switch to automation/introduction of new techniques/machinery — but we are anxious to help you, if we possibly can. It was for that reason that I was authorised/ instructed to offer you the post of . . . .

It is most regrettable that you have declined to accept our offer because if you persist in that refusal, I shall have no alternative other than to terminate your employment. It is not possible to keep you on at your present job; the new job carries less pay but reduced responsibility; and I do ask you to reconsider the position very carefully and to let me know your decision as soon as possible.

NOTE:
*If you force a person into a lower paid job, you are in effect dismissing him. Are you able to prove that the dismissal was 'fair'?*

## 85    Impending dismissal

As you know, we are affected by the current recession in the trade and are likely to have to cut down our payroll, before long. In the circumstances, we are trying to give our employees the maximum possible warning, in the hope that they may find other jobs in the area. If you find one, then we shall be pleased to provide you with a reference.

We are very sorry that the situation has come to the present pass — but it is not of our making.

With our best wishes to you.

NOTE:
*This letter does not amount to a 'dismissal'. If an employee leaves, having been warned of impending dismissal — or, for that matter, that redundancies are on the way — he loses his rights either to redundancy pay or to compensation for unfair dismissal. In the former case, a man*

*has to prove that he was 'dismissed' — at which stage a redundancy will be presumed. In the latter case, he must also show that he was 'dismissed' before his employer has to show that the dismissal was 'fair'. Any employee who jumps the gun does so at his own risk.*

# Chapter 11

# Fair dismissal with notice

In the past, an employee's only protection against the miseries of dismissal was the length of his period of notice. He now has two cushions — redundancy pay — and compensation for 'unfair dismissal', which he can claim whether or not he has been given notice.

It follows that while there are still occasions when it is advisable to give no reasons in your letter of dismissal, it is often wise to be specific, and to indicate your reasons, so that if the employee does make a complaint to an Industrial Tribunal, you will be able to show both reason and consistency and he will not need to request written reasons.

Naturally, if you dismiss an employee summarily you will not say to him: 'If you sue me for damages, this letter indicates the defences which I will raise'. But you should still make those reasons plain in your letter, where possible,

There are circumstances in which you have been told by an employee — or by his union representative — that if you do give notice, you will be taken to the Tribunal. In that case, it becomes all the more important for you to express yourself clearly, concisely and firmly in your letter. This will be taken before the Tribunal — unless, of course, the case is settled before reaching that stage. So take care.

## 86   Dismissal with notice

Please treat this letter as notice to terminate your employment on the . . . , in accordance with your Contract of Service.

NOTE:
*Any employee at any level is entitled to his agreed notice; in the absence of agreement, to reasonable notice; in any event not less than the statutory minimum periods now laid down by* The Contracts of Employment Act, 1972, *as amended by the Employment Protection Act: after four weeks, one week's notice; after two years, two weeks, after three years, three weeks; and so on adding a week a year up to twelve weeks after twelve years.*

## 87 Dismissal of director with reasonable notice

I am instructed to give you notice to terminate your service with the company. As no period of notice was agreed with you when you were appointed to the Board of the company, you are entitled to reasonable notice. As it is the wish of all your colleagues on the Board that the company should act towards you in as generous a manner as possible the period of notice will be . . . .

Please forgive the formality of this letter, but from your viewpoint as well as that of the company, it is as well to give this notice in a proper form.

## 88 No accrued holiday pay where dismissal for misconduct

Thank you for your letter. You have received everything to which you are entitled. I would refer you to the written particulars of your contract of employment, supplied to you in accordance with *The Contracts of Employment Act, 1972.* You will see therefrom that where the company dismisses an employee as a result of his misconduct, the employee forfeits any right, which he would otherwise have, to accrued holiday money. As you well know, you were dismissed for serious misconduct and we are not prepared to waive our normal rule on this occasion.

## 89 Lack of 'capability' – insufficient 'skill'

Unfortunately, the series of unhappy accidents in which you have recently been involved have made it plain that you no longer possess the skill necessary for the carrying out of your work. It is therefore with the greatest regret that I must ask you to treat this letter as giving you notice, to terminate your employment on the . . . . You will appreciate that you are entitled under your contract of employment to . . . weeks notice.

I would only add that were it possible to find other work for you within our business, we would have been happy to do so. Unfortunately, no such work is available.

We wish you success in the future.

NOTES:

*1    If an employer wishes to show that dismissal was 'fair' he must show one of the specified reasons, or some other 'substantial reason'. The first such reason given is one which 'relates to the capability . . . of the employee for performing work of the kind which he was employed by the employer to do'.*

*2    'Capability' is defined as meaning 'capability as assessed by reference to skill, aptitude, health or any other physical or mental quality'.*

*3    When an employee is dismissed because he does not possess the requisite skill, this is very often in no way his fault.*

*4    Even if you can prove one of the specified reasons, you will still have to pay compensation, if the employee suffers loss as a result of his dismissal, unless you can show that the dismissal was 'fair'. The Tribunal will consider whether 'in the circumstances the employer acted reasonably or unreasonably as treating that reason as a sufficient one for dismissing the employee; and that question shall be determined in accordance with equity and the substantial merits of the case'.*

*5    In other words, a Tribunal will ask: Was the dismissal fair in all the circumstances? Did the employer act 'reasonably'?*

*If you dismiss a man because he did not possess the requisite skill, then it may be unreasonable to do so if there is other work available for him — so it is wise in the letter to indicate that such work could not be provided. And in all such cases (as in the ones now following) I advise the maximum possible generosity in the periods of notice actually given — which, in my opinion, should (out of both kindness and for tactical reasons ) exceed the minimum required in the circumstances.*

## 90    Lack of 'qualification'

Unfortunately, due to the introduction of the new machinery/equipment, you are no longer qualified to carry out your duties. We have offered you the opportunity to undergo a training course, at our expense, so as to equip you to do your work in the new circumstances, but you have declined to accept our offer.

In the circumstances, please treat this letter as notice to terminate your contract of employment as at the . . . . By giving you . . . weeks notice — instead of the . . . weeks, as required by your contract of employment – we hope that this will enable you to obtain other work, for which you remain qualified. We thank you for your co-operation during the time that you have been with us.

NOTES:

*1 Lack of 'qualification' may be a good reason for 'fair' dismissal – normally with notice. 'Qualifications' are defined as meaning 'any degree, diploma or other academic technical or professional qualification relevant to the position which the employee held'.*

*2 In industries in which there are frequent technological changes – and even in offices or businesses where computers are introduced – this ground of dismissal is fairly common. It is unlikely that a Tribunal would regard lack of qualifications as forming a reasonable ground for dismissal unless the employee has (where possible) been given the opportunity of acquiring the qualifications he needs. The longer his service with the company, the more important it becomes to allow him to obtain the necessary training – or at least, in the letter of dismissal, to indicate why such training was not undergone.*

## 91   'Capability' and 'qualification' combined

As discussed with you, when you called on me this morning, I regret very much that your health, combined with your lack of technical qualification, have forced us to terminate your services. In the circumstances, please treat this letter as notice, terminating on . . . .

NOTES:

*1 If there has been an oral discussion, then by all means refer to it. It shows that you have at least taken the trouble to see the employee – and this sort of opening may be used in all similar circumstances.*

*2 If you have more than one reason for the dismissal, say so. If you come before a Tribunal and wish to add reasons which were not set out in your original letter, you may find your case disbelieved.*

## 92   Lack of 'aptitude'

I am sorry that you do not possess the aptitude necessary

to deal with the tasks allocated to you. I hope that you will be successful in finding other work elsewhere, more in your line. As I told you this morning, the company will not require your services after the . . . of this month.

NOTE:
*You do not need to go into details — but if there are specific, vital tasks with which your employee could not cope, then you may wish to say so in your letter.*

## 93  'Physical or mental quality'

We had all hoped that you would manage to cope with your job — but this has proved impossible. So I must give you notice terminating your employment on . . . . If you would like to discuss this or any other matter with me, please do not hesitate to call on me in my office.

NOTE:
*It is sometimes kind to say little — and most Tribunals will accept this as a reason for putting little into a letter. You may not wish to tell an employee that he is 'getting beyond it' — or that some physical or mental incapacity prevents him from doing his work properly. Still less may you wish to put this into writing. But in those circumstances you should keep a note on your file, attached to the letter. This could be merely a memo, for yourself — or for those who succeed you. It could be a note addressed to your superior. Thus:*

## 94   Note of reasons, to superior

I enclose herewith a copy of a letter which I have today handed to Harry Smith. The unfortunate chap is still suffering from . . . . He cannot do his job properly. Indeed, his lack of concentration is proving a danger to other employees. But I have thought it best not to say too much in this letter. I do not want to upset him — he is a good man.

I hope that you will also approve of my having given him a good deal longer notice than is strictly required.

NOTE:
*Be sure to keep a copy of all letters, notes and memoranda. Careful*

*filing now can save both money and worry at a later stage. Documents win cases. Remember – you may be forced to reveal at any hearing nearly any document that is relevant, however private.*

## 95 Misconduct

I have now had to warn you on at least . . . occasions about your carelessness. This not only causes danger to yourself but also to fellow employees. In the circumstances, I feel that I have no alternative other than to terminate your employment forthwith. I enclose herewith your pay in lieu of notice – although I think it right to point out that having regard to the persistent and habitual nature of your misconduct, I take the view that the company would have been entitled to dismiss you summarily. However, it is appreciated that there are mitigating circumstances in your case, and we do in particular know that you have not been in good health. So, *without prejudice to the company's rights,* I am pleased to be able to enclose a cheque herewith in the sum of £ . . . , details of which are contained in the attached slip. You will appreciate that this also includes your accrued holiday pay as at the date when your notice terminates.

NOTES:

*1    It is vital to appreciate that where you give notice or pay in lieu, in circumstances in which you would have been entitled to dismiss summarily, this should be stated in your letter – for your own protection.*

*2    By all means give details of the misconduct, at greater length, if you wish. The letters which now follow briefly indicate the sort of minor misconduct which would have led, before the Act, to dismissal with notice – and which you must now hope would be sufficiently 'habitual' or 'persistent' to enable you to satisfy a Tribunal, if necessary, that it was 'fair'.*

*One reason which may warrant 'fair' dismissal 'relates to the conduct of the employee'. This will not mean any 'misconduct' – we are all capable of having an occasional 'off day' – and any employee may be guilty of a momentary slip or an occasional misdemeanour. To warrant 'summary dismissal' – with neither notice nor pay in lieu – misconduct must be sufficiently serious as to amount to a 'repudiation by the employee of his contract of service'. A Tribunal is likely to regard a reason 'relating to the conduct of the employee' as warranting dismissal* with notice, when it is somewhat less serious than that which warrants summary dismissal — but not much less. You must prepare your letter of dismissal accordingly.

## 96   Poor timekeeping

I have now warned you on at least . . . occasions that your failure to arrive at work on time was disrupting our production. I have also told you that if this continued, I would have to give you your notice. I must now do so. Your employment with the company will terminate on . . . .

I would only add that we do fully appreciate your difficulties, as you live so far from the plant. It is for this reason that we have been exceptionally patient in your case.

## 97   Alternative — extended lunches

Despite frequent warnings, you have seen fit to return late from lunch — culminating this week with your being over . . . late, on . . . days. In the circumstances, I enclose herewith your pay in lieu of notice. We shall no longer be requiring your services.

NOTES:

*1   Warnings may not of themselves be enough to warrant dismissal. But if you have warned, say so.*

*2   Subject to the new minimum two weeks' pay under a 'basic award', compensation for 'unfair dismissal' is only available to compensate ex-employees for financial loss suffered (including, now, loss of redundancy entitlement.) If your secretary finds other work during the period of notice represented by her pay in lieu — or, of course, by such period of notice as you see fit to give her — then she will no more get compensation than she would otherwise obtain damages for summary dismissal.*

## 98   Redundancy

As we indicated to you some time ago, it has become inevitable that your department must be closed. You will therefore be dismissed and made redundant as from . . . . I enclose herewith a calculation of the redundancy pay to which you will become entitled.

We all greatly regret this end to our long and happy association — and I wish you good luck in the future.

## 99 Secrets

I am very sorry that we have been unable to obtain the necessary clearance for you — and in view of the top secret work which we are now carrying out, I regret that I have no alternative other than forthwith to give you your severance pay, equivalent to the period of notice prescribed in your contract of service. The company cheque herewith also includes accrued holiday money. Details as to the manner in which the sum is arrived at are attached hereto.

Please return the company's car to our transport depot at . . . , not later than . . . , being the date when your notice would otherwise have expired.

I would like to add my personal regrets — but you will appreciate that this is a matter entirely beyond my control, or, indeed, that of the company.

NOTES:

*1 Dismissal will normally be fair if 'the employee could not continue to work in the position which he held without contravention (either on his part or on that of his employer) of a duty or restriction imposed by or under an enactment'.*

*2 Apart from security problems, this ground will probably apply most often if you employ a foreigner, whose work permits expire.*

*3 You should, of course, consider whether you would not have other work in your concern, suitable for the employee in question, and in which his employment would not be 'in contravention of a duty or restriction' imposed on you. You will still have to prove that — 'in accordance with equity and the substantial merits of the case' — you acted reasonably in dismissing the employee.*

## 100    Denial that dismissal is because employee intends to join union

Thank you for your letter. It is not correct that you were dismissed because of your intention to join the . . . Union. The reasons for your dismissal are set out in my letter to you of the . . . . Any employee of this company is fully entitled to join an independent union, as he sees fit. Your dismissal was completely irrespective of your intentions regarding union membership.

## 101    Redundancy — other employees kept on

I agree that there is a redundancy situation in the plant and that other employees who could have been dismissed have in fact been kept on. But this does not mean that you were dismissed 'unfairly'. I suggest that you consult your union representative.

As you know, we are doing our best to cope with a substantial decrease in trade, and I am only sorry that it has been necessary to dismiss a portion of our work force. I do hope that you will succeed in obtaining other work, at an early date.

NOTES:

*1   If it is shown that 'the circumstances constituting the redundancy applied equally to one or more other employees in the same undertaking who held positions similar to that held by the dismissed employee, and who have not been dismissed by the employer', then the dismissal may be regarded as 'unfair', even if the man was redundant.*

*2   If your employee is dismissed as redundant after only a comparatively brief period (perhaps two and a half years) — so that his redundancy pay is comparatively small — and is then out of work for (perhaps) two years — he would probably be much better off to get his remedy for unfair dismissal.*

## 102    Pay in lieu — no reason stated

Your employment with the Company will terminate on the . . . , expiry of . . . days/weeks/months from your next pay day, the . . . . I enclose herewith your appropriate pay in lieu of notice; your accrued holiday entitlement; and your documents.

NOTE:
*See Chapter 13 – written reasons must now be given, at employee's request.*

## 103 Take notice – with regrets

I must regretfully inform you that I am required (by the Board) to give you notice to terminate your employment by the above company. According to your contract, you are entitled to only the minimum periods as laid down by *The Contracts of Employment Act, 1972,* as amended. As you have been with us over four weeks but less than two years, that entitlement is seven days' notice. But I am pleased to extend that period to fourteen days, in your case.

NOTES:
*1 This letter still gives no reason for the notice. It is best used in cases where there has been no misconduct, but where lack of 'capability' or 'qualification' is relied upon (see later in this Chapter). Of course, if you do rely upon misconduct, it is not wise to send a letter which shows cordiality.*

*2 The fact that a contract of service provides for a period of notice never prevents you from giving more. Good employers often do so – and nowadays, generosity of this sort is not entirely altruistic in any case where the employer may have difficulty in proving that he dismissed 'fairly'. After all, he may have to pay compensation in the long run – and he is meanwhile not only giving both appearance and substance to his statement that he acted 'fairly in all the circumstances', but he is also giving his employee further paid time within which to find alternative employment. An employee remains (as before) under an obligation to mitigate his loss, as best he can.*

## 104 Dismissal – no notice required

I am instructed to give you notice, terminating your employment as from the end of this week. You will appreciate that your contract of employment provided that you were entitled to minimum periods of notice as prescribed by *The Contracts of Employment Act, 1972,* as amended. As you have been with us less than 4 weeks, you are not, strictly speaking, entitled to any notice at all. However, we hope that by giving you the best part of a week, this will enable you to obtain alternative employment.

## 105   Notice to terminate contract of employment — of executive

I must ask you to treat this letter as notice terminating your employment in accordance with your contract, at the end of the period of . . . months from . . . , your next pay day.

NOTES:

*1   A variety of letters of dismissal are offered in this book — please see Index. You must consider in each case whether or not to include details of the reasons for the dismissal.*

*2   The employee's rights accrue only if he is 'dismissed'. However harshly or kindly that dismissal is effected, if 'the contract under which he is employed by the employer is terminated by the employer, whether it is so terminated by notice or without notice . . . or if under his contract of employment he is employed for a fixed term and that term expires without being renewed under the same contract . . .' or if he leaves when he is entitled to do so because of his employer's conduct, he is dismissed.*

*3   You could probably give notice commencing from the date of the letter if you serve letter on the recipient that day. But it is preferable to do so from the next day.*

## 106   With kindness

I am very sorry that it has become necessary for me to give you notice, in accordance with the terms of your contract. Your contract will therefore terminate on the . . . .

I do hope that you will be able to obtain alternative employment, at an early date — and if I can be of help to you in any way, please do not hesitate to let me know.

NOTE:
*After a letter like this, it will be impossible to allege successfully that the employee was dismissed because of any misconduct.*

## 107 Notice by employee to terminate contract earlier than expiry of notice

I hereby give notice to terminate my contract of employment on the . . . , which is a date earlier than the Company's notice to me . . . dated the . . . is due to expire.
With best wishes.

NOTES:
*1 An employee may jump the gun by giving written notice to his employer, to terminate his contract. There is no rule (as in the case of redundancy payments – Chapter 21) under which the employer has power to serve a counter-notice, requiring the employee to stay on until his period of notice expires.*

*2 There is no specific 'prescribed form' for an employee's letter in the above circumstances – any words will do. In general, the briefer the letter, the better. But note: If the reason why the employee wishes to leave before his notice expires is that he proposes to take on another job, his loss as a result of the dismissal will be greatly reduced, and if he obtains other work at the same or at a higher rate of pay, it will disappear altogether. He may then have been unfairly dismissed, but he can only get a 'basic award' – two weeks' pay at up to £80 a week plus his lost redundancy entitlement. Anyway, he must 'mitigate his loss' – as in the case of any other contractual breach. Hence, if he is taking a job at a lower rate of pay, the following letter is suggested:*

## 108 Employee jumps the gun – to obtain lower paid job

I am happy to say that I have obtained another post, and I shall therefore be leaving prior to the expiry of the period of notice which has been given to me by the Company. My new employment starts on the . . . , and I shall therefore be leaving on the . . . .
Unfortunately, I shall not be earning the same salary/

receiving the same pay/remuneration/commission/terms, as I
was receiving while working for your Company. The above
notice is without prejudice to any claim which I may here-
after find it necessary to bring, for a basic or a compensatory
award for unfair dismissal.

NOTE:
*The employee must still give the amount of notice required by his
contract of service.*

## 109 Allegation that employee has failed to 'mitigate his loss'

I was concerned to learn that you had rejected the offer of
employment made to you by . . . . Where an employee is dismissed, he is bound to mitigate his loss, if he reasonably can.
You have been given the opportunity to keep that loss to the
minimum — and if you see fit to carry out your threat and to
institute proceedings for 'unfair dismissal' (as, of course, you
are fully entitled to do), not only will the Company deny that
your dismissal was 'unfair', but it will also contend that you
have failed to mitigate your loss as you could have done.

## 110 Employee's reply — alternative job not reasonably comparable

I agree that I have been offered a job by . . . . But my
status, responsibility and pay would not be comparable to
those which I enjoyed while with the Company. I appreciate
that it may be difficult for me to replace my former position
with one which is as satisfactory, but I am certainly not prepared to down-grade myself, without at least a very firm
effort to re-establish myself at a reasonably comparable level.
Incidentally, if I were to accept a lower paid job without
seeking a better one, I suspect that you would then criticise
me for not having taken more energetic steps to mitigate my
loss.

NOTES:
*1   While an employee who seeks either damages for wrongful dismissal
or compensation for unfair dismissal must do what he can to keep his*

*loss to the minimum, this does not mean that he must take either the first job offered to him or one which would result in a vast change in his status. To take an obvious example, a Member of the Board need not accept work as a lift attendant.*

*2 Naturally, the question as to whether a dismissed employee has acted reasonably is one of fact, depending on all the circumstances of the case.*

## 111 Allegation that dismissed employee has brought about his own downfall

I fully appreciate how you feel. But the circumstances of which you complain were, in our view, entirely brought about by your own actions. In particular, I would refer to the following:

(a) . . .
(b) . . .
(c) . . .

I am sorry that the situation has reached this unhappy state. It is not of the Company's making.

## 112 Reply to allegation of 'contributory' actions

I vehemently deny that the alleged or any actions on my part have caused or contributed to the situation which led to my unfair dismissal by the Company. The facts are as follows:

(a) . . .
(b) . . .
(c) . . .

NOTES:

*1 If the employer's letter gives details of the allegations, then the employee's reply should do the same. Conversely, if the employer's letter is brief and unparticularised, a simple denial will do. This would be the same as the above draft, without the second (or the numbered) paragraphs.*

*2 It must be re-emphasised that when the executive – or any other employee – is attempting to protect his position, the basic rule remains the same: He is not bound to put anything into writing, but if he does so, he will find that a Tribunal is more likely to accept his case. On the other hand, anything he does commit to paper must be thoroughly accurate and carefully thought out.*

3   *It follows that if a letter is likely to find its way to Court, it is often wise to have it drafted by a solicitor – even if it is signed by the actual or potential litigant. There is no law which says that lawyers' letters must be signed by them. In practice, there are many occasions when they simply advise on the letter which the client should write – or draft that letter for his signature. So if you receive a well-drafted letter – either from the Company or from an employee – you may well suspect (correctly) the hidden hand of the lawyer.*

# Chapter 12

# Exclusion from unfair dismissal protection

Certain categories of employee are excluded from protection under the unfair dismissal provisions. These include wives and husbands, those outside Great Britain or on board ship, people above retiring age and part-timers.

The current minimum working hours of part-timers necessary to qualify for protection under the unfair dismissal provisions is 16 hours, or 8 hours after 5 years' service, as from 1 February 1977.

\* \* \*

## 113 Part-time employees

As you work for us under a contract which 'normally involves employment for less than 16 hours weekly', you could not under any circumstances qualify for compensation for unfair dismissal. By all means consult your solicitors, as you suggest. To assist them, I enclose herewith a list of the actual hours which you have worked during the past 52 weeks.

NOTES:

*1   Here is yet another incentive to employ part-timers − for less than a normal 16 hour week.*

*2   If a part-timer is employed occasionally − or seasonally − for more than 16 hours a week, provided that his 'normal' working hours are less than this maximum, he will not get compensation for 'unfair dismissal', under any circumstances.*

*3   After five years continuous employment, the part timer is covered if he works 8 hours a week.*

## 114   Part-time — over 16 hours at Christmas

I agree that during the Christmas season you worked well over 16 hours — but this was an abnormal situation. Your work normally involves employment for less than 16 hours a week. In the circumstances, quite apart from our vehement denial that you were unfairly dismissed, it is our view that you could not conceivably obtain compensation for unfair dismissal against the company.

## 115   Part-time — special pressures

Although you were good enough to put in a full working day during the recent rush job, you were normally employed for less than 16 hours a week. In the circumstances, your claim for compensation for alleged 'unfair dismissal' cannot possibly be accepted.

I would add that in any event your dismissal was because of the manner in which you carried out your job, and was not 'unfair', in any sense of that word.

## 116   Five years' continuous employment — 8 hours work

Having now worked with the company for over five years, I am covered by unfair dismissal protection because I normally work over 8 hours a week. In the circumstances, I would invite you to reconsider your decision not to pay me compensation for unfair dismissal; I am putting in a written application for a basic and for a compensatory award, so as to protect my position; I shall be pleased to discuss the matter with you — or, in due course, with the conciliation officer; and I look forward to hearing from you as soon as possible.

## 117   Wives — and husbands

I agree that as a result of our unhappy matrimonial disputes it became impossible to employ you any longer in my business, and you were dismissed accordingly. But I am told that where the employer is the husband or wife of the employee, no remedy for 'unfair dismissal' could be obtained, even if the dismissal were (as I deny) unfair.

NOTES:

*1 The above exception applies where you employ your wife – but not where your company does so. It protects the individual and not the corporate employer.*

*2 The equivalent exception for 'close relatives' was removed by the Employment Protection Act.*


## 118 Small businesses

You were not dismissed unfairly. In any event, I am told that the Trade Union and Labour Relations Act excludes anyone employed in an undertaking which, immediately before the effective date of the termination of employment, employed less than four people who had been continuously employed for not less than 13 weeks. We have only ever had three people in our business.

NOTES:

*1 This exclusion will disappear – probably in 1977 – thanks to the Employment Protection Act.*

*2 The above exception is intended to exclude small businesses. It matters not, though. whether employees are 'employed at the same place . . . or at different places'. So employees who may actually work in a place with only a couple of colleagues may still be protected by the Act, provided that the business employs, in the aggregate, four or more people.*

*3 Those who normally work less than 16 hours a week (or 8 after 5 years' service) are not included in the reckoning.*


## 119 Employees outside Great Britain

I appreciate your feelings about your dismissal – although I cannot agree that you have been unfairly treated in any way. In any event, under your contract of employment you ordinarily worked outside Great Britain and in the circumstances there can be no question of a successful claim by you for compensation for unfair dismissal. I am sorry that our relationship should have to end on this note.

NOTE:
*The 'unfair dismissal' provisions do not apply 'to any employment where, under his contract of employment, the employee ordinarily works outside Great Britain'. This does not include people who 'ordinarily work' in Great Britain but are required to do jobs abroad — even if they are overseas for some considerable time. There will, of course, be many borderline cases.*

## 120   On board ship

I appreciate that you were employed to work on board a ship registered in the UK. But the Trade Union and Labour Relations Act provides that where the employment is wholly outside Great Britain or the claimant is not ordinarily resident in Great Britain, he is to be registered as a person who under his contract of employment 'ordinarily works' outside Great Britain. You have not only been employed wholly outside Great Britain but are ordinarily resident, I understand, in . . . . In the circumstances, even if (which is denied) you would otherwise be entitled to compensation for unfair dismissal, you come within one of the exclusions provided by the Act.

## 121   Above retiring age — man

You were dismissed after reaching the age of 65 and in the circumstances there is no possible question of compensation for 'unfair dismissal'. We would like to point out, in any event, that we kept you on beyond retiring age because of our high regard for you — and we feel that we have acted more than fairly in your case. And we hope that on reflection you may agree.

## 122   Above retiring age — woman

Once a woman attains the age of 60, she is no longer protected against 'unfair dismissal'. So as you were beyond retirement age when you were dismissed, the unfair dismissal rule cannot help you.

In any event, I cannot agree that you were dealt with unfairly. We in fact kept you on as long as we possibly could. And you were given more than the required period of notice when we decided that you would have to leave us.

I am sorry that I cannot be of help to you.

NOTE:

*The upper ages are the normal retiring ages applicable in the business, or 65 for men, 60 for women. There is no lower age limit (for redundancy pay, you have to be at least 20 – having continuously served for two years after reaching your eighteenth birthday). The absence of a lower age limit is particularly relevant when considering the rights of apprentices.*

# Chapter 13

# Written statements of reasons for dismissal

The Employment Protection Act requires employers to state in writing their reasons for dismissal — if an employee of 6 months standing makes a written request for such reasons. Until the Act, an employer could dismiss without stating reasons — sometimes in the hope that such reasons would appear, after the employee had gone, e.g. ex-colleague says: 'I am glad that you got rid of John Smith. Did you know that he . . .', followed by a series of revelations of misdemeanours which could be revealed about an ex-colleague, but not in the form of a 'grass' on a current fellow servant.

Naturally, if the employer was sued for damages for wrongful dismissal, i.e. where he was allegedly not given his proper notice or pay in lieu, or where he claimed compensation for unfair dismissal, whether or not his notice was adequate, the employer who wished to avoid payment had to give reasons. But by then, he could have assembled his weaponry at his leisure.

Reasons may have to be stated clearly and in advance. This requires considerable care. Naturally, if there has been previous correspondence or (in particular) any written warning of intended dismissal (see Chapter 10), this should be referred to. And in any event, while the employee will be entitled to advance written particulars of the reason why he is to lose his livelihood, these may be used in arrear — against the employer, in a claim for damages or compensation. Therefore the writing must be produced with great care.

Conversely, if the written reasons are sufficiently precise or imprecise (that is, giving room for manoeuvre, if necessary), they may not only help the employer to win his case but avoid that case altogether. If the employee can see that the employer's defences are visibly and provably impenetratable, he may prefer to avoid battle.

Here are some suggested written statements — for especially careful adapting to the circumstances.

\* \* \*

## 123  'Incapability'

You have asked me to put in writing the reason for your dismissal.

As you know, you have not been coping with your job as you used to. We accept that this was due to advancing years/ your ill health – but making all possible allowances and putting up with the situation for as long as we could, we eventually came to the reluctant decision that we could not retain your services.

With kind regards.

## 124   Ill health or old age – brief

The reason (as requested by you) for your dismissal was (as you know) that your capability for carrying out your work had been severely affected by age and ill health.

NOTE:

*1   There is likely to be guidance or a code of practice, put out by the Advisory, Conciliation and Arbitration Service – if in doubt, enquire from the ACAS whether this is yet available. But whatever instructions come from above, all that will be required is that you state – clearly and effectively – the reason for the dismissal. You will not be forced to write a book about it. Better to be criticised for brevity than to destroy your case through excess wordage.*

*2   If you are depriving an employee of his livelihood, then you should not be allowed to do so without giving him the opportunity to protest, to appeal, to know your alleged reasons. Which is fair.*

## 125   Technical qualification

When we modernised our administration, we tried to train our existing employees to do the work in the new way – and most of them managed to adapt themselves. Unfortunately, you did not. As you neither had nor are able to acquire the necessary technical qualifications for coping with the work, we felt that we had no alternative but to give you your notice.

## 126   Conduct

The reason for your dismissal was your conduct. Briefly,

the company's main complaints were:

 *(a)* . . .
 *(b)* . . .
 *(c)* . . .

### 127 Illegal to employ

You have been given your notice because it is illegal for us to employ you. Your work permit has expired and in the circumstances it is not possible for us to keep you on without breaking the law.

### 128 Redundancy

The reason for your dismissal was that you were redundant. The reason why you have not received redundancy pay is that you had not been employed for the minimum two years. The minimum six-month period of continuous employment to which you refer applies only to the protection provided by the Trade Union and Labour Relations Act for people who are unfairly dismissed. It does not apply to a right to redundancy pay.

### 129 Denial of entitlement to written statement

Under the Employment Protection Act, you are only entitled to a written statement for the reasons for your dismissal if you have been continuously employed for at least 26 weeks ending with the last complete week before the effective date of the termination of your employment. You were only with us for . . . weeks — and therefore you are not entitled to a written statement. Nor, of course, are you protected by the unfair dismissal rules in the Trade Union and Labour Relations Act.

I would only add that it is denied that you were in fact dismissed unfairly, as alleged or at all.

## 130   Reasonable to refuse — breach of confidence

We are not willing to provide a written statement of the reasons for the termination of your employment because to do so would involve us in a breach of confidence.

## 131   Reasonable refusal — medical

Save that the dismissal was on medical grounds, we are not prepared to provide the written statement that you request. If, as you threaten, you present a complaint to an Industrial Tribunal — as you are fully entitled to do — we shall maintain that our refusal to give further details was in the circumstances wholly reasonable.

NOTE:

*If a Tribunal finds that a written statement was unreasonably refused, then the employee will be entitled to the equivalent of two weeks' pay by way of compensation. But if you can satisfy the Tribunal that your refusal was 'reasonable', you will be in the clear. Reasonableness (as usual) is a question of fact.*

## 132   Reference to written warning

You were given written warnings of intended dismissal on the following dates:
(1) . . .
(2) . . .
(3) . . .
In those letters, I clearly stated the conduct complained of and that if this continued, the company would have no alternative other than to dismiss you. The conduct did continue and you were accordingly dismissed.

## 133   Alternative — reference to written warning

In reply to your letter of the . . . , requesting written reasons for your dismissal, I must refer you to my letter dated . . . . In that letter, I warned you that if the conduct therein complained of persisted, you would be dismissed.

You did not mend your ways. The company therefore
carried out its stated intention.


## 134   As warned — but additional reasons

Thank you for your letter requesting written reasons for
your dismissal. You were dismissed because in spite of my
letters to you dated . . . and . . . , you persisted in the conduct
therein complained of. In addition, the situation was made
worse by the following matters:
1    You were late at work on the following occasions . . . .
2    You failed to attend work on the following occasions,
     and did not produce a medical certificate. . . .
3    . . . .

# Chapter 14

# Demotion — and dismissal

An employee who is prepared to accept demotion is agreeing to a variation of his contract of service. He will not then be able to claim that he has been 'dismissed' — so he will have no claim to compensation for 'unfair dismissal'. Conversely: Demote with care. To reduce a man's status . . . his money . . . his future employability . . . could cost the company as much as £11,760.

Letters of demotion are potentially perilous.

\* \* \*

### 135 Concerning agreed demotion

I confirm our conversation — in which we agreed that you were not coping successfully with your job as . . . and that it would be better for all concerned — and in the interests of both yourself and the company — if we were to lift the burden of responsibility which has now rested on you for so long.

In the circumstances, it was agreed by us both that as from the . . . , you will serve as . . . at a salary/wage of £ . . . — and I feel sure that you will be much happier with this new arrangement. If you wish to see me in connection with the move or with your new job at any time, please do not hesitate to contact me.

With my best personal regards to you.

### 136 Demotion offered — no alternative

For reasons which I discussed with you, we are no longer prepared to keep you on in your present position of . . . . I fully appreciate the difficulties which you have had and am very sorry that this decision has become inevitable.

However, I am happy to confirm that we are prepared to move you across to the post of . . . — although necessarily not on quite the same terms. If you accept this change, your pay would be £ . . . per week/month — your period of notice will be . . . weeks/months; but in all other respects, your terms will be the same as previously.

I do hope that you will accept the alternative position. If not, then I am afraid that you must treat this letter as notice to terminate your employment on . . . . You will appreciate that you are, strictly speaking, entitled to only . . . weeks/months notice — and the notice which I am now giving you is much longer. But I would like to emphasise once again that the company will be happy to retain you in its service, in a job which would impose less heavy burdens on you.

Please would you let me know your decision as soon as possible.

### 137   A move — which equals demotion

I am writing to confirm our conversation about the opening of the company's new office/plant/premises/department. The company is anxious to make use of your considerable experience and knowledge and to put you in charge of the new enterprise. It is true, as you pointed out, that you would be supervising/managing less people than at present — but there would be no change in your remuneration or other terms of service. In the circumstances, I earnestly hope that you will agree to this move.

We have carefully considered your suggestion that the move be for a trial period, and are agreeable to this if necessary. But we would point out to you the disadvantages from your point of view. The element of permanence provides stability for all concerned.

I look forward to hearing from you,
With best wishes.

NOTE:
*However you may dress it up, the 'move' changes the employee's job — and is a dismissal in law. If you cannot obtain his agreement, then you either leave him where he is or, if you insist upon shifting him, then he will be entitled to regard that insistence as the destruction of his present contract of service. If he decides to claim compensation for unfair dismissal, then the burden of proving fairness will rest upon you.*

## 138   Refusal of demotion

I have carefully considered your suggestion that I should accept less responsibility — but after anxious thought, I must reject it. I have served the company loyally and well for . . . years; I have received no complaints — oral or written — concerning my work; and while I appreciate that it might suit the company's short-term interests that I be moved across into the position suggested, I respectfully disagree that the company would benefit in the long run, and in any event I am not prepared to accept what amounts to a demotion/serious loss of status.

I am sure that on reconsideration you will understand my decision — and I assure you that I will continue in the future, as in the past, to devote my energies to the company's service. With best wishes.


## 139   Confirming agreed demotion — elderly manager

I was very pleased to have been able to tell you that the company has found a niche for you as its . . . . You have served the company loyally and well for many years and I believe that this new post will bring you not only security but also satisfaction. I confirm that your revised terms of service are as follows:-

1    Remuneration: £ . . . per week/month/year.
2    Holidays increased to . . . weeks per year — and holiday pay pro rata, when your employment terminates for whatever reason.
3    Otherwise, on the same terms as previously.
With my best wishes to you.

# Chapter 15

# Admonition, warning, reproof and rebuke

One of the less happy jobs of every executive with subordinates working under him is the meting out of reproofs — which may be done orally on the traditional carpet, or in writing — probably so as to have the copy available as evidence. And the more elevated the subordinate, the greater the remedy he is entitled to win, if he is eventually dismissed 'unfairly'.

The letters that follow are designed as honest expressions of opinion, intended to produce results from the recipient or, at worst, a good impression on a tribunal or Court. They are written with one eye on the business and the other on the law. Some are alternatives to letters in Chapters 10 and 11.

\* \* \*

## 140   Mild reminder

May I remind you of our conversation? You did promise to ensure that . . . . I do hope that you will not forget.
With best wishes.

## 141   Mild rebuke

You did assure me that you would . . . . But this has not been done. Please would you have it put in hand without further delay?

## 142   Explanation, please

The Chairman asked you some weeks ago to . . . . But despite your assurance that the job would be carried out without further delay, it does not appear to have been done. What is your explanation, please?

## 143   Appeal for mending of ways

As you know, I am concerned for your position in the
company — and have been doing all that I can to turn away
the wrath of the . . . . But I am no longer having much success
in this. Please would you now ensure that . . . .

## 144   Excuses unacceptable

I have noted the excuses which you have presented to the
Board, for your failure to do . . . . In view of . . . , these are
totally unacceptable. In the circumstances, please would you
now . . . .

## 145   Time limit

The promised reorganisation of your department has now
taken . . . weeks/months, and is still not complete. I am
asked by the Board to inform you that they insist upon the
completion of the job within the next . . . days/weeks/by the
of this/next month.

## 146   Tearing off strips

The patience of the Board is now exhausted. The following matters require your immediate attention:
   *(a)* . . .
   *(b)* . . .
   *(c)* . . .

NOTE:
*Once you write details, these must be both accurate and provably so.
It may be that you will receive a letter in reply — but the chances are
that you will either get action or an oral retort. Your rule should be:
Either keep your rebukes to general terms or ensure that they are fair,
warranted, provable — and in moderate terms. An undignified loss of
control resulting in the vocal harangue will happily go unrecorded. Its
written equivalent can kill a case.*

## 147   Warning

The Board has noted with dismay the failure of your department to balance its accounts/complete its stock check/ meet its norm. I am instructed to warn you that if there is any recurrence, the most serious consequences will inevitably result.

NOTE:
*When employers can prove that they have given adequate warnings to dismissed employees, they seldom obtain compensation for unfair dismissal. And even if they do win their cases, the amount of compensation is generally reduced — the tribunal holds that the sacked man has 'contributed' to his own state of unemployment. So letters of warning are exceedingly important.*

## 148   Second warning

May I refer you to my letter of the . . . , in which I warned you of the inevitable consequences of your failure to . . . . Please may I have an immediate explanation — together with an assurance that there will be no further delay in . . . .

## 149   Final warning

I am instructed by the Board to give you one final oppor- tunity to carry out . . . in accordance with . . . .
Unless you comply with these requirements by . . . at the latest, the company will replace you with a . . . who is both willing and able to carry out the duties which have been en- trusted to you.

## 150   Dismissal — with reminder of warnings

I must now refer you to my letters of the . . . , the . . . , . . . and . . . , and to the warnings therein contained. The work/stock taking/job evaluation/. . . has not been completed, satisfactorily or at all. In the circumstances, your employ- ment is hereby terminated with effect from . . . . You will shortly receive the company's cheque in respect of all money due to you as at the date hereof, including salary and accrued holiday pay.

We trust that you will find some other post which suits you better, and are indeed sorry that our association must end in this manner.

NOTE:

*1 The employment has been terminated without notice – but it may well be that the company would prefer to give notice or pay in lieu.*

*2 Even when dismissing summarily and after many warnings, it does no harm to attempt to end the association on good terms. Hence the final sentence.*

# Chapter 16

# An executive's letters

Inevitably, a book of this sort is designed for executives in their business capacities. If, for instance, a man has to hire and fire, he must do his job as well and as fairly as he can – even if sometimes he finds it distasteful.

Similarly, the Trade Union and Labour Relations Act and the Employment Protection Act are law – and the executive must cope with them not only from his viewpoint as an employer's representative, but also from his own, as employee – however mighty.

Here, as an antidote to some of the miseries doled out to others, are some letters (additional to those scattered through this book) which the executive may like to use and to adapt for his own purposes, if he is dismissed. Naturally, the object of the exercise is to ensure that his dismissal is 'unfair' – and that he receives a handsome, tax-free sum if he cannot get other work. Remember – applications must still be made, wherever practicable, within three months from the date when the employment terminates. Delay too long and you may lose your rights.

\* \* \*

## 151 Claim by dismissed employee for compensation

I was shocked to be dismissed. The pay in lieu of notice which I received has in no way compensated me for the loss arising out of my dismissal. I have been unable to obtain other work at anything like the equivalent status or pay, and in the circumstances, I shall have to seek my remedy from the Industrial Tribunal.

I am advised that the burden of proving that the dismissal was 'fair' rests upon the company. I am also advised – and am confident – that this is a burden which the company will be unable to discharge.

I shall be pleased, in the circumstances, to receive an admission of liability from you. I shall then be prepared to discuss terms. We can, if necessary, call in a conciliation officer to approve them.

If this matter is not dealt with swiftly and satisfactorily, then I shall have no alternative other than to lay my complaint before a Tribunal.

This is indeed an unhappy ending to a long association.

NOTE:

*You may, of course, prefer to put the matter in the hands of your solicitors – and if there is much money involved, this may be wise. Thus:*

## 152   Threat to instruct solicitors

As you have not seen fit to make any substantial offer of compensation for my unfair dismissal, I have decided that I must put the matter in the hands of my solicitors. I have now been out of work for . . . . I have therefore lost £ . . . . As I have a wife and children to keep, I can delay my claim no longer.

I repeat: Unless I hear from you by return with a sensible and substantial offer, I shall pass the matter to my solicitors.

## 153   Denial of allegations made by employers

I am in receipt of your letter in which you see fit to allege that I have been dismissed for misconduct/lack of qualification/lack of aptitude. This allegation I strenuously deny. By any standard, my dismissal was as unfair as it was unexpected. Unless I hear from you with an offer of a very substantial payment, I shall bring a claim for unfair dismissal before the Industrial Tribunal.

NOTE:

*Just as it is important for employers to put their case on to paper as soon as possible, so it is vital for the employee to do the same. If you are dismissed in writing, then answer the letter – and keep a copy of the answer. Deal with any allegations made, as briefly and lucidly as you can.*

## 154   Executive unfairly dismissed

My dismissal has been unfair, in every sense of that word. I have been unable to find alternative employment. In the

circumstances, I shall apply to the Industrial Tribunal for
my full remedies.

It would, of course, enable me to mitigate my loss considerably if I were to obtain other work. Perhaps you would
bear this in mind, when you are next asked for a reference
for me. Meanwhile, I am informing prospective employers
that my . . . years of service with the Company are likely to
provide the best reference that I can get in the circumstances.


## 155   Passing the buck

Before I dismissed James Brown, I discussed the matter
with the Company solicitors/the Personnel Director/Mr . . . .
We both appreciate that there were risks involved in taking
this course, and that we might end up having to pay compensation for unfair dismissal. However, it was felt that this was
a risk worth taking in the circumstances.

With best wishes.

NOTE:
*In all borderline cases involving 'unfair dismissal', management should
confer – and, in general, advice should be taken either from a superior,
or from the Company's solicitor – or both. This is, of course, a form
of buck passing – but it is entirely legitimate. When you deal with unfair
dismissal, there is (potentially at least) over £10,000 at stake! and if
you are trying to cope with an actual or potential industrial dispute,
even an hour's break in production may cost the company a small
fortune.*

*Still, it is as well to do any buck passing with appropriate dignity –
and to attempt, where possible, to take your fair share of responsibility
and more. The above letter is intended to strike a sensible balance.*


## 156   Refusal to resign

I know that I have been overruled. I appreciate that I am
in a minority of one on the Board, but I adhere to my view
that the step which it is proposed to take is not in the interests
of the Company.

I shall not resign.

NOTE:
*Never resign unless you have actually got a better job to go to or unless you could prove that you were forced out, and hence dismissed 'constructively' (see Chapter 9). Only if you are dismissed can you hope to get a remedy for unfair dismissal – or redundancy pay.*

## 157 Refusal to contract out of right to claim compensation for unfair dismissal on expiry of fixed term

Thank you for your letter, suggesting that – in return for my long expected increase in salary – I should contract out of my possible right to claim compensation for unfair dismissal, if the company decides not to renew my employment when the present term comes to an end.

I am sure that if you look at this matter from my point of view, you will appreciate that this is not something that I could possibly do. I appreciate that the company is not bound to increase my salary, as I am on a fixed-term arrangement. However, the Managing Director has made it quite plain to me on numerous occasions that – having regard to the completely unexpected and enormous increase in the cost of living and the fall in the value of money – it is unreasonable to expect me to continue to work as I am, on the basis of the agreed salary. Equally, it is not reasonable to expect me to give up my potential statutory rights against the company.

In the circumstances, could you kindly arrange for me to see the M.D. personally?

Meanwhile, you may be sure that I shall continue to use my best endeavours on the company's behalf.

NOTES:
*1   Meet the Managing Director face to face, and you will probably get better results than you could do through any correspondence.*

*2   When you turn down a suggestion, it is important to do so in an amicable and dignified manner. After all, you will be continuing to work for the company, at least until your term does expire. You do not want to give anyone any chance of showing that you have given grounds for 'fair dismissal'. Hence,*

*3   Always state that the company has the assurance of your loyalty, support, conscientious work, etc., etc.*

*4    You can only contract out of your right to unfair dismissal remedies if you have a fixed-term contract of two years or more (Chapter 4).*

## 158    Denial that executive 'ordinarily works outside Great Britain'

It is true that I have been employed by the company outside Great Britain for the past six months. It is not correct that I 'ordinarily work' outside the UK. My overseas visit was extraordinary — not a normal part of my work. In the circumstances, I am advised that I am entitled to rely upon my statutory protection against 'unfair dismissal'. From my point of view, that is just as well — since you have seen fit to dismiss me, I have not been able to obtain alternative work. My loss is therefore enormous.

I hope that you will now deal with this matter speedily.

NOTE:
*See page 91.*

## 159    Claim for compensation — not redundancy pay

I note that you say that I am being 'made redundant'. If I am dismissed as redundant, then that would be thoroughly unfair — and I shall take such steps as I may be advised in order to protect my position generally, and in particular in order to claim compensation for unfair dismissal.

Perhaps you will now reconsider the matter.

## 160    Denial that lack of qualifications a 'reasonable' ground for dismissal

I am astonished that you should have seen fit to dismiss me for alleged lack of qualifications, without giving me the opportunity to acquire such qualifications. I appreciate that the new computer which you have introduced into the office has affected my work, but I was and remain fully prepared to take such courses as may be necessary in order to acquire the technical qualifications which I shall now need. You gave me no such opportunity, but instead have given me my notice.

In the circumstances, it is quite clear that I have been dismissed — and in my view, completely unfairly. I would ask you to be good enough to reconsider this matter — and in particular my wish to undergo training, in order to cope with the new machinery and methods.

I look forward to hearing from you at your earliest convenience.

NOTE:
*It is not enough to show a reason relating to 'capability' or 'qualifications or 'conduct'. The law also requires that the employer show that he acted 'reasonably'. When disputing 'fair' dismissal, you should always allege that the employer was 'unreasonable' in the action he took. If that denial is made from the start, it is more likely to be accepted at the end. In any event, even if the claim will be settled in due course, it is important to put your case on record. As important when you are acting for yourself as when you are doing your duty for your company.*

## 161 Denial that employee has mitigated loss

I note your claim — which is disputed, in its entirety. In any event, I have seen no evidence that you have made any or any sufficient efforts to obtain alternative employment, and hence to mitigate your loss.

In my view, any loss which you may have suffered has been due not only to your own conduct while you were in the company's employment, but to your own inactivity thereafter. In the circumstances, any claim for compensation or damages will be contested.

NOTE:
*There remains a difference between a claim for damages for wrongful dismissal and for compensation for unfair dismissal. But presumably — as so much more money can be obtained in a claim for compensation — under the Act — claims for damages will disappear as such, becoming incorporated into unfair dismissal proceedings before Industrial Tribunals.*

## 162    Reply to allegation of 'contributory' actions

I vehemently deny that the alleged or any actions on my part have caused or contributed to the situation which led to my unfair dismissal by the Company. The facts are as follows:

   *(a)* . . .
   *(b)* . . .
   *(c)* . . .

NOTES:

*1    If the employer's letter gives details of the allegations, then the employee's reply should do the same. Conversely, if the employer's letter is brief and unparticularised, a simple denial will do. This would be the same as the above draft, without the second (or the numbered) paragraphs.*

*2    It must be re-emphasised that when the executive – or any other employee – is attempting to protect his position, the basic rule remains the same: He is not bound to put anything into writing, but if he does so, he will find that a Tribunal is more likely to accept his case. On the other hand, anything he does commit to paper must be thoroughly accurate and carefully thought out.*

*3    It follows that if a letter is likely to find its way to Court, it is often wise to have it drafted by a solicitor – even if it is signed by the actual or potential litigant. There is no law which says that lawyers' letters must be signed by them. In practice, there are many occasions when they simply advise on the letter which the client should write – or draft that letter for his signature. So if you receive a well-drafted letter – either from the company or from an employee – you may well suspect (correctly) the hidden hand of the lawyer.*

## 163    Claim for compensation – with details of loss

Thank you for your letter, specifying alleged grounds for my dismissal. These I do not accept. I was unfairly dismissed. Even if (which I deny) I was guilty of the alleged failure to obey instructions, it was certainly not reasonable to treat such failure (which, I repeat, I deny) as sufficient grounds for terminating my employment. You appear to forget that I have been with the company for . . . years.

In the circumstances, unless I receive a substantial offer from you, I shall bring a claim before the Industrial Tribunal, to compensate me for the very considerable loss I have suffered. This comes within the following categories:

1    Loss of salary/wage – at £ . . . per week, and continuing.
2    Loss of the following fringe benefits:
 *a* subsidised meals;
 *b* use of company car;
 *c* sickness insurance;
 *d* share option scheme;
 *e* pension rights;
 *f* . . .

In addition, I have had to move to London. The costs incurred have been as follows:
 1 . . .
 2 . . .

I have thought it best to place these facts on record, at the earliest possible opportunity. I shall be pleased to hear from you within the next seven days, failing which I shall place the matter in the hands of my solicitors.

This is indeed a very unhappy ending to a long and loyal period of service to the company.


## 164    Refusal to leave prior to 'dismissal'

I appreciate the warning which you have been good enough to give me, concerning forthcoming redundancies. However, I am not prepared to resign under any circumstances. You will appreciate, I am sure, that if I were to do so I would jeopardise my right to redundancy pay – accumulated as a result of many years of loyal and enthusiastic service for the Company.

NOTE:

*1 'Never resign'. . . well, hardly ever . . . . And at least not unless you have a better job to go to and/or you can prove that you were forced into resigning and hence that you were 'constructively dismissed'.*

*2 However, once you have been dismissed, i.e. given your notice, telling you that you will have to go very shortly, you may be able to jump the gun. if you do it properly (see Letter 108).*

## 165   Offer of re-engagement

In accordance with the order made by the Industrial Tribunal, I am pleased to offer you re-engagement by the company, in the capacity of . . . at a salary of £ . . . , i.e. on the terms specified by the Tribunal.

Kindly let me know at your earliest convenience whether this offer is acceptable to you.


## 166   Acceptance of re-engagement

Thank you for your letter offering me re-engagement on the terms set out therein. Your offer is accepted and I shall be pleased to attend for work on . . . .


## 167   Refusal of re-engagement

Thank you for your letter offering me re-engagement by the company. First, the terms set out are not those recommended by the Tribunal. They differ in the following respects:

   *(a)* . . .
   *(b)* . . .
   *(c)* . . .

(In any event, having regard to the thoroughly unpleasant manner in which I have been treated by . . . , I do not feel that it would be possible for me to return to working in the same department/under the supervision of Mr . . . . If you are able to offer some alternative arrangement, then I will of course be only too pleased to consider it. Meanwhile, you may be sure that I am continuing my efforts to obtain alternative employment and hence to mitigate the loss caused to me by your unfair dismissal.)

NOTE:
*It is vital in a letter of this sort to say why you are not prepared to accept the offer of re-engagement — particularly if you can show that the offer does not accord with the terms recommended by the Tribunal. It is also important to show that you are attempting to keep your loss to the minimum.*

## 168    Complaint of harassment

I wish formally to record my regret at the treatment which I have been receiving during recent months. In particular:
*(Insert details of treatment complained of)*
In the circumstances, I am finding it increasingly difficult to achieve the results which I seek, for the benefit of our company. I would be grateful if I could discuss this matter with you at your early convenience.

NOTE:
*It is not good enough simply to have a discussion with the Chairman. It is vital to be able to prove your complaint, if necessary. If your discussion takes place first − whether by accident or design − the following letter may help:*

## 169    Confirmation of complaints made orally

It was good of you to spare me so much of your time, in order to discuss my part in the company's business. It may be helpful if I confirm the precise matters which have been causing me so much concern. They are as follows:
*(Insert details of complaints)*
I would be grateful for anything that you can do in order to put matters right. At the moment, and until we can get our organisation back on to a level keel, the company's business and its future prosperity are equally imperilled.
With best wishes.

NOTE:
*It is always as well to emphasise your own good intentions. This is doubly so when you have been receiving letters of complaint. Some sample replies to such letters now follow:*

## 170    Denial of complaint

Thank you for your letter. I completely deny the allegations which have been made against me by . . . . After my . . . years of hard work on the Board, it is most unjust that anyone should have made such allegations against me. I can only think that an effort is being made to oust me from the Board.

This effort will be fiercely resisted. I have no intention whatsoever of resigning and I can only emphasise that I have been,
remain and will continue utterly devoted to the interests of
our Company.

## 171   Retort to letter of complaint

I was most distressed to receive your letter of the . . . . I do
not know who has seen fit to give you the information which
forms the basis of your allegations. It is completely untrue. I
utterly refute in particular the following:

    1 . . .
    2 . . .
    3 . . .

The situation is in fact as follows:

    1 . . .
    2 . . .
    3 . . .

I regard the attempt to oust me from the Board as absolutely shocking − and totally unfair.

If you think that any useful purpose would be served, I
shall be pleased to discuss these matters with you. As you
know, I have the greatest of respect for you personally and
am only sorry that you have been dragged into this sordid
controversy. Meanwhile, I shall continue to perform my
duties and I trust that my efforts will not be frustrated by
any further interference.

NOTES:
*1   The introduction of the word 'unfair' is important − in the world
of dismissals, it has only one meaning − a potential £11,760.*

*2   It is important, where possible, to separate off the Chairman from
the Board − and to give him the chance to move in your direction,
without losing personal prestige or face. Another alternative:*

## 172   Stress on personal friendship with chairman

I have enjoyed and appreciated working with you over the
past . . . years. Your letter therefore came as a particular
shock to me. I have, if I may say so, the greatest possible

respect for you – and I deeply regret that you have been
drawn into the current personal controversy.

I absolutely deny the allegations that have been made –
in particular:

1 . . .

2 . . .

May I suggest that we now meet to see whether we cannot
get matters sorted out, before the Company – whose interests
we both hold so dear – is torn apart?

NOTE:

*The emphasis in all these letters rests upon your devotion to the Company's interest – and your determination not to be ousted.*

## 173   Brief denial – and request for meeting

Your letter came as a deep shock to me. The allegations
made against me are utterly without foundation. I would
welcome the opportunity to discuss them with you. Could
you spare me, perhaps, an hour before the meeting on . . . ?

## 174   Even briefer retort

No. These unfounded allegations just won't do. The
attempt to oust me from the Board will fail. I will not
willingly resign – and any dismissal would be grossly unfair.

NOTES:

*1   A really brief bullet of this kind sometimes has killing effects. But it must be absolutely on target.*

*2   If you are* forced *to resign you will be 'constructively' dismissed.*

## 175   To managing director – response to complaints

You are quite right – it has not been possible for me to
carry out my work with as much dispatch as I would have
wished. But the fault in this is not mine. I am desperately
under-staffed/the equipment ordered has not been supplied/
I have been refused the necessary equipment required . . . *(or*

*as the case may be).*

I would add that I bitterly resent the attempt to place the blame for the current difficulties at my door. In the present difficult circumstances, we are producing results which are a good deal better than the Company is entitled to expect.

However, I am very anxious indeed to satisfy you — and, above all, to produce thoroughly efficient results. Would you therefore be kind enough to arrange for me to have the necessary additional staff/to be supplied with the following equipment, as previously requested . . . *(or as the case may be).*

I shall be pleased to discuss these matters with you at your convenience.

NOTES:

*1   By all means offer to discuss the matter orally — but first get your allegations into writing. Apart from impressing (if necessary) a Tribunal, this approach often has a thoroughly salutory effect on the Board.*

*2   Remember to keep a copy — at home? A handwritten memo or note should be photocopied.*


### 176   To managing director — asking that the matter be raised at board meeting

As you know, I do my best to shield the Board from ordinary matters of day-to-day administration. But the criticisms that are now being made both of me and of my department have gone beyond the stage at which I can deal with them on my own. They are creating an atmosphere of tension and are interfering with my attempts to reorganise
. . . .

In the circumstances, I would be pleased if you would agree to my placing this matter on the Agenda of the next Board Meeting. I look forward to hearing from you.

With my thanks in anticipation.

NOTE:

*The fact that you are fighting back — or even the suggestion that the matter may be raised at a Board Meeting — often has a lively effect. The MD is quite likely to call your persecutor in to see him. You may even find that there is a genuine and successful attempt to solve the difficulty, behind the scenes. Hence the following drafts:*

## 177   Agreement to meeting

Yes, I fully agree that it would be better to sort this matter out behind the scenes. But I must put firmly on record my disquiet at the unwarranted allegations which Mr . . . has seen fit to make against me.

Anyway, I shall be pleased to meet you on . . . at . . . .

## 178   Agreement to see chairman

I am always sorry to burden the Chairman with personal problems, but if you think that his intervention would help in the present case, I shall be very pleased to see him. However, I trust that the correspondence will be placed before him and that he will know that the allegations made against me are firmly rejected.

Perhaps you might also indicate to him that there appears to be an unhappy combination of executives seeking to drive me into the wilderness. As I consider that they are not acting in the best interests of the Company, I have no intention of leaving my post under fire.

## 179   Confirming satisfactory discussions

You were right — talks were indeed called for. I hope that now that we have had our frank discussion, we can once again work together as a team. I am particularly pleased to confirm agreement on the following specific points:

    1 . . .
    2 . . .
    3 . . .

Without wishing in any way to labour the point, or to prolong the previous misunderstanding, I would like formally to record the fact that Mr . . . withdrew unreservedly the allegations made against me in his letter/notes of . . . .

## 180   Apology accepted

I happily confirm that I was only too pleased to accept the apology which you were good enough to give me at our meeting. I now look forward to working together with you, in harmony, as we did before the recent contretemps.

With best wishes.

NOTES:

*1   An apology (like a contract) may be made orally or in writing. The oral variety is far more common and avoids loss of face. But (again like contracts) the oral word is far easier to contradict than the written statement. As you are unlikely to get a written apology, you can yourself confirm the nature of your conversation.*

*2   The above letter is one of thanks and is one which removes the knife from between the commercial shoulder blades. The recipient is unlikely to object to it.*

*3   As in the case of so many of these personal letters, it is generally better to have them handwritten. But make a photocopy for your own records.*

## 181   Meeting unsuccessful

It was indeed good of you to spare so much time to meet the Managing Director and myself last . . . . I am only sorry that this meeting failed to resolve the unhappy situation.

Having given the matter further reflection, I can still find no justification whatsoever for the allegations which have been made against me. The threats of dismissal were particularly unfair, as the defects in the accounts/administration/ my office are in no way of my making. They are, as we discussed, entirely caused by . . . .

In the circumstances, I shall continue to do my best to serve both the Company and yourself with all my energy. I only hope that, despite the attitude taken up by Mr . . . at our meeting and previously, he will not make my work impossible.

Once again, my thanks to you for your courtesy and patience.

NOTES:

*1   Presumably, this letter will be shown to the Managing Director. It is hardly likely to improve the situation – and may even precipitate your dismissal. But you may regard your departure as inevitable – in which case it is vital to have your case on paper, before the documents are placed before the Court.*

*2 This letter (as opposed to the last one) should be typed. It should be made formally clear that you intend to do battle. This may drive away the wolves. As Stalin said to an Eastern diplomat, shortly before his death: 'The Russian peasant may be illiterate, but he is also wise. He does not argue or moralise with the wolves who approach his village. He shoots them. Knowing this, they keep away.' You might even try the following:*

## 182 Any dismissal would be unfair

It is quite clear that efforts are being made to oust me from my position — and hence, of course, from my livelihood. The allegations that are being made against me are grossly unfair and completely untrue. They are being made in order to protect others.

During our conversation, you asked me whether I proposed to substantiate my allegations concerning improprieties of which I informed you. I am perfectly capable of doing so; the documentary evidence is available; but I have no wish either to exacerbate matters or to create any further ill feeling. However, I am sure that you will appreciate that I have every intention of fighting back, if I am forced to do so.

Finally, I would like to emphasise once again my untiring loyalty to the Company. My work will continue to be devoted to the Company's interests.

NOTES:
*1 This sort of letter is dynamite. Use it sparingly and adapt it carefully to suit your purposes.*

*2 Note in particular that the swipe from the rear is generally more effective than the assault from the front. The above letter suggests that the writer does not wish to use the ammunition available to him . . . that he has no desire for ill-will . . . that he does not wish to be forced to substantiate allegations made orally. This is a mature and sensible approach — particularly when combined with the renewed assurance of loyalty to the Company's best interests.*

*3 If you ever do put allegations into writing, they will almost certainly be libellous. Even though the occasion will undoubtedly be privileged, you may well be accused of 'malice'. So you are generally far better off not to make allegations against other executives or employees. Indeed, if you emphasise your wish to avoid recriminations, it goes a long way to rebut any suggestion of malice.*

## 183    Refusal to resign

I was shocked to receive your letter, suggesting that I should resign. This I will not do. I have no reason to do so. I have served the company well in the past and will bend every effort to continue so to do in the future,

## 184    Are you intending to dismiss?

I have found the treatment you have accorded to me of late to be quite inexplicable. If it is your intention to dismiss me from the company's service, then I will be pleased if you would so inform me. Otherwise I shall continue to serve the company in future, as I have in the past.

# Chapter 17

# References

You are not bound to provide references. If you do so and you know the basic rules, though, you have nothing to fear — even if the reference is unsatisfactory or incorrect.

Speak ill of the person referred to and you defame him. If the defamatory statement is made orally, it is slanderous; if it is in writing or some other permanent form, then it is a libel.

In practice, there are three reasons why you need have no worries about a defamation action arising out of a defamatory reference:

1 The person defamed is unlikely to obtain evidence of the defamation — after all, why should the recipient of the references pass on the evil tidings?

2 The person defamed would have to spend his own money on the litigation — there is no legal aid. And any lawyer would tell him not to bother, not merely because of the risks involved (which Oscar Wilde discovered) but because of the defences open to the giver.

3 There are two main defences to this sort of action:

   *a* Justification — that the statement was substantially true. You cannot complain if someone takes from you a good character which you have not earned. On the other hand, a justification plea which fails leads almost always to increased damages — after all, the unkind statement has been repeated to a wider audience.

   *b* Qualified privilege. Unlike the MP speaking in Parliament or Judge, Counsel, witness or litigant in Court, the privilege is not 'absolute'. It is 'qualified' — by the rule that if it can be shown that the reference was given out of malice — from a desire to harm the person defamed, rather than a wish to assist the recipient — then the defence will be defeated.

Still, defamation actions arising out of uncomplimentary references are almost unheard of. You may give them with impunity. If you are afraid that you may be charged with malice, though — then defame by telephone. Slander is even harder to prove than libel.

The real danger lies in statements which are incorrect — particularly trade references. You 'owe a duty of care' to the recipient. He is entitled to rely upon your reference, even if he made no payment for it. Therefore you must not be negligent.

If, then, you give a good reference to a man who deserved a bad one — perhaps because you got the name wrong; or (more likely) if you mislead the recipient of the trade or professional reference by saying that he is worthy of credit when you knew or ought to have known of his sad financial state of lack of credit-worthiness — you could be in trouble.

Here, though, a 'disclaimer' provides a watertight defence. You should take a leaf out of the bank manager's book and never give (nor permit your subordinates to provide) a reference without a disclaimer — saying that the reference is given 'without legal responsibility'.

\*    \*    \*

### 185   Trade reference — with disclaimer

We are pleased to confirm that we have been suppliers of Messrs Smith Ltd for . . . years. They have paid their accounts promptly and we have no reason to suppose that they would not be worthy of the credit which you are proposing to give them.

This reference is given without legal responsibility.

### 186   Company sound — but disclaimer

We thank you for your letter of . . . concerning Messrs Smith Ltd. We believe that company to be well managed and financially sound.

While we are pleased to oblige with trade references, all references are given on the basis that no legal responsibility can be accepted.

### 187   Trade reference — unsatisfactory — with disclaimer

We thank you for your request for a reference for Messrs Smith Ltd. We trade with that company on a cash basis only. This reference is given without legal responsibility.

NOTE:
*A disclaimer of responsibility will free you from liability in respect of negligent misstatements, but not (of course) from potential libel actions.*

*The disclaimer is addressed to the recipient – the libel action would be brought by the person defamed.*

## 188    Unsatisfactory reference for ex-employee

We confirm that Mr Black worked for this company from . . . to . . . . He was dismissed for misconduct/as unsuitable/ because . . . .

While we are pleased to provide references for former employees, all references are given without legal responsibility.

## 189    Least said

I confirm that Mr Black was employed by my company from . . . to . . . .

NOTE:

*Silence speaks. If you do not wish to say too much, then say little. And if you receive a reference of this kind and want further and better particulars, telephone the sender.*

## 190    Request for written references

### *John Brown*

The above named has applied to us for the position of . . . . We understand that he was employed by you, and in the circumstances, would be extremely grateful if you would kindly give us any information which may affect our decision as to his employment. In order to simplify matters, we are appending hereto a brief questionnaire. If you would be good enough to complete the same we would be most appreciative. Naturally, we shall be very pleased to return the courtesy, if at any further date we can be of assistance to you.

With our thanks in anticipation of an early reply,

*Sample questionnaire*
Name of Applicant:      John Brown
Position applied for:         . . .
1    What was the date of the commencement of the appli-

cant's employment by you?

2    In what position was he originally employed?

3    Kindly detail any promotions or demotions

4    Upon what date did the applicant leave your service?

5    Kindly indicate circumstances in which employment terminated.

6    Did you find the applicant:

    *a*    In every respect, honest and reliable?

    *b*    Satisfactory in his relationships with members of the Board?

    *c*    Satisfactory with his relationships with subordinates?

    *d*    Well informed concerning:

        (i)   . . .

        (ii)  . . .

        (iii) . . .

7    Would you consider him suitable for the position applied for, as indicated above?

8    Have you any further comments which would be of help to us, in deciding whether or not the applicant's request for the above employment should be accepted?


NOTES:

*1    Under Paragraph 6(d), you should insert any particular qualities required for the particular post.*

*2    You may find from experience that there are certain employers who like to fill in a questionnaire of this sort – and others who do not. If in doubt, a telephone call to the employer or personnel manager concerned may be worthwhile.*

*3    It is usually wise and thoughtful to enclose a stamped, self-addressed envelope. And you may wish to send a copy of the questionnaire, for retention by the referee.*


### 191    Asking for telephone reference for company secretary

We understand that Mr David Evans was employed by you until recently as your Assistant Company Secretary. He has now applied to the above company for a similar position, and we would be extremely grateful if you could give us some guidance as to his reliability, honesty, efficiency, and as to his relationship with other employees, both those whom he supervises and those under whose supervision he comes.

If I do not hear from you within two or three days, then I shall telephone. It may be that it would prove more convenient to discuss this matter orally — and if so, then please do not trouble to reply to this letter, I shall be in touch with you shortly.

With my thanks in anticipation of your kind co-operation.

NOTE:
*When asking for a reference, you should give the ex-employer the benefit of the doubt — and presuppose that they will know their law and be careful in the information they give to you. So oral references are often worth obtaining. But in case you wish to receive a written reply, the previous draft incorporates most of the questions which you may want to ask. Naturally, you will strike out those that do not apply and adapt the remainder, as necessary.*

## 192   Please telephone

Thank you for your letter concerning Andrew Hammill. If you would care to give me a ring, either at the office or at my home (telephone . . . . .) I shall be pleased to discuss this man with you.

Trusting that you are keeping well and with kind regards.

NOTE:
*Although a statement is just as defamatory if made orally as in writing — and where a person is defamed concerning his occupation, no actual financial loss need be proved by him, if he is to recover damages — the proof of slander is infinitely more difficult than that of libel (which, by definition, is in a permanent form). Consequently, it is often preferable to give a reference orally — and, conversely, often easier to obtain an accurate and helpful reference if you speak to the ex-employer in question, rather than writing to him. Alternatively, you could write the previous letter.*

## 193   Reference for former company secretary

Thank you for your letter concerning Mr Talbot. He was employed by the company from . . . to . . . . I regret to inform you that he left after a dispute with the Board.

This reference is given in strict confidence without legal responsibility on the part of the writer or of the company.

"THIS LETTER SETS OUT OUR FIRM'S POLICY ON
DISCRIMINATION IN BLACK AND WHITE ... "

# Part Three

# DISCRIMINATION, WOMEN'S AND MOTHERS' RIGHTS — AND RACE DISCRIMINATION

# Chapter 18

# Equal pay and discrimination

The Sex Discrimination Act amended the Equal Pay Act. A term is now implied into the contract of every woman employee that she will be treated on an equal basis to men — in particular, that she will receive equal pay for work or for work rated on an equivalent basis.

\* \* \*

A person discriminates against a woman . . . if

'*(a)* on the ground of her sex he treats her less favourably than he treats or would treat a man or,

*(b)* he applies to her requirements or conditions which he applies or would apply equally to a man but —

> *(i)* which is such that the proportion of women who can comply with it is considerably smaller than the proportion of men who can comply with it and

> *(ii)* which he cannot show to be justifiable irrespective of the sex of the person to whom it is applied, and

> *(iii)* which is to her detriment because she cannot comply with it'.

Equally, a man's 'marital status' must not affect his treatment. Nor must there be discrimination against a man or against married people in the field of employment. Nor must you victimise a person who seeks to exercise his rights under the Sex Discrimination Act.

After this opening salvo, the Act turns to discrimination in the employment field. Bearing in mind the increased temptation to discriminate against women in appointment to executive or managerial posts (see Chapter 19) and the rules on the reinstatement of mothers after child-birth, Section 6 of the Sex Discrimination Act, is important:

'It is unlawful for a person, in relation to employment by him at an establishment in Great Britain, to discriminate against a woman —

> *(a)* in the arrangements he makes for the purpose of determining who should be offered that employment, or

> *(b)* in the terms on which he offers her that employment, or

> *(c)* by refusing or deliberately omitting to offer her that employment.'

Again, he must not discriminate in connection with promotion, transfer, training or any other benefits, facilities or services — or 'by dismissing her, or subjecting her to any other detriment'.

Exceptions: Women employed 'for the purposes of a private household' or where neither the employer nor any associated employer has a payroll not exceeding five people (leaving his home employees out of the account). And you may also discriminate in connection with terms of employment relating to 'death or retirement' — actuarily, women live longer and are not necessarily entitled to the same pension opportunities.

With deadpan (or unconscious) humour, the Act makes one remarkable exception. You are entitled to discriminate in connection with the employment 'where sex is a genuine occupational qualification for the job' (*sic*). Your secretary, for instance?

There are other exceptions in Section 7. For instance:

1   Where the 'essential nature of the job calls for a man for reasons of physiology (excluding physical strength or stamina) . . . or for reasons of authenticity . . .'. Curiously, being a man is not a genuine occupational qualification for the job for reasons of physical strength. You must treat each 'person' who applies on his or her merits. Stakhanovite ladies may enter traditionally male areas — as they have done in other (often less advanced) countries.

2   You may employ a man where it is necessary so to do 'to preserve decency or privacy'.

3   Where 'the nature or location of the establishment makes it impracticable for the holder of the job to live elsewhere than in premises provided by the employer', then you may employ men if you wish.

4   Hospitals, prisons and other 'establishments for persons requiring special care and supervision' and where the inmates are male are normally excluded.

5   Providers of welfare, educational 'or other similar personal services' which are 'most effectively provided' by men are excepted.

6   So are jobs held by men because of legal restrictions.

7   Where a job is one of two held by a married couple.

8   Finally: where the job is 'likely to involve the performance of duties outside the United Kingdom in a country whose laws or customs are such that the duties could not — or could not effectively — be performed by a woman'. Your sales representative in Saudi Arabia, for instance.

Part 2 of the Sex Discrimination Act (which covers discrimination in the employment field) is reproduced in Appendix 1. Now follow sex discrimination precedent letters.

\* \* \*

## 194   Denial that pay 'unequal'

My colleagues and I have given careful consideration to your allegation that you and other women employees in our office/accounts department are not being paid on the same basis as men.

We do not employ men in those departments, doing the categories of work which are the subject of your complaint. However, this is the result of chance, not design; when recruiting for posts in these departments, we select people irrespective of whether they are men or women (or, for that matter, without regard to their marital status); and we are satisfied that the rate which we are paying you and your colleagues is the same as that which we would pay men, if and when male applicants for these jobs are successful in obtaining them in the future. In other words we are paying the rate for the job, irrespective of sex and in the circumstances, while we have given full and careful consideration to your claim, we find no merit in it.

## 195   Work rated on equivalent basis

The work that you are doing is rated on an equivalent basis to similar work performed by men in our . . . department. There is therefore no justification whatever for your allegation that you are being paid at a lower rate because you are a woman. For many years, this company has prided itself on treating people fairly and on an equal basis, totally irrespective of their sex. We were therefore all the more disturbed at receiving your complaint; we have examined it with care; and we were pleased to find that it is unjustified.

## 196   Other companies' rates irrelevant

It is, we understand, correct that certain women are paid more by other companies in the district — but the circumstances are not the same. Other terms of work are less satisfactory/they do not have the same canteen facilities and other fringe benefits/their working conditions are far less pleasant/ they have not been hit by the current recession in the trade in the same way as ourselves/they are in a different sector of the industry/their pay structure is very different to ours (or as the case may be).

We pay women in our business the rate for the job — which is not assessed on the basis of their sex, but with regard to other terms of service and to what the company can afford.

## 197   Equal Opportunities Commission — consultant

We have taken your allegation of unequal treatment very seriously, although we regard it as unwarranted. We have therefore sought the advice of the Equal Opportunities Commission and as soon as we have any news for you, we will immediately be in touch again.

With best wishes.

## 198   Application to Equal Opportunities Commission for advice

Further to our telephone conversation, I am enclosing herewith correspondence which passed between the union and our company, concerning alleged failure to grant equal pay/ failure on the part of this company to comply to its obligations under the Equal Pay Act/Sex Discrimination Act.

After the most anxious consideration, we consider that we have complied with our obligations, in the spirit as well as to the letter. However, we shall be pleased if a representative of your commission would call upon us so as to discuss the matter and so as to attempt to resolve the current dispute in an amicable and fair fashion.

## 199 The Advisory, Conciliation and Arbitration Service — discrimination in appointment?

I was pleased to speak to you by telephone and am sending you herewith as promised, the correspondence in the matter of the alleged discriminatory practices by this company in connection with the non-employment of men/women in our ... section/operation/plant/shop (*or as the case may be*). As I told you, there is no discrimination in the above regard. (*Alternatively:* the company does employ only men/ women in the above job because . . .). In any event, we will be grateful if you or one of your colleagues will call upon us as soon as possible, in order that we may receive your advice in what may otherwise turn into a complicated dispute.

NOTES:

*1   Whether to call in ACAS or the Equal Opportunities Commission is a matter of judgement — and often of personal contact.*

*2   It is almost always preferable to speak to ACAS or the Commission by telephone in order to set up the help you want. Equally it will save time and problems if those who are to assist you are given the necessary documents in advance.*

*3   For further details and precedents concerning ACAS, see Chapter 23.*

## 200   Sex — essential qualification for job

We have carefully considered the representations made to the company by your union, alleging that we ought to open up the . . . job function to women. Having regard, however to the essential nature of the work/to the need to employ men in that job for reasons of authenticity/to . . ., we consider that the carrying out of the work by men is an essential qualification for the job. We have also written to your union to explain our view.

NOTE:

*The Courts will have to decide when sex is 'an essential qualification for the job', to use the Act's remarkable phrase. Meanwhile, the only certainty is that to be a female is to have an essential qualification for Bunny Girls.*

*Chapter 19*

# Women and married
# executives—complaints

Women executives and managers who are already in their jobs may be
grateful for the new legislation. They are entitled to equal pay; non-
discrimination; maternity pay; and to reinstatement in their jobs after
childbirth — in exactly the same way as any other woman employee.
They are, though, far more vulnerable than shop floor employees,
whose reinstatement rights will cause far less trouble to management,
if only because (if you will pardon the expression) women 'turn over'
so much faster than men. At higher levels, there is lower turn-over and
those who decide on employment policies may discover that the problems of dismissing replacements are such that they prefer, where
possible, to employ men — even where they cannot successfully maintain that 'sex is an essential qualification for the job'.

Anyway, there is no point in women executives having rights unless
they know how, where and when to exercise them. They will need
letters.

\* \* \*

## 201  Equal Opportunities Commission — help required

I would be obliged for your advice, followed, if necessary,
by your active help — in connection with my complaint
against my employing company/firm, details of which are
attached hereto. Please would you write to me at my home
address. I would be pleased to call upon your appropriate
officer, if this would be the best way to deal with the matter.
For obvious reasons, I do not want my employers to know
of this approach, at the present stage.

NOTES:
*1 The address of the Equal Opportunities Commission is: Overseas
House, Quay Street, Manchester M3 3HN (Tel: 061-833 9244).*

*2 The Commission will, of course, deal with any enquiries on a
confidential basis. You can then discuss with the appropriate official
the action which the Commission may be prepared to take in your case
— which may be advisory; conciliatory; or even the appropriate assistance*

*with necessary litigation required to enforce your rights, by going to an industrial tribunal.*

## 202 Complaint — equal pay

I am sorry to have to trouble you about this matter, as it only affects myself/a few of your staff/one category of employees/it really should have been sorted out without the need to come to you. However, as I am anxious to have the dispute dealt with speedily and without causing further ill will, I know that you will not mind my approaching you/ putting details of our conversation into writing.

In my view, I/women employed as . . . in the office/ accounts department (*or as the case may be*) are not receiving equal pay for the work that they are doing. They are being paid less than men doing equivalent work/work graded on an equivalent basis.

I trust that this matter can be rectified at an early date and send you my thanks in anticipation.

## 203 Own pay unequal — protest

After all these years of loyal service to the company, I am sure that you know that I make no unnecessary complaints or protests — and that I am totally devoted to the success of the business. It is therefore with regret that I find myself impelled to write to you concerning my own pay/terms of service. In particular, it seems clear that I (and, incidentally , . . .)/other women employed in a similar capacity (*or as the case may be*) find myself being treated less favourably in connection with terms of service/payment/promotion/transfer/ opportunities for advancement/training, than my men colleagues, working in a like capacity.

I have tried to raise this matter privately and informally but without success. I would therefore be grateful if you would be kind enough to arrange for this complaint to be fully investigated — and I shall, of course, be only too pleased to discuss it with you.

NOTE:
*In practice, women executives and managers may be loath to risk their*

*positions in this way. But if a letter of this sort is followed (within at least any reasonable time) by dismissal, then the reason for that dismissal will be clear enough to enable the woman to obtain her remedy; and if she finds herself forced out of her job – pushed into resigning – then the existence of this letter will be great help to her, if she seeks to show that she was constructively dismissed.*

*An alternative to this approach would be a quiet word with the Equal Opportunities Commission or with ACAS.*

### 204   Married man – discrimination alleged

I am writing directly to you in the hope that you will be kind enough to intervene, to avoid any further ill will or the perpetuation of a problem which could lead to anxiety not merely for me but also for the company. This letter is a confidential one; if you would like me to discuss it with you, then I shall be pleased to do so; but I hope that in any event you will understand that my complaint is one which I only make to you or at all after prolonged and anxious consideration.

I was appointed as . . . on . . . . I have worked very hard for the company and the results of my efforts/department show, I think, the products of this work – and, of course, of the team-work which I have been able to engender from my colleagues and subordinates. If proof be required, then I enclose herewith letters of thanks/congratulation from . . . , . . . and . . . .

It was therefore with great surprise that I found that another person/other persons had been promoted over my head. Having regard to remarks made to me – and to the absence of any other reason – I can only think that I was held back because of my marital status/I am a bachelor. Not only does this situation cause ill will, but it is, of course, an apparent breach of the Sex Discrimination Act.

As I said, I would be very grateful if you could look into this complaint – and I send you my warm thanks in anticipation.

NOTE:
*This letter, of course, could easily be adapted to the needs of a woman who considers that she has been held back on the ground of her sex. But the Act gives no protection to single people ('gay' or otherwise).*

# Chapter 20

# Mothers' replacements

When a mother leaves to have her baby and you appoint a replacement, it is essential — where there is any real possibility of that mother exercising her right to return — so to inform the replacement. Otherwise, if the replacement stays with you for six months or more, she (or he) will be protected by the unfair dismissal rules and dismissal of the replacement will be 'unfair'. You may then even be ordered to reinstate the replacement — and will certainly have to pay compensation (a basic award of two weeks' pay (maximum £80 per week), as the minimum; £11,760 at the most).

\* \* \*

## 205 Warning — job temporary if mother returns

I write to confirm that we shall be pleased to employ you as . . . on the terms attached hereto/which will shortly be sent to you. You will be replacing Mrs Brown, who has left to have her baby but who intends to return to work after the baby is born. She is entitled to exercise this right at any time within 29 weeks from the date of her expected confinement, which is . . . — with an additional four weeks, if she is not then fit enough to come back.

You will appreciate that Mrs Brown is under no obligation to return; and, indeed, intervening circumstances may prevent her from doing so. I am sorry that your job must therefore be initially on a temporary basis — but we believe that it is in fact unlikely that Mrs Brown will come back, despite her stated intention; and if she does so, then we will make every effort to fit you into our organisation in another and equivalent position.

Despite the uncertainty — which is inevitable and a direct result of the Employment Protection Act provisions — we all hope that this will be the start of a long and happy association between us and that you will do very well in your new position.

With best wishes.

## 206    Alternative confirmation – replacement temporary?

I confirm our discussion in which we agreed to appoint you as a replacement for Mrs Brown, who is leaving to have her baby; and we made it plain that Mrs Brown may exercise her right to return to her job, as provided for by the Employment Protection Act. She has notified the company of her intention to return; and in those circumstances, we are informing you in accordance with the Act that your services may have to be terminated, if and when Mrs Brown carries out her intention. However, we do not think that the situation is likely to arise; and if it does, we shall do everything possible to continue your employment. In any event, for the first . . . weeks of your employment (which commences on the . . . – the date when Mrs Brown is leaving us), your employment will be subject to four weeks notice on either side.

In spite of all the above – which I am bound to set out, for the company's protection – I do hope that you will not only enjoy your job but that it will prove to be the start of a long and happy association between the company and yourself.

With kind regards.

NOTE:
*Just as the mother has four weeks extra after the 29th week in which to return to her job if she is still not fit, so you have four weeks within which to hold off the mother who wants to return, so as to make her place available for her. And you must give notice to your replacement. The fact that a person is a replacement gives you no right to terminate his (or her) services, without proper notice.*

## 207    Replacement – accepts that mother may return

I, . . . of . . . confirm that I accept the position of . . . with . . . Ltd, on the terms set out in the written particulars/letter of appointment dated . . . . In particular, I confirm that Mr/Mrs/Miss . . . has explained to me that I will be replacing Mrs/Miss . . . who has left/will be leaving by reason of pregnancy or confinement and that in the event of her returning to her job, the company will reserve the right to terminate my appointment. I further confirm that Mr . . . has given his assurance that in the event of Mrs/Miss . . . returning to work, he will make every effort to find a reasonably suitable alternative position for me, with the company/or with one of the companies in the group.

(Signed) . . . . . .

(Dated) . . . . . .

NOTES:

*1 The assurance of the company's promised effort to find alternative work is not one which is in fact enforceable at law, but it may help to induce someone suitable to take on the position of replacement.*

*2 It is irrelevant so far as the maternity provisions of the Employment Protection Act are concerned whether the mother to be is married or unmarried, or even for that matter whether she leaves to be confined or to have an abortion.*

## 208 Intention to return − request for writing

I have been informed by your Personnel Manager that you are expecting a child, and I send you warm congratulations.

In accordance with the normal policy of this company, I must ask you to inform me in writing if you intend to return to the company's service, after your confinement. Details of your statutory rights are sent herewith.

## 209 To all women employees − notice of intention to be in writing

I am writing to you − along with all other female employees − to inform you that, in accordance with the provisions of the Employment Protection Act, the company hereby requests that any notice of intention to return after childbirth be given in writing. If you may wish to return, please let me know, and I will be pleased to explain your statutory rights.

NOTE:

*Section 35(2)(c) provides that the mother shall not be entitled to exercise her right to return unless 'she informs her employer (in writing if he so requests) at least three weeks before her absence begins or, if that is not reasonably practicable, as soon as reasonably practicable . . .'*

*that she intends to return to work with her employer. There is no requirement that this request be made in any particular form or at any special time. There would therefore seem to be no reason why the request should not be made, in the case of all existing employees, by letter – nor, indeed, in any revised terms of service which may now be prepared as a result of the provisions of the Employment Protection Act, combined with the Health and Safety at Work Act. The following additional term could be slotted into place in a contract, rather than included in a letter:*

## 210   Additional written particular – request for writing

I confirm that the following term should be added to the written particulars of your contract of service:

Any woman who is absent for work by reason of pregnancy or confinement and who intends to return to work thereafter is hereby requested to state such intention in writing, if practicable, at least three weeks before leaving.

## 211   Statement of intention – for pregnant employee

Kindly complete the form at the foot of this letter and return a copy of it to your Personnel Manager (*or as the case may be*).

I, . . . do/do not intend to return to my job, following my absence due to pregnancy or confinement.

NOTES:
*1   Any woman who knows her rights – and in particular that she has nothing to lose by stating an intention to return – is unlikely to say that she does not wish to come back. If she says that she does intend to return and she changes her mind, her employers will acquire no rights against her. If she says that she does not intend to come back, then she burns her boats.*

*2   Rather than sending the above letter, it is better to deliver it by hand. You should tell the employee of her right to return; assure her that if she states that she does not intend to return and then changes her mind, you will still do your best to find a place for her in the company; but ask her to be good enough not to say that she intends to come back if she has no such intention because of the difficulties that this will inevitably create not merely for the company but especially for her replacement.*

*3 You may, of course, sit tight and hope for the best – providing no written document at all – particularly if you have previously requested a written statement of intention. If that written statement is contained in a letter which sets out the employee's rights, she can hardly be heard to say that she did not know of them and hence that it was not 'reasonably practicable' for her to state an intention within the required time. However, in the absence of a written request, the employee who fails to state her intention at least three weeks before leaving to have her baby is likely to avoid trouble with the time element because:*

a    *She may allege that she told someone in the firm other than her immediate superior or personnel officer – and this claim will be hard to disprove.*

b    *She may say that she told her immediate superior or personnel manager – and he may (or may not) have forgotten the conversation – but she is more likely to be believed.*

c    *Following precedent (unfair dismissal cases, in particular), if she did not know of her rights, then it may be held not to have been 'reasonably practicable' for her to have stated her intention. So writing of the above kind is both sensible and fair, and good tactics.*

## 212   Request for written decision – with explanation of rights

As I expect you know, the Employment Protection Act gives you the right to return to your job at any time within 29 weeks of your confinement (with the possible extension of 4 weeks, in the event of illness), provided that you state an intention to do so, where reasonably practicable, at least three weeks before you leave. I understand that you will be leaving shortly in order to have your baby, and in writing to congratulate you, I also would be grateful if you would let me know whether or not you do intend to come back to your job. If you have no such intention, I would be very grateful if you would say so. If you change your mind, then we will do everything possible to find a position for you. But obviously, it would not be fair on your replacement to con-

sider that the job may be a temporary one, if in fact you do
not intend to come back.

In the circumstances, I would be grateful if you would fill
in the form at the bottom of this sheet, and return it to me
at any convenient time.

With best wishes.

I do/do not intend to return to my job after being away due
to my pregnancy and/or confinement.

NOTES:

*1   You might prefer to omit congratulations, if the expectant mother
is unmarried. The protection afforded by the Act is not confined to
legitimate confinements. The law (not for the only time) is concerned
with reality, not morality.*

*2   If you can prove that this letter was not only written but also
received, then if it is not returned, the intended mother will certainly
have known her rights; you will have requested notification of intention
in writing; and her chances of finding an excuse for not complying with
your requests are remote.*

### 213   Job open — but in different department

I thank you for your letter notifying me of your intention
to return to work on the . . . . I confirm that your job will be
open to you — and that you will be working in the . . .
Department/office. Please report to . . . at . . . a.m.

Looking forward to seeing you and with best wishes.

NOTE:

*A mother is entitled to return to her 'job' — which means, to do work
of the same nature and quality in the same place — but not, it would
appear, necessarily working for the same individual or in the same room.
For instance, if she was previously employed as a secretary, then she
must be taken on again as a secretary — but not necessarily working
for the same man. It is arguable, though, that where a woman is a
personal secretary or assistant, it is not the same 'job' if she is working
for someone else, albeit in the same place.*

## 214   Reminder – of intention to return

Before leaving to have your baby, you informed us that you intended to return to your job. We have not heard from you and in the circumstances, are we to take it that you no longer intend to do so? Please would you let me know – I enclose stamped addressed envelope herewith.

Hoping that you are keeping well and with best wishes.

NOTE:
*The Act includes no provision for revocation of intention – but a reminder of this sort could form a useful step in normal procedures. You could, on the other hand, properly wait until the 29 weeks have passed – in which case the mother's right to return expires.*

## 215   Right lost through delay

You telephoned my office this morning stating an intention to return to your job, having had your baby. Our records indicate that more than 29 weeks have passed since your confinement. In the circumstances, we regret that we were unable to keep your job open for you.

NOTE:
*You are under no legal obligation to help the mother in the future.*

## 216   Intention not stated

I am sorry but we do not have a vacancy at present. Nor can we reinstate you in your old job because we engaged a replacement. I must remind you that you did not state your intention to return to your job after having your baby, either at least three weeks before leaving, or in writing (in accordance with paragraph . . . of your terms of service/ our letter dated . . . requesting a written statement of intention) or at all.

If you would like us to keep your name on our list for possible future vacancies, please will you let me know.

Wishing you well in the future and with our renewed regrets that we are unable to assist you at present.

## 217    Written request for written statement ignored

In my letter to you dated . . ./included in your wage
packet on the . . . , I specifically requested that if you wished
to be reinstated in your job after having a baby/any mother
who wished to be reinstated in her job after having her baby
should state her/your intention to return in writing, whenever practicable not less than three weeks before her absence
for pregnancy or confinement began (in accordance with the
rules laid down in the Employment Protection Act). We
received no such notice of intention; and in the circumstances, your job was not held open for you.

Nevertheless, we will try to find a vacancy for you at some
future date, if you wish. Please would you let us know about
this?

## 218    Position redundant

I have received your message that you wish to return to
your job. Unfortunately, since you left to have your baby
we had to close the department in which you formerly
worked. We have looked for an alternative position which
would suit you, but I regret to tell you that there is none.

In the circumstances, as you have been employed continuously by the company for more than two years, you will be
entitled to a redundancy payment, and I have asked our
accounts department to make all appropriate arrangements.

Naturally, we are all very sad at this departmental closure,
but the current recession/shortage of orders for our goods/
(*or as the case may be*) made this inevitable.

With best wishes.

NOTES:
*1   No woman who has been employed for less than two years is en-
titled to return to her job after childbirth; and every woman who has
been employed for two years or more is entitled to a redundancy payment.*

*2   It is not enough to show that the employee cannot be replaced in
her old job because of redundancy; you must also show that you have
done your best to replace the mother in a reasonably suitable alternative
job – otherwise she will be both 'redundant' and 'unfairly dismissed'
(with all the potentially expensive consequences which that involves).*

## 219 Not qualified — insufficient service

Thank you for your letter. You are not in fact entitled to maternity benefits — either maternity pay or reinstatement in your job — because by the beginning of the 11th week before the expected week of your confinement you had not been with the company for the statutory minimum qualifying period of two years.

## 220 Not qualified — left too early

To qualify for reinstatement in her job, a mother must remain at her job until 11 weeks or less before the expected date of her confinement. You left more than two months before that date.

In addition, had you not been able to stand/carry out your normal duties, we would have been pleased to find you an alternative job that did not require standing/you would have been able to do in spite of your condition.

In the circumstances, you were replaced in your position and I regret that we cannot make a job available for you.

NOTE:

*If a mother is dismissed before the beginning of the 11th week before her expected confinement, then — if the dismissal was as a result of her condition — she retains rights both to reinstatement and to maternity pay. If, however, she leaves voluntarily before that date, without being dismissed, it seems that she loses both her remedies.*

## 221 Notice to return — impracticable

Thank you for your letter. It was not reasonably practicable for me to give notice of my intention to return for the following reasons:

1 I did not know of my rights under the Act;
2 I was in any event in hospital and not in a fit state to look after my affairs; and
3 I did not know at the time that the reason for my indisposition was pregnancy.

In the circumstances, I look forward to hearing from you that my job will be made available, in accordance with the

Employment Protection Act. And I shall be very pleased to return to my loyal and energetic service to the company.

With my best personal regards to you.

NOTES:

*1   It is likely that — by reference to decisions on what is or is not 'reasonably practicable' in connection with the giving of notice of claim for remedies for unfair dismissal, within the time limit (three months from termination of employment) — that reason (1) above will be conclusive.*

*2   Reason (2) above should suffice — provided that the illness really did prevent the giving of notice of intention — which would be arguable.*

*3   Reason (3) above is worth including — but is the least likely of the three to be upheld.*

*4   Naturally, any of the three reasons which is not applicable in your case should be excluded.*

# Chapter 21

# Race relations

Whether race relations is a field in which Parliament can effectively interfere is a question of argument and philosophy. Employers must cope with whatever Parliament produces — and a new production has (as we go to press) passed through Parliament.

*The Race Relations Act, 1976,* has not yet been published — so a fuller Chapter and greater detail must await the next edition of this book. However, we can now record that the new Act 'makes fresh provision with respect to discrimination on racial grounds and relations between people of different racial groups'. It amends and strengthens the 1965 and 1968 Race Relations Acts and it establishes machinery for the enforcement of the Race Relations legislation which runs along very similar lines to that already existing under the Sex Discrimination Act.

Direct discrimination is banned against a person of a particular racial group on the ground of his 'colour, race, nationality or ethnic or national origins'. 'Nationality' is new. There is still no reference to religion, although, on the wording of this section, discrimination against Jews is almost certainly covered.

Part 2 of the Act deals with discrimination in the employment field. It now becomes unlawful for a person 'in relation to employment by him at an establishment in Great Britain, to discriminate against another —

*(a)* in the arrangements he makes for the purpose of determining who should be offered that employment; or

*(b)* in the terms in which he offers him that employment, or

*(c)* by refusing or deliberately omitting to offer him that employment.'

Access to opportunities for promotion, transfer or training 'or to any other benefits, facilities or services' must not be afforded or withheld on grounds of racial discrimination. Nor must an employee be 'dismissed or subject to any other detriment' on such grounds.

Employment agencies, vocational training bodies, the Manpower Services Commission, the Employment Services Agency and the Training Services Agency are specifically covered. So is discrimination against contract workers — as opposed to people who are actually on your payroll.

It will be unlawful for a partnership of six or more partners 'in relation to a position as partner in the firm' to discriminate on racial grounds − although partnerships of one to five people may still select on whatever grounds they wish. Trade unions and employers' associations are also covered by the Act. And it becomes unlawful for those who confer authorisation or qualification to discriminate in this way.

Matching the Equal Opportunities Commission, which already seeks to help women to get their rights, the 'Commission for Racial Equality' will establish Codes of Practice; conduct investigations; seek information; and assist those who are discriminated against.

Enforcement of the Act against defaulting employers will (as in Sex Discrimination and Equal Pay cases) be via complaints to Industrial Tribunals.

If a complaint of discrimination is established the tribunal may make a declaration; it may order the payment of compensation; and it may make a 'recommendation' that the employer take within a specified period such action as the tribunal considers 'practicable for the purpose of obviating or reducing the adverse effect on the complainant of any act of discrimination to which the complaint relates'. Failure to comply with the recommendation may lead to further compensation.

There is much more in the Act − including Part 8, making it an offence to 'incite to racial hatred'. Nor need the prosecution prove any 'intent' to incite.

There are exceptions to the rules − as where a person's race or colour is 'an essential qualification for the job' (Chinese cooks − but not Chinese waiters, it seems). And 'discriminatory advertisements' are outlawed.

Racial discrimination may be very expensive − especially as a person who is dismissed unfairly on grounds of his race may obtain his remedy even though he has not been employed for the usual six months qualification period.


## 222   Race relations − denial of discrimination

We were extremely upset to receive a letter from your Commission alleging discrimination by this company, which has always prided itself on the entire lack of prejudice which governs its policies.

It is denied that Mr Smith was 'discriminated against' on the grounds of his 'colour, race or ethnic or national origin'. We declined to employ him because we did not regard him as suitably qualified for the work concerned.

We are passing your letter to our solicitors, Messrs . . . and
. . . . If there is any further correspondence in this matter,
kindly address it to them, for the attention of their Mr . . . .

## 223  Facilities not refused because of colour

*Confidential*

It is denied that we refused to supply the goods/facilities/
services concerned to Mr Jones by reason of his colour. At
the material time, he was drunk/atrociously rude to our
manager/abusive to me personally/asking for goods/facilities/
services to be provided to him outside hours/when the business
was shut/ which we did not have available.

We are passing your letter to our solicitors, Messrs . . . and
. . . . If there is any further correspondence in this matter,
kindly address it to them, for the attention of their Mr . . . .

## 224  Invitation to Commission to send in officer

There was no discrimination on our part. But there is
clearly a misunderstanding, which we would be happy to
clear up. Perhaps one of your officers would call and see our
managing director?

## 225  Complaint of discrimination

We are making this formal complaint to the Commission
for Racial Equality Board in accordance with the Race Relations Acts, because we are convinced that our employee,
James Jones, has been discriminated against on the ground of
his colour. This most excellent man sought housing accommodation from Messrs . . ., on the new estate at Redville. Having
been told by telephone that several houses were available,
immediately he appeared at the office of the estate agents, he
was assured that all accommodation had been sold. This was
patently untrue, as the various 'For Sale' boards bore witness.

Would you kindly look into the matter?

Mr Jones is a most excellent, reliable, diligent and kindly
person and we have every confidence that his complaint is

justified. We have asked him to countersign this letter by way of written authority from him to make the complaint concerned.

## 226    Written authority for complaint to Commission

I, James Jones, of . . . in . . . , hereby authorise my employers, Smith Ltd, of . . . in . . . , to make complaint on my behalf in connection with unlawful discrimination against me by . . . Ltd, estate agents, of . . . in . . . .

(Signed) . . . . . . .

## 226a    TUC Equal Opportunities Clause

'The parties to this agreement are committed to the development of positive policies to promote equal opportunity in employment regardless of workers' sex, marital status, creed, colour, race or ethnic origins. This principle will apply in respect of all conditions of work including pay, hours of work, holiday entitlement, overtime and shiftwork, work allocation, guaranteed earnings, sick pay, pensions, recruitment, training, promotion and redundancy (nothing in this clause is designed to undermine the protections for women workers in the Factories Act).

The management undertake to draw opportunities for training and promotion to the attention of all eligible employees, and to inform all employees of this agreement on equal opportunity.

The parties agree that they will review from time to time, through their joint machinery, the operation of this equal opportunity policy.

If any employee considers that he or she is suffering from unequal treatment on the grounds of sex, marital status, creed, colour, race ot ethnic origins, he or she may make a complaint which will be dealt with through the agreed procedures for dealing with grievances.'

" I FIND THE BOOK INVALUABLE IN DEALING WITH TRADE UNIONISTS___ ! "

# Part Four

# EMPLOYMENT PROTECTION

# Chapter 22

# Introduction

*The Employment Protection Act, 1975,* covers a vast area — ranging from the establishment of the Advisory, Conciliation and Arbitration Service on a statutory basis to the disclosure by employers to independent trade unions of appropriate information, during the course of collective bargaining; from guarantee payments for workless days to the notification of trade unions and/or of the Secretary of Employment in respect of intended redundancies.

The Part which now follows includes all the miscellaneous areas of the Act — but excludes changes in the unfair dismissal protection and women's rights, which are dealt with in Parts 2 and 3, respectively.

# Chapter 23

# The Advisory, Conciliation and Arbitration Service

The Advisory, Conciliation and Arbitration Service is now established on a statutory basis. Every employer and manager who is liable to run into employment difficulty on any scale — whether large or small — should know of the powers and responsibilities of the Service, which can do so much to achieve that splendid object — the avoidance of disputes and litigation.

ACAS was born out of the Commission on Industrial Relations and fathered by the Department of Employment. But it has long been totally independent. One of its top officials recently stated that never at any time has the Service been leaned on by any Government Minister, at any level. It is respected by all sides of industry for its independence. This is the touchstone of its ability to assist — an ability, greatly enhanced by the Employment Protection Act, which sets out its functions.

Section 4: 'The Service shall, if it thinks fit, on request or otherwise, provide without charge, to employers, employers' associations, workers and trade unions such advice as it thinks appropriate on any matter concerned with industrial relations or with employment policies'.

The Service is not bound to advise; it may do so of its own volition or on the request of any party; it is not permitted to make any charge; and its field of operation is as wide as can be conceived. The individual matters include:

1  The organisation of workers or employers for the purpose of collective bargaining.
2  Recognition of trade unions by employers.
3  Machinery for the negotiation of terms and conditions of employment, and for joint consultation.
4  Procedures for avoiding and settling workers disputes and grievances.
5  Questions relating to communication between employers and workers.
6  Facilities for officials and trade unions.
7  Procedures relating to the termination of employment.
8  Disciplinary matters.
9  Manpower planning, labour turnover and absenteeism.

10    Promotional and vocational training, recruitment and retention of workers.
11    Payment systems, including equal pay and job evaluation.

If you require advice on any of these matters — from the dismissal of one employee to a massive worry about the recognition of a trade union — do not hesitate to contact ACAS.

The Conciliation officers who provide the advice are a highly trained body, ranging of course in experience from new appointments to industrial conciliators of long standing. Conversations with personnel chiefs and trade union officials throughout the country, suggest that very few people regret seeking the advice of ACAS. It has two special advantages: it is free and you do not have to follow it.

If the advice does not produce a settlement, ACAS may then conciliate.

Section 2: 'Where a trade dispute exists or is apprehended, the Service, may at the request of one or more parties to the dispute or otherwise, offer the parties to the dispute its assistance with a view to bring about a settlement'.

Naturally, conciliation depends upon consent. 'We spend much of our lives dragging channels of communication between people who do not know how to talk to each other', a conciliator told me. ACAS provide industrial catalysts of a high order. Their success rate with incipient disputes is in the region of 50 per cent — a massive saving in industrial chaos and a huge avoidance of loss to industry, employers, employees and the country alike.

Third, the Service may arbitrate. Like any other arbitration, it can exist only because the parties agree in advance to accept the decision of an independent arbitrator, who acts as a judge in their cause. His decision is enforceable in the same way as that of a judge.

Commercial arbitrations have considerable disadvantages. They are often as expensive as litigation — in building disputes, for instance, the evidence may be paraded with the same mass of documentation by the identical skill and highly paid lawyers as if the matter were before an official referee. But arbitration is often an acceptable and thrifty way of dealing with industrial disputes and of avoiding industrial action.

Section 3: 'Where a trade dispute exists or is apprehended, the Service may, request that one or more parties and with the consent of all the parties to the dispute, refer all or any of the matter to which the dispute relates for settlement', by arbitration. Unlike advice or conciliation which may be provided at the request of one party, arbitration can only proceed 'with the consent of all the parties to the dispute'.

ACAS may appoint one or more persons to deal with the arbitration, but it is not entitled to appoint one of its own conciliators. Alternatively, it may refer the dispute to the Central Arbitration Committee (which now replaces the Industrial Arbitration Board).

Advice; conciliation; arbitration — and the catalyst Service also creates new Codes of Conduct. Like the Highway Code on the road or the Code of Industrial Relations Practice (with its requirement that you must give, whatever practicable, written notice of intending dismissal) ACAS codes regulate good industrial relations practices. Examples: the Code dealing with the time off which should reasonably be given to trade union officials for the purposes of industrial relations activities and (above all) the Code which guides employers as to the information which they must disclose to independent, recognised trade unions during the course of collective bargaining.

ACAS codes (like the rest) are not binding in law. But in any civil or criminal proceeding in which a breach of the Code is relevant, that breach (may and almost certainly will) be brought in evidence against those who have offended against it.

Whether dealing with actual or possible disputes over the recognition of trade unions (in connection with which ACAS is at the centre of a new procedure); when working out new payment systems or manpower planning policies — whatever the problem, if it concerns good industrial relations, ACAS can help you. Know of that help — and use it. To do so, you will need letters.

\* \* \*

## 227   Collective bargaining — advice sought

We wish to extend collective bargaining arrangements within our plant/company. Please would you arrange for one of your officers to call upon me as soon as possible in order to advise as to how this object may be accomplished.

## 228   Industrial dispute — experienced officer needed

I regret to inform you that we have now reached a deadlock in a dispute which is likely to lead to industrial action. As this could cause a total halt in our production and the laying off of large numbers of people, please would you arrange for a most experienced officer to assist with advice and, if necessary, with conciliation, at the earliest possible opportunity. This letter is being delivered by hand.

NOTE:

*If you need the help of a particularly experienced person, do not hesitate to say so. You may be fortunate already to have a contact with an individual Conciliation Officer, thus:*

## 229   Industrial dispute — particular officer needed

### *Urgent*

I regret that the issue that I discussed with you concerning . . . has not been resolved and it is now likely that an official strike will be called. Your services are most urgently required and I would be most grateful if you would contact me personally forthwith. I shall send this letter by hand and await word in my office.

Many thanks for your assistance in the past and in anticipation of the earliest possible response to this request.

## 230   Negotiating machinery — overhaul needed

We are not satisfied with our negotiating machinery — and nor are the various trade unions concerned. However, we are having difficulty in reaching agreement and the assistance of your Service would be much appreciated by all concerned. Please would you contact me as soon as possible.

## 231   Trade union facilities

We cannot reach agreement with the . . . Union concerning the various facilities sought by them for extending their membership/calling meetings in working hours (*or as the case may be*). We would appreciate your guidance and help in sorting out this problem.

## 232   Unfair dismissal — advice required

We are suffering greatly from absenteeism and our disciplinary procedures will have to be invoked. We know that allegations are bound to be made of unfair practices — however carefully and fairly we proceed. Perhaps you could spare a few minutes at your earliest convenience to help us to establish some sort of procedure that will be both manifestly fair and accepted as such by the trade union?

## 233   Redundancy planning — advice

I confirm our telephone conversation when I told you that we are going to have to create redundancies. Please would you call by as soon as possible to help us to establish a procedure which will both operate fairly and enable the company to make the best of a bad situation.
With many thanks.

NOTE:
*By all means telephone the Service or an individual officer with whom you have the appropriate relationship. Confirmation in writing, though, is often advisable.*

## 234   Job evaluation — advice

We are proposing to instruct work study engineers to consider our pay structure and to do full job evaluation studies. Before giving them instructions, however, we would greatly appreciate your advice as to the best way to proceed.
With our thanks and best wishes.

## 235   Equal pay dispute

The . . . Union is alleging that its women members employed as . . . in our . . . are not receiving equal pay for like work to that done by men in other businesses. This we deny. However, we will greatly appreciate your advice and guidance as to how this matter may be resolved on an amicable and fair basis.

## 236   Enquiry invited

A most serious industrial relations situation is arising in

our business. This may be summarised as follows:

1 . . .
2 . . .
3 . . .

We would greatly appreciate your advice as to how this matter should now be dealt with and we also officially request an enquiry into the question in issue in accordance with the powers given to the Service by Section 5 of The Employment Protection Act.

We look forward to an early reply and with my thanks in anticipation.

NOTE:

*Section 5 gives the Service power 'if it thinks fit' to enquire into 'any question relating to industrial relations generally or to industrial relations in any particular industry or in any particular undertaking or part of an undertaking'. The findings may or may not be published – but will certainly have great weight. Before you ask for an enquiry, make sure that you are prepared to accept its outcome. Otherwise, remember the famous advice given by a factory inspector, asked whether it was wise to consult his Service. He quoted an ancient proverb: 'Love work; hate tyranny; live righteously; and do not let your name get too well known to the authorities'. This proverb is more applicable to the factory man and the tax man than to ACAS – but is nevertheless worthy of thought.*

## 237   Codes of Practice – request for copies

We understand that the Code of Practice on . . . is/is likely shortly to become available. Would you kindly arrange for a copy to be sent to me, with an invoice if necessary.

Would you also please arrange for the appropriate person to inform me as to the current arrangements for me to be put onto the mailing list in respect of publications which are of concern to my company and which may from time to time be produced by your Service.

My thanks in anticipation.

## 238   Conciliation request – victimisation

I am afraid that we have reached deadlock in connection

with the dismissal of the convenor of the . . . Union. For
reasons which we have explained to you, we are not prepared
to take him back; and the union is determined not to permit
its members to return to work unless we do reinstate him.
They allege victimisation — which we deny.

Could you please see whether the time has now arrived
when conciliation might be possible? Alternatively, we will
be prepared to consider arbitration, if this would be acceptable to the union.

Your early attention to this request would be most
appreciated.

NOTE:
*Letters individually addressed presume a relationship with a particular
conciliation officer. Otherwise, refer direct to the Service — preferably
after preliminary enquiries made personally or by telephone.*

## 239   Arbitrator required

I am pleased to inform you that the . . . union has agreed
that we go to arbitration in connection with the dispute
concerning . . . . The question now arises: Whom do we
appoint as arbitrator?

I appreciate that your Service does not itself appoint ar-
bitrators from its own ranks, but perhaps you would arrange
for someone to contact us immediately, to assist both sides
to agree on an appropriate and acceptable person to arbitrate
upon a dispute which, I would remind you, is causing severe
disruption in production and much hardship to individual
employees.

## 240   Arbitration urgent — chaser

You kindly promised that you would contact . . . with a
view to seeing whether he would be prepared to act as
arbitrator in the current dispute between our company and
the . . . Union. It is now . . . days/weeks since our meeting
and we have heard nothing further from you. The situation is
getting serious. Please would you contact me, at once?

With many thanks and best wishes.

## 241    Arbitration requires submission — to union

We note that you are prepared to submit to arbitration but that you are not prepared to agree in advance to accept the arbitrator's decisions.

We must respectfully point out the essence of an arbitration is the prior acceptance by all parties concerned of the decision of the arbitrator — and while we are prepared to proceed to arbitration, this can only be on the basis that you, like ourselves, must agree to accept the judgement of the independent arbitrator.

The alternative would be to set up some sort of court of enquiry — which we do not feel would meet the purpose — which is, of course, to achieve a resolution of the unhappy dispute which at present divides us.

I look forward to hearing from you.

NOTE:

*In a dispute involving ASLEF (The footplatemen's union) and British Rail, the union agreed to arbitration on the strict understanding that it would not commit itself in advance to acceptance of the arbitrator's award. Sensibly, the arbitration proceeded — but in fact it was a Commission of Inquiry, whose decision was in fact accepted. It is sometimes a mistake to worry too much about formalities, when results are required. Flexibility is essential — and ACAS is a marvellously flexible body, with wide powers sensibly used.*

## 242    Thanks — to ACAS

We are all very grateful to you for the help which you gave to us in resolving the dispute with the . . . Union. All sides are convinced that the settlement is fair and reasonable — and it is clear that had you not intervened so effectively and patiently, industrial action would have been inevitable and grave harm would have been caused to the company and to all who work for it.

I am sending a copy of this letter to the chairman of ACAS.

NOTE:

*Do not forget to give thanks where it is due — and, where appropriate, to let that thanks be known to those upon whom the individual depends for his position — and his prospects of promotion. Thanks cost nothing*

*– but they help to cement a friendly relationship which has been useful to you in the past and which you may require again in the future.*

# Chapter 24

# Recognition of trade unions

As discussed in the previous Chapter, the Employment Protection Act established an entirely new system for dealing with recognition disputes. With the Advisory, Conciliation and Arbitration Service (ACAS) in charge; with the emphasis on attempts to reach agreement, it set up the new procedures where negotiation has failed.

Section 11: 'A recognition issue may be referred by an independent trade union to the Service by written application in such form as the Service may require'.

Only an independent trade union, i.e. not one under the direct or indirect control of the management may apply. The employer may, however, ask ACAS to advise or to conciliate on the issue — so in practice either party may call on the Service to intervene and to help.

'Recognition' is defined as 'recognition of the union by an employer, or two or more associated employers, to any extent, for the purpose of collective bargaining'.

Suppose that a 'recognition issue' arises between you and a trade union representing, perhaps, only a proportion of your work force — an issue, that is, 'arising from a request . . . for recognition . . . including, where recognition is already accorded to some extent, a request for further recognition'. You are not prepared to accede to the request. The union may call in ACAS which 'shall examine the issue . . . consult all parties who it considers will be affected by the outcome of the reference and . . . make such enquiries as it thinks fit'.

ACAS will do its best to have the issue settled by agreement and 'where appropriate, will seek to assist such a settlement by conciliation'. The reference may be withdrawn at any time by notice in writing.

If the issue is not settled and the reference is not withdrawn, then ACAS will produce a written report setting out its findings and any advice — including any recommendation for recognition and the reason for it. ACAS is not restricted in its power to recommend. The recognition may apply, for instance, to the whole of the unit or part of it; to some description or descriptions of workers or to all of them; to one or more 'level or levels'. It may also be subject to conditions.

In the course of its enquiries, ACAS 'shall ascertain the opinions of workers to whom the issue relates by any means it thinks fit' — including a formal ballot. Section 14 provides the procedures for such a ballot.

If ACAS recommends recognition but the union considers that the recommendation has not been complied with, then at any time within a period of two months from the date when the recommendation became operative, the union may make a complaint to ACAS. The complaint will be that the employer 'is not taking such action by way of or with a view to carrying on negotiations as might reasonably be expected to be taken by an employer ready and willing to carry on such negotiations as are envisaged by the recommendation'. Once again, ACAS must attempt to settle the matter by conciliation.

If conciliation then fails, the union may apply to the Central Arbitration Committee — the body set up by the Act which replaces the Industrial Arbitration Board. If the Committee finds the complaint wholly or partly well founded, it will make a declaration, and the right of the individual worker to have recognition accorded to his trade union will then become embedded in the contract of employment of that worker. Failure at that stage to accord recognition may lead to an action (including proceedings for an injunction) for breach of the contract of service — an action which may be brought in the High Court at present but, when the additional provision of the Employment Protection Act is brought into force transferring disputes regarding contracts of service to the (steadily more omnipotent) industrial tribunals, the complaint will (like most others under the Employment Protection Act) duly end there.

These rules are now in force. The wise employer will keep as far away from any procedures other than conciliation as he reasonably can. He will also comply, where necessary, with recommendations of ACAS. In order to do so, he must watch his documentation with care.

\*   \*   \*

## 243   Agreement to recognition

I am happy to confirm that the Company is pleased to grant recognition to your union, for bargaining purposes, as follows:

1   At the following plant/plants: . . . .
2   In respect of the following description/descriptions of workers: . . . .
3   The above recognition to be general/in respect of the following specified matters: . . . .
4   At all/the following levels: . . . .

My colleagues and I trust that this agreement will represent not merely the continuation of our happy relationship with you and your colleagues and your union as in the past, but the start of an intensification of that relationship, for the benefit of those whom you represent as well as for that of the Company.

With best wishes.

NOTE:

*The categories set out in (1) to (4) above are those specified in Section 12(5) – being those which must be specified in any recommendation for recognition made by ACAS.*

## 244   Refusal of recognition

The management has given most careful consideration to the request of your union for recognition in respect of. . . .

As only about . . . per cent (number) or workers in the plant/workshop/category concerned have joined your union, we do not feel that it would be appropriate for the company to recognise your union for bargaining purposes. However, we have a completely open mind as to the future; as you know, no impediments are placed in the way of your seeking to extend your membership; and we will be pleased to re-consider the matter in due course, if and when your efforts to increase your membership are crowned with success.

With best wishes.

## 245   Request to ACAS – recognition advice

I would be grateful if you would call upon me at your earliest convenience. A recognition issue has arisen which is likely to give rise to a dispute and your help with advice and, if necessary, with conciliation would be most apprecia-ted.

NOTE:

*Repeat: While it is only the trade union which can set the recogni-tion procedures in train, there is no reason why management should not ask ACAS for advice or conciliation on a recognition issue.*

## 246   Consultation arrangements

I note that you wish to consult with the company in connection with the recognition issue referred to you by the . . . Union. I am instructed by the Board to assure you of the full co-operation of the company. Please contact me at your early convenience to make the appropriate arrangements. And if and in so far as you feel that an enquiry is necessary, we shall be pleased to assist in any way.

The above is without prejudice to the view which we have expressed to the union, namely that recognition would not be justified on the basis of its present membership within the plant/office (as the case may be) within which recognition is sought.

## 247   Submission of written evidence

I enclose herewith copies of all documents relevant to the enquiry which you are proposing to hold into the current recognition dispute in our works/. . . department. I have also summarised the main contentions of the company, and I have pleasure in also enclosing that summary herewith in the hope that it will be of assistance to you.

NOTE:
*The Act contains no provision for the submission of documentary evidence as such. However, the sending of such evidence as above has two advantages: It concentrates the managerial mind on the preparation of the evidence and hence of the company's case; and it helps to elucidate the issues for ACAS, in a way that can only assist the company's case — assuming that the case is worthy of assistance, and if it is not then the preparation of the documents will help to make that clear and to reveal its weaknesses. Recognition of weaknesses is necessary not merely so as to fight a case in the best manner but especially so as to know when not to fight and when to propose or to accept a sensible compromise.*

## 248   To ACAS — for promotion of agreement

Section 12(3) of the Employment Protection Act requires the Service to have regard 'to the desirability of encouraging the settlement of the recognition issue by agreement' and provides that ACAS shall, where appropriate 'seek to assist such a settlement by conciliation'.

It may be helpful if I state at this early stage that the company would be very pleased to settle the matter by agreement; that in so far as you or any of your colleagues are able to assist in the promotion of such an agreement, we shall be obliged to you; and that, if necessary, we are prepared to accept conciliation.

## 249    Recognition agreement after dispute

I am happy to confirm the agreement arrived at between your trade union and my company, which has happily put an end to the recognition dispute. The terms of the agreement are as follows:

1    The company agrees to recognise your union for bargaining purposes in respect of . . . employees working in our office/workshop (or as the case may be).
2    Your union forthwith to call off its work to rule, so that full production may be resumed immediately.

With best wishes.

## 250    Denial of failure to comply

I understand that the . . . Union has complained to your Service that the company has allegedly failed to comply with your recommendation dated . . . , concerning recognition of that union. This allegation is wholly denied. We were, are and will remain willing to recognise the union for bargaining purposes. What we are not prepared to accept is a closed shop. The union negotiates on behalf of its own members and we are following your recommendation in both letter and spirit.

By all means visit us at an early opportunity. We shall be pleased to discuss the matter — but not to give greater rights than those resulting from your recommendation.

Chapter 25

# The right to belong

An employee is entitled by law to belong to an independent trade union, i.e. one that is neither dominated nor controlled not influenced by employers. The Certification Officer decides whether or not a trade union is 'independent' and if he certifies that a union is independent, that decision is final (see Chapter 26).

It is unlawful to discriminate against or to dismiss an employee for seeking to belong to or to take part in the activities of an independent trade union. Indeed, whereas normally an employee who seeks unfair dismissal protection must be continuously employed for six months, there is no such time limit where the dismissal is on grounds of trade union membership or activities.

Conversely, an employee is not entitled as of right to belong to or to take part in the activities of a non-independent trade union. Those staff associations which are 'tame' — or 'sweetheart' unions, as they are sometimes called — are not protected.

In closed shop situations, the only people who are entitled not to join a trade union are those who have a 'religious objection' to trade union membership. Jehovah's Witnesses and Seventh Day Adventists, for instance, may successfully opt out. No such 'conscientious objection' as would have sufficed under the Industrial Relations Act can now excuse a person from membership.

\*   \*   \*

## 251  Right to belong — alleged

I write to protest at the discrimination from which I am suffering, because I am seeking to belong/take part in the activities of an independent trade union, namely . . . . As I am exercising my proper, lawful entitlement, I trust that you will ensure that this discrimination ceases. The matters about which I complain are in particular:
  1 . . .
  2 . . .
  3 . . .

## 252 Right to belong – conceded

Thank you for your letter dated . . . . You are indeed entitled to belong to the . . . Union. I have made enquiries regarding your allegation of discrimination, all of which are denied. However, I will be pleased to discuss these matters with you if you will call on me at my office at . . . a.m./p.m.
Dealing with the allegations of discrimination in turn, my investigations have revealed the following:-

1 . . .
2 . . .
3 . . .

I shall look forward to seeing you.

NOTE:
*It is always useful to record in writing the answers to allegations which have themselves been made in writing.*


## 253 Right to belong – denied

I am in receipt of your letter dated . . . , and clearly you are under a misapprehension. You have by law the right to belong to and/or to take part in the activities of any independent trade union. You are seeking to build up a staff association which has not been certified as independent. However, I will be glad if you will call on me to discuss the whole matter.


## 254 Closed shop – right to remain outside denied

I write to confirm our conversation. You do not wish to join the . . . Union, with which the company has made a closed shop agreement. Unfortunately – whether you or I like it or not – you have no legal ground for remaining outside. Your objection may be 'conscientious' but it is not 'religious'. In the circumstances, if you adhere to your refusal to join the union, I fear that I shall have no alternative other than to terminate your employment.

## 255    Religious objection to closed shop

In write to confirm that you have registered any objection
to joining the . . . Union, on the ground that you are a
Jehovah's Witness/Seventh Day Adventist/ and that you have
a religious objection to trade union membership. You are
within your legal right in relying upon such an exception to
the general rule which exists in a closed shop situation, and I
am informing the trade union concerned accordingly.

## 256    To trade union – religious objection

I confirm that I have interviewed Mr George Pritchard, as
you requested. So far as I can ascertain, he is genuine in his
adherence to the religious beliefs of the Jehovah's Witnesses/
Seventh Day Adventists/. . . , and has a sincere religious objection to trade union membership. He therefore comes
within the statutory exception and we cannot impose membership upon him.

With best wishes.

# Chapter 26

# Certification to trade unions

Unions always were registered — even before the Industrial Relations Act. Those who were not on the register set up under the Friendly Societies Acts lost all sorts of benefits, including tax reliefs.

Under the Industrial Relations Act, those reliefs — and many other benefits — were reserved for unions which did not remove themselves from the register kept by the Registrar of trade unions. When Parliament referred to a 'trade union' in the Industrial Relations Act, it meant only one which was on that particular register. But in practice, the Registrar was noted neither for the number of unions over whose activities he theoretically presided nor for the interference with the union's rules which he in practice imposed.

With the demise of the Industrial Relations Act, the Registrar — symbol of a theoretical servitude hated by the trade union movement — was likewise abolished. But unions remained registered. The Chief Registrar of Friendly Societies held the register. His main functions are now transferred to the 'Certification Officer'.

The Certification Officer maintains a list of trade unions, duly certified by him as 'independent'. His certificate is absolute evidence of that independence and is of immense value to unions, many of whose rights under the Act depend upon their being both independent and recognised. 'Sweetheart' and 'tame' staff associations are excluded from most of the new statutory benefits.

To be 'independent', a union must be free of control — direct or indirect — by or on behalf of the employer. Usually (but not always) this yardstick is finance. Who pays the piper?

A union which wishes to register may apply to the Certification Officer, sending a fee of £21 (or such other fee as may later be prescribed by regulations). Address: Certification Officer, Vincent Square, London SW1 (Telephone 01-828 7603).

Once an application is received, the Certification Officer must determine whether the trade union is independent — and if so, he will issue his certificate. If not, then he must give his reasons and the aggrieved trade union may appeal. The appropriate forms should be obtained from the Certification Officer, if and when the occasion arises.

When deciding whether or not a union is 'independent', the Certification Officer 'shall make such enquiries as he thinks fit and shall take into account any relevant information submitted to him by any person'. The employer is a 'person'. Most of the correspondence with the Certification Officer will inevitably be carried out by or on behalf of the trade unions concerned, to whom the above information should where necessary be provided. Employers may require these precedents:

1   Supporting application for certification.
2   Opposing it.
3   Sitting firmly (and with rugged and terrified independence) on the fence.

*   *   *

## 257   Certification application — supported

### *Re: Trade Union's Application for Certification*

I am pleased to confirm that, to the best of my knowledge, information and belief, the above union is totally independent. Certainly in so far as its dealings with our company are concerned, it receives neither direction nor (still less) control from the company or any of its directors, managers or other officers; nor does it receive any financial support from the company, direct or indirect.

## 258   Application opposed

### *. . . Union's Application for Certification*

I have been informed that the above union has applied for registration as an independent trade union. I feel bound to inform you of the following matters which may influence your decision and no doubt of which you will wish to take account:

1   The company has made the following payments to the union during the course of the past . . . months/years:-
2   The union's officers include . . . .
3   The company entered into an agreement with the union on the . . . , a copy of which is annexed hereto.

In the above circumstances, this company does not regard the union as independent.

## 259 Non-committal evidence

Thank you for your letter dated . . . . The information you require is as follows:

1 . . . .
2 . . . .
3 . . . .

### 259a Appeal against refusal to certify

We acknowledge receipt of your decision to refuse certification to the above named union and we wish to appeal against that decision. Kindly accept this letter as notice of that intention and supply us with any further forms and information.

NOTES:

1 *A trade union which is refused certification has a right of appeal to the Employment Appeal Tribunal. An objector to a successful certification (usually a TUC-affiliated union) has no such right.*

2 *The certification office is at Vincent House, Hide Place, London SW1 (telephone: 828 7603).*

3 *Appeal forms (for this and all other purposes) available from the Employment Appeal Tribunal, 4 St James's Square, London SW1Y 4JB.*

4 *Time limit for appeal against certification – 42 days; other appeals – 42 days from date of entry in the register.*

*Chapter 27*

# Disclosure of information*

In the long run, the most far reaching and important sections of the Employment Protection Act are those requiring the disclosure of information.

1    Disclosure is only required to independent trade unions — not to any union which is directly or indirectly under the control of the management.

2    Disclosure is only required at the union's request. Wise employers will anticipate requests and do their best to keep their unions well informed — but the law will not force information on the workers.

3    Information will be required during the course of collective bargaining — and not for the purposes of individual negotiation.

4    Information must be given which is 'material' for the purposes of collective bargaining — but that is just about everything, ranging from the company's current profits or losses; from the state of the order book to the likelihood of expansion or redundancies; from the profitability of a single plant or section within that plant to the current finances of the entire company or group of companies, at home or abroad.

The Act requires the employer to disclose not only information in his own possession but also in the possession of any associated company — that is, the parent, holding or sister company (and not a company with which the employer is associated for business purposes). There appears to be no restriction on whether the associated employer (for this purpose) is at home or overseas — and independent trade unions may seek all information from all branches and sections of the 'undertaking' — anywhere.

However, the Act also lays down a series of exceptions. For instance, information need not be given about an individual, without his consent; if it is confidential to others; if the giving of the information would affect national security or be contrary to some enactment; and above all, if disclosure would cause serious harm to the business.

How these massive exceptions are to be interpreted must (as we go to press) await the emergence of the ACAS Code on the subject (and which, by the time you read and use this chapter, should be available in its formal form on request). Meanwhile, do not be fooled by the parliamentary silence concerning disclosure into thinking that all is simple. On the contrary, all is very complicated indeed. The silence

*Expected Spring 1977.     *178*

arose because, with the tightening up of one exception — these sections were lifted bodily from the Industrial Relations Act.

Finally, note:

1 If you cannot reach agreement on disclosure, ACAS will intervene; if necessary, make recommendations and, if those are not followed, refer the matter to the Central Arbitration Committee. Failure to comply will then result in the employee's right to the information in question being implied as a term in his contract of service.

2 The company secretary and/or accountant is likely to have to produce information far quicker and in much greater detail than that required by the Companies Act. However, he has two extra bolt holes. He need not give inspection of the books nor provide copies of any document other than one prepared for the purpose of disclosing the information — and if he can show that the time and cost involved in preparing the information sought would be out of all proportion to its value to the recipient.

\* \* \*

## 260 Refusal to disclose — against interests of national security

I am in receipt of your request for information concerning .... I regret that it would not be proper for me to disclose this, having regard to the classified nature of the work in the department concerned. Such disclosure would be against the interests of national security. I am sure that on reconsideration you will agree with this.

Nevertheless, if you would care to meet me to discuss this matter, I think that I can provide you with sufficient information for your purposes, without going beyond the bounds of my proper authority — and I would be pleased to meet you at any mutually convenient time.

## 261 Refusal — information supplied in confidence

The information which you request was communicated to the management in confidence, and in the circumstances I regret that it cannot be disclosed.

We have already revealed to you a great deal of information — and it is hoped that you will now be able to proceed with the negotiations. If there are any further matters which can be disclosed without betrayal of a confidence, I shall, of course, be pleased to co-operate with you. We are only too anxious that our negotiations should be carried on in the most frank and friendly manner.

With best wishes.

## 262   Refusal of information relating to an individual

I am sorry. You ask for information relating to payments made to specific individuals. At your request, I consulted them to see whether they would be prepared to have their salaries or wages revealed — and they have declined. In the circumstances, I am not required or entitled to disclose this information to you.

In any event, the information which you have received should, I hope, be sufficient for the purposes of collective bargaining and the management is only too ready to co-operate with you in the hope of achieving a mutually satisfactory agreement.

I look forward to seeing you, as arranged, at tomorrow's meeting.

## 263   Refusal of information — serious harm

### *Confidential*

The disclosure of [*e.g. the nature of the Company's over-drafts*] would cause serious harm to the Company's interests, for reasons other than its effect on collective bargaining. This information is highly confidential and if its disclosure were to lead to a leak, this would not only seriously affect the Company but also the jobs of the people whom we employ and whom you so ably represent.

I am sorry to have to convey this refusal to you, but I am sure that you will understand the position. If there is any other information which you require for the purposes of the current negotiations, please do not hesitate to inform me.

## 264 Refusal of information prepared for legal proceedings

The information you require was prepared by our accountants specifically for the purpose of defending a legal action brought against the Company by . . . . In the circumstances, the Company is not required to disclose that information. You will appreciate, I am sure, that the legal proceedings concerned are of great importance to the Company and the material to which you refer is privileged in law.

## 265 Refusal — information not necessary for carrying on collective bargaining

The information you request is not necessary for the purposes of collective bargaining. It concerns matters outside the scope of the current negotiations. In the circumstances, I would not feel justified in disclosing it to you.

However, I think that information which may concern you more and which we could probably disclose would be . . . .
May I suggest that we discuss the question of . . . ? I would be pleased to look into the question of . . . with you.

NOTE:
*It is always good tactics — in negotiating with employees, in the same way as in bargaining with potential suppliers or customers — not merely to say no. Use the positive approach, wherever you can. This is both helpful, fair and constructive. Suggest an alternative.*

## 266 Employer's reply to criticisms of statement

Thank you for your letter. I have carefully considered the points you make. My answers are as follows:
1   The information concerning . . . relates specifically to an individual who has not consented to its being disclosed.
2   It would be seriously prejudicial to the Company's interests if the information concerning . . . were to be disclosed.
3   The information requested concerning . . . is highly secret; its disclosure would be against the interests of national security.
Now that you know the reasons for the non-disclosure, I

hope that you will appreciate our difficulties — and that you will accept that we have in fact set out in the statement as much as we properly can, in accordance with not only the Regulations (and the Employment Protection Act), but also in accordance with our firm wish that our employees — including, of course, members of your Union — should have the fullest possible information, consistent with good industrial relations practice.


### 267   No inspection of books

We have been pleased to disclose to you and through you to your union full information concerning the following matters:

     1 . . . .
     2 . . . .
     3 . . . .

However, the Employment Protection Act does not require the company to provide you with a roving commission through the company's books, nor are we prepared to do so.

We will be pleased, however, to provide you with copies of all information prepared for you for the purposes of collective bargaining and we trust that this will suffice for your purpose.


### 268   Cost of collecting information too great

I have, as promised, asked the company secretary to set about collating the information which you required. He tells me, however, that the work involved would be enormous; that the cost of getting the information together would be vast; and that when all is done, the value of the information is unlikely to be very great.

In the circumstances, bearing in mind that the Employment Protection Act says that where the cost of preparing information would be out of proportion to its value in collective bargaining disclosure is not required, I would make the following compromise suggestions:

     1 . . . .
     2 . . . .
     3 . . . .

# Chapter 28

# Redundancy consultation and notification

The new early warning system operates in two directions — that of the trade union and its member; and that of the Secretary of State for Employment.

Where you recognise a trade union for bargaining purposes, you must notify that union of any intended redundancy of any member or members — however few and however many — at the earliest practicable date. Notification (and intense consultation) is essential even if you do not reach the minimum of ten employees at any one establishment whom you intend to dismiss within a particular thirty day period — in which case the Act requires at least sixty days consultation with the trade union concerned. If you intend to make a 100 or more employees redundant at any one establishment within a period of 90 days, then you must give 90 days early warning to the union. Note:

1   You must consult even about the proposed redundancy of one union member or person on whose behalf the union negotiates.

2   When totting up the minimum statutory number for major redundancies, you include both union and non-union members.

3   It is possible that courts will interpret the Section as requiring consultation in respect of non-union members, when a union is recognised as bargaining on their behalf as well as on behalf of its members. There is no doubt whatever, though, that consultation is necessary for those members.

Failure to consult will entitle the *trade union* to apply to an industrial tribunal for a 'protective award' on behalf of its member — that award being the employees remuneration during the protective period, i.e. the period during which consultation should have taken place. If a protective award is not paid, then the member may himself bring a complaint.

This protection is for union members only; it is part of the attempt to strengthen the organised trade union movement and to encourage people to join trade unions; and it can only benefit non-union members indirectly. There can be no question, in any event, of their receiving protective awards.

Still, non-union members will benefit in any case where the employer intends to make ten or more people redundant at any one establishment within a 30 day period (60 days notification) or where he intends to make 100 or more redundant at any one establishment within a 90 day period (90 days warning). The employee gets no money — sanction for failure to comply: fine of up to £400 or a loss of up to 1/10th of normal redundancy rebate.

The object of the exercise, of course, is two-fold:

1    To ensure that employees get the maximum warning of impending disaster, and so to help keep hardship to the minimum.

2    To enable trade unions and/or the Department of Employment to negotiate and/or to assist in efforts to avoid the loss of all or some of the jobs concerned.

\*    \*    \*

### 269   Notification to union of intended redundancy — to members

As you know, we are in the throes of a rationalisation programme which will, we believe, enable us to keep the company on a firm and profitable basis for the foreseeable future. We are happy that we are able to keep redundancies to the absolute minimum. But it now appears certain that we shall have to make two of your members redundant in our . . . workshop. We shall be pleased to discuss these redundancies with you at your convenience.

With best wishes.

NOTE:
*You do not have to select or to name the people whom you intend to make redundant. The choice of job losers may (and normally should) be discussed with the union.*

### 270   Consultation invited — 10 to 99 redundancies

We greatly regret that due to . . . , we have no alternative other than to close the . . . department in our . . . works. We shall do our best to keep the department going for as long as possible and we hope not to have to start the run-down until (*state date — not less than 60 days from date when letter will be received*).

We shall be pleased to consult with you over these proposed

redundancies and I would be grateful if you would contact me at my office as soon as possible. The number of expected redundancies is . . . (*between 10 and 99*).

NOTES:

*1 In the absence of 'special circumstances', notification must be made at least 60 days (or in the case of 100 or more expected redundancies 100 days) before the date of the first of the expected redundancies.*

*2 If you do not know the intended number, then say: about 10 (or as the case may be).*

## 271 Major redundancies – 100 or more

It is with great regret that I must inform you that as a result of the collapse of our home/export market/absolute necessity of rationalising production to remain competitive/ in business, that we shall be forced to close our . . . plant/ department/warehouse/unit. Inevitably, this will cause large scale redundancies, probably in the region of . . . .

We have made every effort to avoid this unhappy situation, and we are still intending to explore every possible avenue of keeping the plant/department/warehouse/unit open. At present though, we see no alternative to closure. And we expect to have to start the run-down in . . . months time (*not less than 3*).

We are giving you this formal notification as required by the Employment Protection Act. But we have always valued the excellent industrial relations that have existed in the plant/ the company – and we shall be pleased to consult with you at the first possible opportunity, to see whether any way can be found to avoid the redundancies or, if that proves as we fear, impossible, then at least to keep any resultant hardship to the absolute minimum.

Please would you contact me immediately at my office?

## 272 Special circumstances – customer insolvent

I am sure that you will have been as shocked and upset as was the Board of this company to learn of the insolvency of . . . Ltd. This collapse has meant that we have had to call a

complete/partial halt to our production/production of . . . .
Unfortunately, this will mean that we will be forced to give
redundancy notices forthwith to not less than . . . employees,
many of whom will be your members.

We are holding an immediate plant/department/works
meeting/meeting with the company/area representatives of
the unions concerned at . . . in . . . . I do hope that you will
be able to attend or if that proves impossible, then to send
your most senior deputy.

I need hardly tell you how distressed we are at this turn
of events — particularly at a time when the company was
making such excellent progress. And we shall, of course, do
all in our power to keep the inevitable hardship that will
result from these unpalatable events to the absolute minimum.

With my warmest personal regards.


## 273   Seasonal work terminates unexpectedly

I regret to inform you that, due to the failure of the har-
vest *(or as the case may be)*, work which we had hoped
would keep our employees busy for another three months
has in fact collapsed. We shall therefore be forced to give
redundancy notices to . . . within the course of the next
seven days.

Please do contact us regarding any steps which might help
reduce any resultant hardship.


## 274   Expected order not obtained

I am afraid that our tender for . . . was not successful; the
work that we had been hoping for has not become available;
and when the present job at . . . is completed in about . . .
weeks time, we shall not be in a position to continue the
employment of . . . . We regret this very much — but the
matter was and is beyond our control.

We shall be pleased to consult with you regarding these
redundancies, at your earliest convenience.

NOTES:
*1   The construction industry is an example of one which is particularly
bedevilled with this sort of problem. It is not clear whether the 'special*

*circumstances' will be interpreted by courts to include those where continued employment depends upon acceptance of tenders. Certainly where the odds against acceptance are considerable, it will be wise to notify unions and (where appropriate) the Minister – even if this results in some employees leaving for a more secure post even before the current job is complete.*

*2 In any event, it is important not only to consult at the earliest opportunity but to have evidence of such consultation.*

### 275   Notification to the Department of Employment

I am instructed to inform you that the company intends to make employees redundant as follows:

1    At our . . . plant, the first dismissals taking effect not earlier than . . . .

2    Through the closure of our . . . office/sales unit, approximately . . . redundancies, taking effect not earlier than . . . .

3    Through the transfer of our Accounts Department from . . . to . . . , commencing on or about . . . .

Please send me your appropriate forms.

### 276   Explanation for delay in notification – unexpected events

I have to inform you that it is the Company's intention to make . . . employees redundant at our . . . plant/office commencing . . . . Unfortunately, it was not possible to notify the Secretary of State through you at an earlier date because of the following events which were both unexpected and beyond the control of the company:

1 . . . .
2 . . . .
3 . . . .

### 277   Denial to union of undue delay

Thank you for your letter dated . . . . It is correct that we were unable to consult with your union about the proposed redundancies more than 60/90 days (*as the case may be*) before the first of these redundancies were due to become effective. The delay was caused entirely by special circumstances beyond our control, and in particular:

    1 . . . .
    2 . . . .
    3 . . . .

That said, the company remains ready and willing to explore any possibility of avoiding all or any of the redundancies and/or of avoiding any hardship which may result to any employee as a result. It would be wrong to hold out any real hope — but we would welcome consultations with you at the earliest opportunity. So do please contact me/the personnel director/. . . as soon as you can.

## 278   A denial of right to protective award

Your member was one of four people whom we unfortunately found it necessary to make redundant. We did consult with you at the earliest practicable opportunity. In the circumstances, if you see fit to apply for a protective award on behalf of your member, the proceedings will be vigorously defended.

We have always done everything within our power to be fair and reasonable towards our employees and to encourage good industrial relations. We are therefore particularly disturbed at this allegation which you have seen fit to make against us.

## 279   Consultation adequate — major redundancy

The period of consultation required in the case of our members was 60 days and not 90 days as stated by you — we did not intend to make 100 people redundant, nor, happily, were we forced to do so.

We consulted with you at the earliest possible opportunity which was in fact more than 60 days before the date of the first dismissal. There can therefore be no substance in your claim for a protective award and any proceedings would be most vigorously defended.

None of this removes our regret that these redundancies

became necessary. And in any event, we shall continue to consult with you in the hope that the hardship caused by the redundancies may be kept to an irreducible minimum.

NOTE:
*You will have to work with the union even after the dispute has been settled. So preserve courtesy, dignity and goodwill – especially in letters which are liable to end up before Tribunals.*

## 280   To Minister – notification adequate

We were disturbed to receive your letter alleging that you did not receive sufficient notification of the redundancies at our . . . plant/office. You were in fact notified at the first reasonably practicable opportunity – which, as it happens, was in excess of the statutory minimum period specified in the Act. The facts are as follows:
1   (*Date of notification*).
2   (*Number of employees to be made redundant*).
3   (*Date of first dismissal*).

## 281   Original intention, less than 10

I write to inform you that in about four weeks we shall have to make approximately 15 people redundant at our . . . plant/office/works. The reason why you did not receive the 60 days notification was that we had originally intended to make only six redundancies. Unfortunately, the collapse of certain orders has forced us to cut our work force by more people than we had intended.

I should add that we shall do everything in our power to ensure that as many redundancies as possible are voluntary; and we would be pleased to see your conciliation officer at any mutually convenient time.

NOTES:
*1   Do not hesitate to call in ACAS – particularly where a dispute is possible.*

*2   You are only obliged to give notice of 'intended' redundancies – and you would claim that in the above case that there were 'special circumstances' which made it impracticable to give the statutory notice even in respect of those whom you intended to make redundant, i.e. less than 10.*

*3 Remember there is no minimum number of people who you are required to consult when trade unions are involved.*

## 282   Intended redundancy — union notification

On . . . I told your representative in the factory of the problem foreseen for employment in the next few months, as a result of a shortage of orders, which could result in up to 70 employees being made redundant. In accordance with the 1975 Employment Protection Act, I gave notice of a 60 day consultation period commencing . . . during which the fullest information would be supplied to you. This letter sets out the circumstances and we shall be pleased to commence consultations with you at your earliest convenience.

### 1   Reasons for redundancy

In spite of intense sales and tendering activity the Division has been unsuccessful in obtaining manufacturing orders to support the 1976 programme. The effect of this is being felt progressively in the . . . Unit, where, when current orders are fulfilled from mid-May onwards, there are no contracts to follow on. Because of this the direct operators involved, as well as some of those on . . . and other support services throughout the factory will be affected.

The problem results from no intake of . . . orders for . . . assemblies usually covered by Stores Orders and obtained by competitive tendering. This complete absence of orders is significant at a time when the . . . has reduced its purchasing because of cuts in Government spending as part of the counter inflation policy.

### 2   Consequential action

As a direct result of the shortage of orders in the . . . Unit it has been necessary to revise the complete manufacturing organisation. The existence of two separate unit management structures can no longer be justified and a single production unit with responsibility for all shop production work now replaces the previous two-unit structure.

This major change means the loss of some indirect jobs in management and elsewhere because of duplication quite apart from the reduction in volume of work caused by the shortage of orders.

Although the effects are most strongly felt in Manufacturing there is a follow-through effect into Quality Assurance, Contracts, Sales and Accounting where diminished workload will also be felt.

Finally, the loss of direct effort means reduced recovery of overhead and all departments have been instructed to economise in manning and other expense areas to ensure the continued viability of the Division in these reduced circumstances. In some instances this means simply keeping within budgeted limits, but where reductions in actual workload are certain, reductions in manning are also inevitable.

### 3   Numbers of employees involved

As far as can be seen at this time the original overall estimate is still substantially correct although the make-up of the total now varies slightly from that originally tabled.

Unless circumstances alter, the number of employees affected in jobs and areas for which unions have rights of representation are:

#### *Direct Employees*

| Job Category | Numbers Affected | Total No. Employed |
| --- | --- | --- |
| (1) | | |
| (2) | | |
| (3) | | |

#### *Indirect Employees*

| Job Category | Numbers Affected | Total No. Employed |
| --- | --- | --- |
| (1) | | |
| (2) | | |
| (3) | | |

### Total of Direct and Indirect

Until employees have been identified by name you should not assume that these numbers represent your members only, but it is possible that at least some of them are in membership with you in appropriate jobs. Similarly, until volunteers have been matched with job categories, it should not be assumed automatically that the numbers quoted will result in enforced redundancy.

In Manufacturing, where the problem is greatest, redundancy selection will, in general, be determined by the association of employees with the specific product lines affected by shortage of work. Within these areas it will be necessary to transfer some employees to other product lines where their skills and experience can be utilised. Where this is not possible it will be the Division's intention to release employees who have reached or passed retirement age and part-time employees in that order. If further action is needed to achieve the reduction required the service of employees will become a major factor in selection for redundancy.

Where contract labour can be suitably replaced by company employees this will be done.

It is appreciated that, for the union, membership is of course a key factor. Equally, the Company must necessarily have regard to the welfare of all employees and to the need for them in their particular jobs. In practice, because of the existence currently of 33 voluntary applications and the high level of union membership among direct employees, it may be possible to preserve both viewpoints without difficulty. Other departments involved will follow the same general rules varying them only when specific circumstances, peculiar to them, make it imperative.

Regarding volunteers, the Division will, where practicable, release them at a mutually agreed date, either during or after the end of the 60 day consultation period, but reserves the right to refuse an application if it is not in the future interest of the Division to approve it whatever the reason.

### 4  Redeployment

In addition to internal attempts to redeploy employees who have been warned of redundancy every attempt will be made to help them find alternative work externally. To do this

close liaison on job opportunities has already been established
with other local employers. The services of the Department
of Employment will also be fully utilised and, for those employees who are willing to consider re-location, use will be
made of the Company's jobs finding facility and redeployment
agency.

A general willingness to consider opportunities by employees and your active support will help to achieve success
in this respect.

## 5    Method of dismissal and timing

Apart from volunteers, no employees will be made redundant
until the expiry of the 60 day consultation period. From that
date onwards groups of employees will become redundant as
work runs out progressively in the period to the end of . . . .
As soon as the employees involved have been determined,
each will receive a letter giving them advanced warning of
redundancy. Not less than 14 days prior to actual redundancy
each will receive a final letter giving the actual date of redundancy.

On that day their employment with the Company will be
terminated and each will receive redundancy payments due
to them from State and Company schemes together with
payments for unused holiday entitlement and money in lieu
of notice. They will also be able to exercise any options open
to them under the Company's Pension Plan where appropriate.

The foregoing provisions will apply if and when redundancy
actually occurs. Unusual efforts are being made to try to get
orders with sufficient work content to render redundancy
unnecessary. If we are successful it will be my pleasure to
inform you of any withdrawal of redundancy notices we are
able to make.

In any event, you may be sure that in the present difficult
and unhappy circumstances, the company will make every
effort to keep hardship to a minimum — and production to a
maximum. It will comply with the spirit as well as with the
letter of the new legislation and will be pleased to consult
with you at every stage.

I will be glad if you would contact me at your early convenience, so that we may discuss both how the redundancies
and their effects may be kept to a minimum and how the
maximum protection may be provided not only for those

employees who have to leave but also for the remainder of the workforce. We greatly regret the necessity for redundancies today and look forward to your co-operation so that we can do whatever is possible to preserve jobs in the future.

NOTE:
*With the exception of the final paragraph — which I regard as an essential addition — and with alterations made so as to disguise the circumstances, this is an excellent example of a letter which was carefully drafted and sent out by a personnel manager.*

# Chapter 29

# Guarantee payments*

If a business goes onto short-time working, salaried staff continue to receive their pay in full. Hourly paid workers and others whose pay depends upon results do not. They may get unemployment benefit, but (in the absence of some special contractual term) have no right to their pay.

The new 'guarantee payments' are designed to give the shop floor a little of that security already enjoyed by their salaried colleagues. It is modest in its extent; it will not effect the vast majority of employers who, happily, do not have to put their work force onto a three or four day working week.

Guarantee payments will be made for 'workless days' — days when employees are laid-off because of a diminution in the work available for them. To qualify for a guarantee payment, the employee must have been on the books for at least four weeks; he must be available for work, if required; and he must not unreasonably refuse alternative work during the workless days — how this will be interpreted in practice (as regards demarcation problems and the like) remains to be seen.

Any workless day caused by an industrial dispute in the employing company or any associated employer will not count. If, for instance, there is a strike in your company or in any of its sister or associated or subsidiary companies and workless days result, no one will receive any guarantee payment. If, on the other hand, you have to put people onto a short working week because of strikes in the businesses of your suppliers or customers, or, for that matter, those who provide you with essential services, e.g. fuel, power or transport, then guarantee payments will become due.

The employer will make all guarantee payments out of his own pocket (as opposed, for example, to half redundancy pay from Redundancy Fund and all of Maternity pay from Maternity Fund). The maximum payable will be up to six days pay at a maximum £5 per day during any one of the four three-month periods commencing 1 February, 1 May, 1 August and 1 November, respectively.

An employee will only be entitled to a maximum of £30 during any of the three-month periods — but if he manages to have his workless

*From 1 February 1977.

days in the last week of one period and the first week of the next, then he could tot up £60 in a fortnight.

The following precedents will apply when guarantee payments come into force.

\*   \*   \*

### 283   Guarantee payment — enclosed

I enclose herewith your guarantee payment for workless days — a total of £30, which is the maximum prescribed by the Employment Protection Act. The six days in respect of which the £5 maximum payment is enclosed are . . . .

NOTE:
*All pay statements must (thanks to the Employment Protection Act) be itemised. One of the items to be set out is the manner in which guarantee payments are arrived at. The object of the itemised pay statement is, of course, to enable the employee to know not merely the total sum paid but how that sum is arrived at.*

### 284   Industrial dispute in works — no guarantee payment

I have received your claim for guarantee payments on behalf of your members. The reason why we had to lay-off men was the industrial dispute in our associated company, . . . Ltd, under the Employment Protection Act, guarantee payments do not become due in those circumstances. (We suspect that this mis-understanding may have arisen because we would have been liable to make guarantee payments had the workless days resulted from industrial action in a company other than our own or any associated company).

### 285   New employees excluded

The reason why Mr . . . , Mr . . . and Mr . . . were excluded from the guarantee payments was that they have been employed for less than the minimum four week period.

## 286 Employees not available

The reason why you received no guarantee payment was that when we wished you to carry out work in our premises on the day in question, you were not available. And you will appreciate that the Employment Protection Act does require employees to be available and to be prepared to help out with other work, in these emergency situations.

## 287 To ACAS — guarantee payments

I will be grateful if you will call upon me at your earliest convenience, to help me sort out guarantee payments due to employees as a result of recent workless days.

The reason for the urgency is that if we cannot reach agreement with the unions on this matter fairly soon, I fear that we shall have a dispute on our hands.

*Chapter 30*

# Insolvency

If you need to use this chapter, your company is unlikely to be able to afford the cost of the book. The new insolvency rules (in force since April 1976) are designed to provide a substantial cushion for employees when (in ordinary terms) their employer goes bust.

First, new items join the 'preferential payments', floating to the top when the assets have been accumulated and the creditors are to be paid off.

Priority debts now include guarantee payments; remuneration on suspension on medical grounds, i.e. in certain cases where the employee is laid off due to breach by employers of the Health and Safety at Work Act etc.; payment for time off; and remuneration under a protective award.

Much more important, though, are the new claims which may now be made from the Redundancy Fund. If the cupboard is bare and the employee does not receive the following amounts, he may claim them from the Fund (up to £80 a week in each case). The Fund itself, of course, receives extra money from all employers to cover its new obligations.

The new rights apply to the following debts, owed by an insolvent employer to his unfortunate employee:

1    Arrears of pay for up to 8 weeks.
2    Pay in lieu of notice.
3    Holiday pay (up to 6 weeks).
4    Basic award of compensation for unfair dismissal.
5    Reasonable reimbursement of fee or premium paid by apprentice or articled clerk.

\*　　\*　　\*

## 288    Claim for preferential debt

I am owed the following:
*(a)* . . . .
*(b)* . . . .
*(c)* . . . .

I claim the above as preferential debts, in accordance with Section 63 of the Employment Protection Act.

If the company/firm does not have sufficient assets to cover the foregoing, then I claim the same and each of the same from the Redundancy Funds, in accordance with Section 64 of the Employment Protection Act.

In addition, I claim the following items under Section 64, which do not rank for preferential treatment:

(1) . . . .
(2) . . . .
(3) . . . .

NOTE:

*1 The above letter should be addressed to the officially appointed Receiver of the company, who will give the necessary forms to be completed and returned. If there is no Receiver appointed, or where no reply has been received within 6 months, applications should be made to the Secretary of State for Employment through the local office of the Department of Employment.*

*2 The employee who believes that he has rights which are not being accorded to him (or which are in doubt) under either of these sections should consult his association or trade union and/or its solicitor or his own.*

Chapter 31

# Itemised pay statements

Until the Employment Protection Act, a pay slip could simply set out the total of the employees money, without any breakdown. With a transitional period to allow for reprogramming computerised payments, the Employment Protection Act will soon require the itemisation of pay statements* — so that an employee will be told in writing, not merely how much he is entitled to receive but also its breakdown. This should avoid disputes. It will enable the employee to study, to consider, and if necessary, to challenge the amount which he is paid — and to make that challenge either personally or through his trade union.

\* \* \*

*From 6 April 1977.

## 289   Itemised pay statement — Board to Company Secretary

I have received complaints from the . . . Union, that pay statements received by its members who are employed by our company, are not fully itemised. Please would you ensure that this situation is rectified as we do not want any difficulties under the Employment Protection Act.

## 290   Individual request for itemised pay statement

I regret that the payments of salary and commission which I have been receiving are accompanied only by a slip setting out the net total. I would be very grateful if I could in future receive itemised pay statements, as required by the Employment Protection Act. I hope that this will not prove a nuisance for the accounts department, but will enable me to check in a proper manner as to the make-up of my earnings from the company.

My thanks in anticipation and kind regards.

## 291 Denial of failure to provide itemised statements

Thank you for your letter. I am sorry that your pay statement last week appears to have set out only the sum paid — But I am assured by the accounts department that this is a rare exception to the general rule. Our pay statements are itemised and we will do our best to ensure that your earnings are sufficiently detailed in future.

With best wishes.

*Chapter 32*

# Time off work *

The best employers are fair and reasonable not only concerning their employee's working arrangements but also in giving them reasonable time off work for trade union and public duties. Sections 57 to 62 of the Employment Protection Act seek to bring all employers up to these standards.

Sections 57 and 58 deal with time off for carrying out trade union duties. Their application will be governed by a Code of Practice which (at the time of writing) is still under preparation by ACAS. This Code will cover not only the amount of time which the employee is to be permitted to take off and the purposes for which, the occasions on which and any conditions subject to which time off may be so taken – but it will provide some sort of guide as to what is 'reasonable in all the circumstances'.

Meanwhile and in any event, while the Code 'will provide practicable guidance' – in general, and in particular connection with time off 'for trade union activities connected with industrial action' – reasonableness will be a question of impression. If a member of an independent recognised trade union considers that his employer has been 'unreasonable', then he may present a complaint to an industrial tribunal. At that stage (which, hopefully, the following letters will help you to avoid reaching), the tribunal will consider what is reasonable in all the particular circumstances of that case. This Chapter can provide the tests and the precedents – you will have to apply them.

Section 57 requires an employer to permit any employee who is an official of an independent recognised trade union (that is, a trade union recognised by him for bargaining purposes) to take time off during working hours for the following two purposes:

'(a)  To carry out those duties of his as such an official which are concerned with industrial relations with his employer and any associated employer and their employee;

(b)  To undergo training in aspects of industrial relations which is –

(1)  Relevant to the carrying out of those duties;

*Required time off for public duties and for redundant employees to seek alternative work is already in force. Time off for trade union activities will become effective when the ACAS Code is approved – probably early in 1977.

*202*

(2)   Approved by the Trades Union Congress or by independent trade union of which he is an official.'
Industrial relations duties — and training for them. Not ordinary trade union duties, unconnected with industrial relations — or training for *them.* There is a grey area, of course, between the two. On the one hand, any employer who refuses time off to a trade union official attempting to sort out a dispute requires an immediate psychiatric examination; on the other hand, time off for building up the trade union or its membership may cause trouble.

As usual, if trouble looms consult ACAS — which will have to produce the Code giving guidance as to occasions on which conditions to which time off may be taken — and also practical guidance on circumstances in which time off must be given 'in respect of duties connected with industrial action'.

A trade union official who has time off for his industrial relations duties (or training for them) would be entitled to his normal pay. There is no equivalent provision giving a right to pay when the employer carries out the obligation under Section 58, to give a *member* (as opposed to an *official*) or a trade union permission to take time off for trade union activities. These activities are:

'(a)   Any activities of an appropriate trade union of which the employee is a member;

(b)   Any activities . . . in relation to which the employee acting as a representative of such union,

excluding activities which themselves consist of industrial action whether or not, in contemplation of furtherance of a trade dispute.'

For these activities — like those concerning the public duties (which now follow) payment is not required — but will often be given.

Section 59 says that an employer 'shall permit' time off during working hours 'for the purpose of performing any of duties' of the following offices:

1   JP
2   Member of a local authority, i.e. local councillor.
3   Member of any statutory tribunal.
4   Member of a Regional Health Authority, Area Health Authority in Scotland, Health Board.
5   Member of the managing or governing body of an educational establishment maintained by a local education authority, e.g. Governor of a State but not of a private school or college).
6   Member of a Water Authority (in Scotland, River Purification Board).

An employee who occupies one of the above public offices will be entitled to attend meetings and do anything reasonably necessary in order to carry out his functions in that public office.

The amount of time off which the employee is to be permitted to take will be such time as is 'reasonable in all circumstances'. Regard will be had to the following:-

'(a)    How much time off is required for the performance of the duties of the office or as a member of that body, and how much time off is required for the performance of the particular duties;

(b)    How much time off the employee has already 'been permitted' in connection with trade union duties (as above) and

(c)    The circumstances of the employer's business and the effect of the employee's absence on the running of that business.'

This time, there will be no Code from ACAS — if you are in doubt, then by all means consult the Service. As usual, any employee who considers that you are not complying with your obligations may bring a complaint to an industrial tribunal.

Finally: An employee is already entitled to reasonable time off if he is made redundant, to search for — and to train for — alternative work. Clearly, it will be unreasonable to prevent him from attending an interview. Whether a particular request for time will be 'reasonable' will depend on all the circumstances.

## 292   Tribunal threat

I write to confirm that I have been invited to accept an appointment as a Justice of the Peace for the County of . . . . Unfortunately, you have refused to give me sufficient time off to sit on the bench — and in view of the Employment Protection Act, I am writing to ask that you be good enough to reconsider this decision.

As a loyal and enthusiastic member of your management team, I certainly have no wish to create any difficulties, but if you persist in your refusal I will be left with no alternative than to bring proceedings before an industrial tribunal on the ground that the time off is reasonable in the circumstances. I do hope that this step will not be necessary and look forward to hearing from you.

## 293   Threat rejected

Thank you for your letter. We are always prepared to give
our employees reasonable time off in order to attend to
public duties, and there is no need to invoke the Employment Protection Act nor, still less, to threaten proceedings
before an industrial tribunal in order to encourage us to comply with our moral and legal obligation. However, I must
point out that we are only bound to grant such time off as is
reasonable in the circumstances; in your case, it is wholly
unreasonable that you should have a day a week/fortnight
(*or as the case may be*) off from work because your absence
would gravely affect the operation of our office/plant/works/
of the team which you head/manage.

We have reconsidered the situation with care, as you requested. I regret that we cannot change our decision.

However, if you would like to discuss the matter further
so that we may explain our reasoning in more detail than is
possible in a letter, please do not hesitate to contact me.

## 294   Redundant employee — time off for interview

I confirm that you are attending interviews for alternative
jobs as follows:

    1 . . . .
    2 . . . .
    3 . . . .

Please let your immediate supervisor know how long you
will need to be away in order to attend those interviews and
time off will be given. We wish you the best of luck in your
endeavours to find other work.

## 295   Redundant — training time off refused

I have carefully considered your application for seven days'
time off in order to train for alternative work. As we are
attempting to run down the department as slowly as possible
and to keep our team together for the purpose, it would not
be reasonable to give you the time off you seek. However, if
you will ask your shop steward to see me I will be pleased to
discuss with him the possibility of making some alternative
arrangement.

### 296    Time off — trade union duties — agreed

Further to our conversation, I am happy to confirm that
the company is agreeable to your having time off, as you
request, during working hours for the following of your
duties as an official of the . . . Union:
   *(a)* . . . .
   *(b)* . . . .
   *(c)* . . . .
May I take this opportunity of saying how much the company appreciates the happy relationship which has so long
existed between your union and its officials and the management — to which I would add that I personally am delighted
in your appointment/renewed election as convener/works
chairman (or as the case may be).

NOTES:
*1    It will be a matter for judgement, in each case, whether it is better
to confirm arrangements in writing or to leave them with the flexibility
which an oral arrangement (like the unwritten British constitution) may
produce.*

*2    The final paragraph — with its emphasis on personal relationships —
is infinitely variable but extremely important in an area in which,
whatever the formal agreements, personal relationships will decide
whether or not industrial relations are satisfactory. It follows that you
should not hesitate to make equivalent additions to any of these
precedents, which will personalise a letter — in any event when there
are words of appreciation or goodwill to be set out. Bear in mind, too,
that letters of this sort are likely to be passed higher up the union line,
so the effect of your words not merely on the official concerned but
on his branch, area or national body should be borne in mind.*

### 297    Unreasonable time off — refused

We have given very careful consideration to your request
for time off during working hours in order to . . ./for the
purposes of . . . .
Having had careful regard to the terms of the Code of
Practice and especially to the problems which will be created
for your colleagues/in your operation (*or as the case may be*)
as a result of your absence, we cannot consider the request

to be reasonable.

However: As you know this company is always ready, willing and anxious to assist, in so far as it can — and if you would call on me, at my office, perhaps we could sort out some mutually agreeable compromise.

With best wishes.

NOTE:

*Once again, remember that this letter may go forward — and if it is not couched in a friendly and kindly terms, it could cause an unnecessary row. Conversely, even a refusal may be laced with goodwill and suggested possible compromise.*

## 298   Training time — agreed

Thank you for your letter concerning the proposal that our Mr Brown should attend a training course organised by ... at ... on the ... (from the ... to the ...). As you have specifically asked that he should attend; as we agreed that the course is relevant to the carrying out of his industrial relation duties; and as the course is approved by the TUC (or: laid on by your union), we shall be happy to arrange for Mr Brown to attend. I am further pleased to confirm that he will receive his normal remuneration while attending the course.

When you are next in this vicinity, do please call by for a chat. There are a number of matters which I would like to discuss with you.

NOTE:

*Where you are agreeing to a request or making a concession, by all means use this as an opportunity to invite further discussion — perhaps on thornier problems.*

## 299   Training time — unreasonable

Thank you for your letter concerning the 10-day course on industrial safety, organised for officials of your union who are also safety representatives under the Health and Safety at Work Act.

While we congratualte you on the course and on the

obvious thoroughness with which this vital topic is to be covered, we would like to draw your attention to the extensive safety training facilities which are already provided by the company. These have included, during the past few months, the following:

*(a)* . . . .
*(b)* . . . .
*(c)* . . . .

In the circumstances — and also bearing in mind the difficulties which the absence of Mr . . . would create in the office/department/section, we do not feel that we can reasonably agree to his being away for such an extended period.

However, we have discussed with him the possibility of his going on a rather more intensive course, if you arrange one in the future — so do please keep us in touch. We are sure that you, like Mr . . . , will understand that while we must decline your invitation to send him on this particular course, we in no way underestimate the importance of the training work which your union is arranging — nor our appreciation for your efforts in the field of industrial safety.

With best wishes.

NOTE:
*Before replying to the letter, you will have discussed the matter with the individual official. Any indication that he has accepted the decision should be included in the letter. If he is dissatisfied, try the following:*

## 300   Refusal — discussions continuing

We have had preliminary discussions with your Mr Jones, concerning the request that he should attend a 10-day industrial safety course provided by your union. Our initial view is that the course is too extensive for the particular requirements of our business — in which not only the accident record is excellent but the dangers are not great. And we also have a special regard to the instruction and training which is already provided and which already includes:

*(a)* . . . .
*(b)* . . . .
*(c)* . . . .

However, Mr Jones is not happy about our decision and as we regard safety training as being of paramount importance, we are having further discussions on the matter with Mr Jones/ with our Safety Committee and with Mr Jones. I shall be in touch with you again shortly.

## 301  Time off for trade union activity — agreed

Thank you for your letter concerning time off for your members, Mr . . . , Mr . . . and Mr . . . , in connection with activities for your trade union. We are agreeable to the arrangements you suggest; we regard these as in accordance with good industrial relations and with the Code of Practice; and we would only add the following cautions;

1  Time off must be confined to . . . .
2  We are sure that your members will bear in mind the following difficulties which may arise because of their specific work . . . .
3  . . . .

With kind regards.

## 302  Trade union activities — refusal

We have given most careful and anxious consideration to your request that Mr . . . , who is a member of your union, should have time off for . . . .

Unfortunately, we are unable to agree to this request for the following reasons:

1  The activities referred to themselves consist of industrial action (in contemplation of furtherance of a trade dispute).
2  Your trade union is not registered as 'independent', within the meaning of the Act.
3  The time off is in excess of that which is 'reasonable', having regard to the relevant provisions of the Code of Practice.
4  To agree to your proposition would result in a wholly disproportionate disruption in the work of the firm/ department/section.

We are sorry that we cannot comply with your request on this occasion, but we would be happy to meet you, if you wish, to see whether some mutually acceptable compromise can be arrived at.

NOTE:
*Have you discussed the position with ACAS, before sending the refusal?*

### 303    Local councillor — refusal

We are indeed in favour of our employees taking an active
part in public life. But we do not consider that — having
regard to the nature of your job and the responsibilities you
bear — it would be possible for you to find that compatible
with the active work required of a local councillor. Naturally,
it is entirely a matter for you whether or not you stand for
office. But we cannot guarantee to give you time off in order
to attend committee meetings and the like. We shall be pleased
to help in any way we can — but we must emphasise that
yours is one of those positions in which availability is vital.

### 304    Threat of complaint

I was most concerned to receive your letter, refusing to
grant me time off from work in order that I may carry out
the duties of a local councillor. I fully appreciate the necessity
for my services to be available and of course the company's
needs would have priority. But I would most respectfully
ask that you reconsider your decision in this matter, not
because of the Employment Protection Act and the rights
given to employees to make complaints to industrial tribunals
in such cases, but in order to preserve the excellent repute of
the company and the good industrial relations which have
proved so important.

I shall be most pleased to come to discuss this matter with
you or any of your colleagues if necessary. But you will
appreciate the importance of this request to me.

NOTE:
*Letters of this sort have to be written with the greatest of tact — but if
the threat of industrial tribunal proceedings (however veiled, as in the
above precedent) leads to 'constructive' dismissal, appropriate letters
are provided in Chapter 9.*

"IT WAS A VERY SAD CASE – HE WAS TRYING TO RETRIEVE A
DRAFT LETTER AND FELL INTO HIS OWN SHREDDER —.!"

*Part Five*

# HEALTH AND SAFETY
# AT WORK

*Chapter 33*

# Introduction

A cynical old MP once advised a new recruit to the Commons: 'Never do good by stealth!'

Under the Health and Safety at Work Act, it is not enough to be good. You must, if necessary, be in a position to prove your virtue. If you are prosecuted for an offence, your defence will almost certainly be: 'I took such steps as were reasonably practicable in the circumstances'. In that case, the Health and Safety at Work Act says: 'Prove it'.

This Part contains samples of the letters which you are most likely to need, when coping with the Health and Safety at Work Act and attempting to avoid trouble. Use and adapt the precedents to suit your circumstances and you will go a long way towards keeping out of trouble.

That is the negative side. The positive is more important. Suppose that your employee refuses to follow the safety rules which you have laid down for his protection. By all means speak to the offender and try to induce him to mend his ways. If that fails, after appropriate consultations with shop stewards or workers' representatives put your complaint into writing. In that way you will not merely protect yourself if you have to prove that you used 'all reasonable persuation and propaganda' to induce the employee to comply with the rules. With luck, the fact that you have taken the trouble to make a written complaint may embed itself sufficiently into the mind of your employee to induce him to be more careful in future.

The Health and Safety at Work Act repeatedly demands that employers take steps that are 'reasonably practicable'. Reasonableness is the key to avoiding trouble. Reasonable care is (once again) essential when using these drafts. They are provided in the knowledge that if properly used, they can avoid headaches, accidents — and, potentially, heavy penalties.

Finally, Section 2(3) of the Act requires you to prepare and whenever necessary to revise written statements of your Health and Safety policy, organisation and arrangements and to make these statements available for your employees.

My thanks to the Health and Safety Commission for their kind permission to reprint their Guidance Notes — and to my friends in industry who have agreed to my publishing their statements, in Appendix 3, as guides to the perplexed.

# Chapter 34

# Health and safety statements

The Act requires that every employee be provided with a health and safety statement. This falls into three parts:

1 *Policy* No problem — the employer's policy is undoubtedly to give paramount importance to the health and safety of his employees at work.

2 *Organisation* You cannot set out your organisation unless you have one. Who is in charge of safety in your business? What part is each level of management expected to play? Have you set up any (and if so what) safety committees?

3 *Arrangements* Each employee is entitled to know what arrangements you have made to protect him. The statement should identify the main hazards faced by the particular employee at his work and state how to avoid them.

Usually, one statement of policy and organisation will cover most if not all employees, even in the largest concern. Statements of arrangements, though, often have to be individual. The Act requires (for the first time) that employers apply their minds to the dangers involved in each job.

The Health and Safety Commission's guidance document on safety statements is set out in full (Appendix 3), followed by samples of some safety statements, in current industrial use.

Next time your factory inspector pays a visit, his first question may be: 'Where is your safety statement?' If you have no statement, you are breaking the law. If your statement is defective, you are asking for trouble. If your statement sets out satisfactory organisation and arrangements and you do not adhere to them, then what defence could you possibly have to a charge that you have failed to take 'such steps as were reasonably practicable' to protect your employees, in accordance with the procedures which you yourself have set out as necessary?

\* \* \*

## 305 Request for statement

I do not appear to have received a written statement of the company's safety policy, organisation and arrangements. I would be very grateful if this could be made available to me at your early convenience.

## 306 To inspector — statement under preparation

I confirm that the safety statement for our new plant at . . . is under preparation. Thank you for agreeing that it is better for us to take a little more time in order to ensure that statement is first class, rather than rushing through a document which may be less effective.

NOTE:
*Factory inspectors are very reasonable — and if a statement is genuinely under preparation, there will rarely be problems.*

## 307 Denial that statement defective

The company's safety statement does indeed set out not only our policy and organisation, but also our safety arrangements. We have to strike a balance in connection with the arrangements. While we must identify the main hazards faced by each person in his job (and we have done so), we must not put in so much that the statement will not be read or understood.

Anyway, we shall be pleased to discuss your comments both with you and with the factory inspector, so that if we are wrong in our view, revised statements can be provided very swiftly.

Thank you for drawing this matter to our attention — and with our best wishes.

# Chapter 35

# Duties to employees

'It shall be the duty of every employer to ensure, so far as is reasonably practicable, the health, safety and welfare at work of all his employees.' Section 2 of the Health and Safety at Work Act codifies, strengthens extends — and moves further into the law of crime — the bulk of the civil law on health and safety at work. Into the bargain, it adds 'welfare' — a word which the Act does not define.

Therefore, it is now a criminal offence, punishable at worst by two years imprisonment and/or an unlimited fine — *not* to ensure, so far as is reasonably practicable, the health, safety and welfare at work of all your employees.

The Section breaks down the duties (again, in most cases) mirroring the civil law by saying that they include the following specific duties: That of:

'*(a)* the provision and maintenance of *plant and systems of work* that are, so far as is reasonably practicable, safe and without risk to health;

'*(b)* arrangements for ensuring, so far as is reasonably practicable, safety and absence of risk to health in connection with the *use, handling, storage and transport* of articles and substances;

'*(c)* the provision of such *information, training, instruction and supervision* as is necessary to ensure, so far as is reasonably practicable, the health and safety at work of his employees;

'*(d)* so far as is reasonably practicable as regards any *place of work* under the employer's control, the maintenance of it in a condition that is safe and without risk to health and the provision and maintenance of means of access to and egress from it that are safe and without such risks;

'*(e)* the provision and maintenance of a *working environment* for his employees that is, so far as is reasonably practicable, safe, without risk to health, and adequate as regards facilities and arrangements for their *welfare* at work.'

The employer, then, is not his employees' insurer. The fact that someone is injured while at work — or suffers ill health as a result of his work — would not of itself make the employer criminally liable, any more than it can of itself make him (or his insurers) liable to pay compensation at civil law. The employer who has taken all such steps as are 'reasonably practicable' to protect his employees and to comply with the law will be in the clear. Unfortunately for the employer (or his manager or executive), though, Section 40 of the Act provides that it is 'for the accused to prove' that he took such steps as were 'reasonably practicable'.

If, for example, you wish to prove that you could not reasonably have been expected to do more than you did, for the protection of your employees, then the burden of proving that contention rests upon your bowed shoulders.

How can an employer discharge this unusual burden? He may be able to give oral evidence (personally or by calling on a colleague, a subordinate or even a superior). Yet the spoken word is always suspect — if only because the human memory is so fallible. The best evidence is always in writing.

Or take Section 3, which (again) codifies the law — this time on an employer's duty *not* to his own employees but to anyone else who may be affected by his work — a visitor, a neighbour, a member of the general public.

'It shall be the duty of every employer to conduct his undertaking in such a way as to ensure, so far as is reasonably practicable, that persons not in his employment who may be affected thereby are not thereby exposed to risks to their health or safety.'

Once again, the Act uses those crucial words: 'So far as is reasonably practicable'.

A visitor — perhaps the employee of a contractor or of a sub contractor . . . a child, brought in by a driver (your own or that of your supplier) . . . a representative or a buyer . . . is injured on your premises. The Inspector's attention is drawn to your activities and you are questioned about your safety organisation and the steps taken to protect that visitor. Could you prove that you had done that which a reasonably prudent occupier of premises would and could and should have done, in the circumstances, for the safety of visitors?

Or suppose that the employee or the visitor is injured through his own failure to comply with your safety rules or procedures. It will not be enough for you to tell the Court: 'I warned him. . . . The protective clothing or equipment was available. . . . The system was a good one. . .'. You would have to prove — positively — that you took all reasonably practicable steps to persuade and to propagandise the employee into making use of the procedures or systems, the equipment or clothing, provided by you.

Once again (as always) the finest formula for the avoidance of trouble with the law lies in the pen in your hands, the pencil poised by your secretary, the dictating machine — in the appropriate letters, duly recorded, copied and filed.

To preserve your own safety from the dire dangers of prosecution and punishment, you must now consider (if you have not already done so):

1   Does your organisation need reviewing or tightening up, to cope with the requirements of the Act?
2   Do your employees and colleagues know of your system — and are they instructed and trained in how to operate it? And
3   Have you the necessary precedents, to be used or adapted to suit those most worthy of twin purposes: The protection from harm of your employees and of others 'affected' by your 'undertaking' — and the protection of your company, firm and/or yourself from trouble under the Act?

\*   \*   \*

## 308   Instructions to department to tighten up safety procedures

The Board has been disturbed to receive a number of complaints regarding the lack of adequate safety procedures in your plant/office/workshop. Bearing in mind the heavy burden of care placed on employers and their managers by the Health and Safety at Work Act — and the potentially stringent criminal penalties which may result from non-compliance — I must insist that you take immediate steps to ensure, so far as is reasonably practicable, that those of our employees who come under your management are not submitted to unnecessary risk to their health or safety.

In particular, but without prejudice to the generality of the foregoing, please take immediate steps to deal with the following:

1   The failure of employees in . . . to wear their safety helmets/spectacles/protective clothing.
2   The removal by employees of guards from lathes/ machinery.
3   The general untidy state of the . . . resulting in obstructions in the gangways.
4   . . . .

Please formally acknowledge receipt of this letter and let me have your assurance that these matters will be dealt with, without delay.

NOTES:

*1   With full responsibility placed on those at fault, and with directors and managers at every level personally responsible in law, it is vital to be able to show, if necessary, that you were not at fault. The above letter makes an excellent start to that worthy end.*

*2   As usual, getting a signature from the recipient has two useful functions. It emphasises to him the importance placed by you on compliance with the rules in general and your requirements in particular; and it avoids any possibility of doubt as to whether or not your letter was both written and received.*

## 309   Report from manager

Thank you for your letter concerning safety measures in my department/office/workshop. I fully recognise that the system is far from perfect. However, as I have explained to you, and through you, I hope, to the Board — on several occasions, it is not possible for me to make other than marginal improvements, for the following reasons:

1    In order to avoid the continued risk of backstrains, we must either be provided with more mechanical lifting equipment or with additional help.
2    In order to obviate the risk with the . . . machine, it would have to be replaced by a . . ./adapted by . . . .
3    To induce my workforce to make proper use of their safety helmets/equipment, I require the full time service of a safety officer/adequate resources made available for safety training.

I am as concerned as the Board with the safety of our employees, and would be very happy to discuss these matters with you. I fully appreciate the importance of the Health and Safety at Work Act and I am doing all that I can — but I do hope that the Board will now give consideration to the need for additional resources to be devoted to the health and safety aspects of our work — and I look forward to hearing from you.

NOTES:

*1   As with master, so with man — writing counts.*

*2   Just as it is possible for the buck to be passed downward — so it may also go up the line. Further precedents in Chapter 52.*

*Chapter 36*

# When the employee causes the accident

Sometimes death or injury at work is due to the fault of management; sometimes because employees will not co-operate — on some building sites, for instance, it is said that workers only don their safety helmets when it starts to rain.

How far, then, can you be held criminally liable under the new Act, if your employee fails or refuses to follow the safety rules? And can *they* be held personally to blame?

The Act not only requires employers to achieve high standards of health, safety and welfare for the benefit of employees, but it also demands that employees shall co-operate in the carrying out of the safety and health measures. Duties placed on them by existing legislation are extended.

Every employer must do what he can to ensure that his employees know of and follow the rules; that all reasonable 'persuasion and propaganda' is used to encourage and persuade them to take proper care of themselves and others; and only if the procedures are sufficiently clear and established is the employer himself likely to avoid prosecution and punishment if an accident occurs or even if the inspector considers that the Act is being flouted.

Here are some suggested procedures, designed to put the maximum fair pressure on employees to look after their own safety and so to avoid accidents to them and their colleagues, and (at the same time) to fend off either civil or criminal liability which may otherwise fall on you. Check this list; keep it by you; follow the suggestions — and you should keep out of trouble.

\* \* \*

1  Check that your employee's *system* of working is safe. When have accidents occurred in the past and why and how can they be eliminated? Are you satisfied that all the equipment or machinery provided for the use of your employees is really adequate and satisfactory?

2  Is your system of training, instruction and supervision beyond reproach — both as regards new and existing employees? And can you, if necessary, prove that system? Is it sufficiently documented?

3   Have you won the approval and co-operation of your employees, individually and collectively, to your safety procedures? Is yours a large enterprise with trade union membership or a staff association? If so, have you consulted the organisation or committee concerned so as to ensure that your employees fully understand and approve of your safety, health and welfare set up – and have you sought their help in the enforcement of the rules? (*Note:* You must comply with the regulations requiring consultation with appointed representatives of recognised trade unions. These 'safety watchdogs' do not bear personal liability arising out of their duty in that capacity – but, if properly harnessed – can greatly help keep the business safe and hence keep management out of trouble with the law. The regulations are new and time will show how they operate in practice. If in doubt, consult your Inspector or the Health and Safety Commission.)

4   The Code of Industrial Practice requires the operation of a fair dismissals system – including, where possible, written warnings. A similar system is now essential, to deal with employees who fail or refuse to follow safety rules or procedures. Watch out for guidance from some future Code of Practice. It will almost inevitably include the following routine, which should be set up without delay:

*(a)*   Speak personally to the employee who is not complying; emphasise the importance of his doing so; warn him of the consequences of failure.

*(b)*   Refer the employee to Sections 7 and 8 of the Act, which require him to take proper care for his own safety and not to interfere with safety equipment and the like – and which render him liable to the same penalties for breach as the employing company or its managers.

*(c)*   If the first effort fails, try again – this time in company with a fellow employee (if union representatives are involved, try to bring the shop steward with you); and this time or the next deliver a written warning; if possible, get a signed duplicate or receipt.

*(d)*   If danger (actual or potential) is being caused not merely to the employee concerned but to others, then emphasise the unfairness of the conduct.

*(e)*   If dangerous behaviour persists, consider dismissal. Factors to be taken into account include:

  *(i)*   The nature and extent of the danger – to the employee himself and to others.

  *(ii)*   The effect of dismissal on good industrial relations.

  *(iii)*   The employee's length of service, degree of responsibility and general conduct. And

    *(iv)*  All the circumstances of the case which might make the dismissal 'unfair', so as to give the employee a right to compensation.

*(f)*  Deliver second written warning, preferably by hand — and once again, if possible, accompanied by a workers' representative. This warning should state:

    *(i)*  If applicable, that further non-compliance will leave you with no alternative other than to dismiss; and in any event

    *(ii)*  Drawing attention to previous warnings; to the rules under the Act; and stating that no responsibility can in any event be accepted by the company in the event of the risk giving rise to injury, loss or damage to the employee. (Note: This disclaimer may be of help in a civil action, but it will not necessarily free the employers from criminal liability. But it does emphasise the seriousness with which the employee's misconduct is regarded).

*(g)*  Consider whether your equipment or system of work requires redesign or change — perhaps to remove employees' objections or so as to make it impossible for the machine or equipment to be used in the dangerous manner complained of. *Typical example:* A noisy operation — and operatives who refuse to wear 'ear defenders'. Can the noise be reduced sufficiently to obviate the need for the ear defenders?

An employer will not necessarily wish to use the above steps in the suggested order. These should be adapted, as best suited to his business and circumstances. But if he follows the rules, it can hardly be said that he did not take 'reasonable steps' to influence his employee. In the event of an accident, he would probably avoid liability — the employee's contributory negligence would be 100 per cent. The employee knew of the dangers; and the employer (or his insurers) could prove their case — so that the responsibility would rest on the employee.

Equally: If the employer is prosecuted either under existing legislation or under the new Act, his defences would be well prepared.

Above all: The Act is not designed to produce actions or prosecutions but to avoid accidents. These procedures will help.

\*   \*   \*

## 310   To trade union representative seeking co-operation

As you know, we are very concerned with the failure of some of your members to wear their safety helmets/use equipment provided for their safety. We appreciate that in the past, the rules have often been treated in a very relaxed way. But clearly this is no longer possible – both as a result of the Health and Safety at Work Act and also (and especially) because of the suffering caused through accidents, many of which could have been avoided, had the rules been complied with.

In the circumstances – and knowing how concerned you are with the health and safety of your members – I would be very happy if you would meet me [Mr . . ., our safety officer, and myself] so that we can discuss the best ways to persuade people to take proper care of themselves.

Looking forward to hearing from you and with all best wishes.

NOTE:

*It is essential to obtain union co-operation – and this must be done on the basis of persuasion, in the interests of members. Any aggressive approach – such as the quoting of Section 7 – is likely to produce a hostile response.*

## 311   To shop steward – for personal approach to member

I have/our safety officer has/spoken to John White on several occasions, because of his failure to wear his safety boots/his insistence upon removing the guard from his machine/the slipshod way in which he risks danger to himself and to others by removing the guard from his lathe. Obviously, it is essential for his safety/and for the safety of others that he comply with the rules – and I am sure that a word from you would be of enormous help. Please would you let me know whether you think it would be best for you to tackle Mr White personally or whether you would prefer to do so together with me; Perhaps you would drop by and see me in my office as soon as possible about this.

With best wishes.

## 312   To shop steward – please accompany me

Once again, I ask for your kind co-operation in connection with a serious infringement of the safety rules – this time by

your member, Mr Jim Smith. I tackled him last week about
his continued failure to wear his safety mask — he will be
lucky if he is not blinded as a result and anyway there is now
a serious breach of the Protection of Eyes Regulations and of
the Health and Safety at Work Act.

In the circumstances, I would be grateful if you would
come with me to see this man, so that between us we may
persuade him to mend his ways — and to retain his eyesight!

I shall be along to see you about this, later in the day.

With very best wishes.

### 313   First written warning — by hand

In spite of our conversation last Tuesday in which you
promised that you would never again leave the guard off
your machine, I was most concerned to observe this morning
that you have again infringed the same important safety rule.
This rule is designed, of course, for your own protection. But
the company is bound to enforce that rule, not only so as to
keep you safe but also so as to protect both the company and
indeed you from possible prosecution under the Factories
Act and/or the Health and Safety at Work Act.

I am writing to you personally as an indication of the
seriousness with which this matter is regarded — and to ask
that you never again cause unnecessary danger to yourself by
removing the guard from your machine.

I am delivering this letter to you by hand [in company with
your shop steward] — please sign the duplicate/carbon/receipt,
which will acknowledge that you have received, read and
understood this letter.

### 314   Record of warnings — to manager

I must inform you that I have had to warn Roger Price for
not wearing his safety spectacles (*or as the case may be*), on
the following occasions, each of which is recorded in a note
on his file:

    1 . . . .
    2 . . . .
    3 . . . .

May I suggest that you now consider what further action
might be taken?

## 315   Request to employee to sign record

I have now had to warn you on four occasions (on the following dates: . . . ), as a result of your failure or refusal to wear your safety spectacles. I have therefore reported the matter to the personnel officer. Please sign carbon copy of this letter to show that you have duly received it.

NOTE:

*As usual, the law does not require the giving of a signature, but it has two effects: It proves beyond doubt that the document was received; and it emphasises to the recipient the importance that you place on the letter.*

*If the employee refuses to sign, a note should be made on the carbon accordingly – and the carbon should be placed on the file. (See also Chapter 39 – on receipts and acknowledgements.)*

# Chapter 37

# Further and final warnings*

The time must come when an employer must lay down the law —
especially the new law on health and safety at work — and must do so in
writing. Oral requests and demands for co-operation in health and
safety measures have failed? The first written warning (as in the previous
Chapter) has been given? Then comes the great problem: What do we
do if the employee continues with his wrongful behaviour?

If the danger is sufficiently great — to the employee or to others —
then you may have to threaten dismissal. But this threat should never
be made idly or if you are not prepared if necessary to carry it out. So
before threatening the ultimate deterrent, consider:

1    Would it be 'fair' to dismiss in all the circumstances of the case?
2    Are you seeking to make an example out of one person when the
     practice is widespread?
3    Have you really tried all reasonable persuasion and propaganda to
     induce the employee to comply — so as to treat dismissal as the
     very last resort?
4    What would be the results of the dismissal on good industrial
     relations?

There are, then, two sorts of second or further written warnings.
Some contain a threat of dismissal — others do not. A variety of such
letters now follows.

\*    \*    \*

## 316    Second warning – simple

I have been told that in spite of my letter to you dated . . .
you are still, on occasion, removing the guard from your
machine. I hope that this information is incorrect because —
as I both explained and wrote to you — any further infringement of the rules could lead to serious consequences.

*For general 'dismissal' letters, see Part 2.

# 317  Regrets at breach of undertaking

As a result of my letter to you dated . . . , you undertook
to comply in future with our safety rules and in particular
. . . . This you have failed to do and I must now warn you
that if you again cause danger to yourself/and to others in
this way, disciplinary action will have to be taken.

NOTE:
*You are, of course, not bound to state the nature of the disciplinary*
*action which you have in mind. A generalised warning not only gives*
*scope for the employee's imagination but leaves your options open.*
*However, if you propose taking a specific step, then it may be prefer-*
*able to say so. Thus:*

# 318  Suspension

Once again and in spite of my letter to you dated . . . , you
have seen fit to smoke in close proximity to inflammable
materials. This behaviour cannot be tolerated and unless I
receive your immediate assurance that there will be no further
repetition, I shall have no alternative other than to suspend
you for a period of a fortnight without pay, in accordance
with the company's rules. This letter is being delivered by
hand and I shall be glad if you will immediately call on me
in my office.

NOTE:
*If your disciplinary rules do not provide for suspension, do they need*
*revision? Clearly, the threatened action must be in accordance with*
*your contract with the employee concerned.*

# 319  Dismissal warning – safety

After repeated oral requests that you wear your safety
helmet/ear defenders, and in spite of my warning letter to
you dated . . . , you are continuing to ignore the safety rules
– which are, of course, designed to protect you. Especially
as a result of the Health and Safety at Work Act, it is not
possible for the company to ignore these breaches of rules
any longer. I must warn you that if you again fail to wear

your safety helmet/ear defenders, I shall feel bound to give you your notice/terminate your employment.

I trust that you will now treat this matter very seriously and that you will not put me in the position of having to take this very unpleasant step.

Please sign the duplicate of this letter, so as to acknowledge not only that you have received it but that you have understood the seriousness of the position.

### 320   Dismissal — danger to others

You have chosen to ignore the repeated requests of your shop steward and myself that you keep the guard in place on your lathe, so as to avoid causing danger not only to yourself but to your work mates. You have not taken heed of the warning contained in my letter dated . . . — nor have you complied with your repeated promises to obey the safety rules. In the circumstances, I must now warn you that any further breach of this rule — which, I repeat, is necessary both for your safety and for that of other employees — will result in my having to dismiss you.

As you know, dismissal is regarded in this company as an absolutely last resort. We have all tried our best to persuade you to co-operate in taking reasonable care of your own health and safety and that of your colleagues — but so far we have failed. We cannot permit any continued failure.

### 321   Protective clothing must be worn — or else

If employees do not wear protective clothing, they are liable to suffer dermatitis — and we cannot guarantee that they will not suffer serious personal injury in the long run. As I explained to you in my letter dated . . . , it is vital that all employees wear the protective clothing provided — and breach of this rule cannot be permitted.

In spite of that warning — and despite also the entreaties of your shop steward/foreman/departmental manager — you are still not wearing your gloves/coat/apron.

As you have ignored so many polite and friendly requests, I am now forced to warn you that any further failure will inevitably lead to your dismissal. I would be very sorry to have to take such serious action — please do not remove my alternatives.

## 322   Forklift truck — driver warned

I have now warned you — both orally and in writing — of the dangers involved both for you and for your colleagues in the way in which you are handling your forklift truck. In particular:

1    You are riding on the truck, when it should be controlled only on foot.
2    You are manoeuvring the truck far too close to the edge of the dock.
3    . . . .
4    . . . .

As this behaviour is risking injury to yourself and/or to others, I must now warn you that any further breach of the rules will force me to give you your notice.

I would be very sorry to have to dismiss you — and I hope that you will now appreciate the seriousness of the position and comply with the rules — not merely because the Health and Safety at Work Act so requires, but for the sake of your own safety and that of others who work with you.

## 323   Pallets not carefully stacked

If a stack of pallets were to fall, injury or even death could easily result. I have had to warn you — both by word of mouth and in writing — of the slovenly way in which you have sometimes been stacking.

As you know, I have now received a complaint about your stacking from Mr . . . . The Board have therefore instructed me to refer to my letter to you dated . . . , complaining about your carelessness; and to warn you that any further complaint will lead to your dismissal.

## 324   Further infringements at own risk

It is true that your continued failure to wear your safety mask endangers only your own safety. But you are in breach of Section 7 of the Health and Safety at Work Act and are liable to be prosecuted; you are taking risks which are wholly unnecessary and which could bring disaster to you and to your family; and because you are such a valued and long serving employee, your behaviour worries us very much.

Once again — and repeating what I wrote in my letter to you dated . . . I must ask you to comply with the safety rules. I must also warn you that the company can accept no responsibility whatsoever, if you continue to behave in such a reckless and dangerous manner.

Please sign the enclosed receipt to show that you understand the situation.

NOTE:
*The fact that you said no responsibility is accepted will not, of course, free you from such responsibility. In civil law, there should be no problem — you have taken all reasonable steps to persuade and to propagandise your employee into complying with the law. But under the Health and Safety at Work Act, the question will still remain: Have you taken such steps as are 'reasonably practicable' to avoid danger — and if so, can you prove it? This letter should do the trick — provided, of course, that the practice complained of is not sufficiently dangerous. A balance must be struck between the degree of danger and the employer's wish not to dismiss the employee.*

### 325   Too dangerous to tolerate

I am sorry — but we cannot permit you to continue . . . . This practice is far too dangerous, for your colleagues as well as for yourself. I repeat the warning given to you in my letter dated . . . . But this time I must add a further warning: If at any time your conduct is repeated, I shall have no alternative other than to terminate your employment.

### 326   To union — asking for support in dismissal

Whatever our differences on other matters — and I am happy to think that these are not great — we share the same concern for the health and safety of those of your members who work for our company. It is therefore with great regret that I must tell you that your efforts and ours to induce your members to use their protective clothing/not to remove guards from machines have failed. Because the practice is so dangerous — and especially in view of the Health and Safety at Work Act and the penalties contained in it — we shall have no alternative other than to dismiss those members who are risking their own lives and limbs — and those of their colleagues/ workmates if the practice continues. We have now sent out final warnings. This letter is to keep you in touch; to ask that you renew your efforts to persuade your members to take care; and to thank you for your support in our efforts to reduce to an absolute minimum the toll taken by accidents in our enterprise.

With best wishes.

## 327 Warning to all employees

I am writing to you — and to all other fitters/operatives/ shop floor workers/furnace men (or as the case may be), to remind you of the grave danger caused to you/and to your colleagues/workmates by the deplorable practice of . . ./by the continued failure of some employees to keep guards on their machines/stack pallets with sufficient care/operate fork-lift trucks with due regard for their own safety and that of others. I am instructed to warn all employees concerned that they are not only in breach of the company's rules but also the Health and Safety at Work Act. In the circumstances, any continuation of the practice by any individual may lead to the termination of his employment.

This letter is being sent on my responsibility, but with the knowledge of all relevant trade unions — who are as concerned as we are to avoid any unnecessary accidents, and who recognise the unnecessary risks at present caused.

I trust that you will take this warning very seriously.

NOTES:

*1 It is always advisable to obtain the full co-operation of all relevant trade unions. This helps to exert pressure on their members, for their own sakes — and, of course, to avoid undesirable effects on industrial relations.*

*2 It is best to address serious warnings of this sort to individual employees — and, where possible, to obtain receipts for the letters (see*

*Chapter 39). Alternatively (but second best) they could be put in wage
packets. Third (and worst) they could be exhibited on the appropriate
notice boards.*

## 328   Final warning – general

I am writing to you and to all other employees employed
in . . ./on . . . to issue a final warning that anyone found
smoking in our . . . shop/. . . area will be dismissed instantly
and without notice. Leniency has been exercised in the past –
but in view of the Health and Safety at Work Act – and of
the considerable danger caused by this practice, not merely to
the smoker but to anyone else affected – employment will be
terminated forthwith in all future cases.

Please treat this warning seriously. It is given with the full
knowledge and approval of all relevant trade unions – who
are as anxious to preserve safety in our works as we are.

NOTES:
*1   No threat should be made unless you are prepared, if necessary, to
enforce it.*

*2   I repeat: Dismissal must be regarded as a last resort, when all else
has failed. To be regarded as 'fair', it muse not only be preceded, where
possible, with warnings – it must not be used as an excuse for
victimisation or 'picking on' individuals whom you would be happy to
dismiss for other reasons.*

*3   The employee who does not follow safety rules might be held to
have been dismissed 'unfairly', but his compensation is almost certain
to be reduced, to take account of his own irresponsibility for his own
downfall.*

## 329   Denial that employer's general duty has been breached

I accept that it is the duty of every employer to ensure, so
far as reasonably practical, the health, safety and welfare at
work of his employees. But it is also the duty of employees.

I am passing your letter to the company's insurers for their attention, but I cannot hold out any hope of your obtaining the sort of compensation which you apparently have in mind.

NOTE:

*If insurers are to be involved, either deny liability or say nothing. Admission may be a breach of the contract of insurance.*

# Chapter 38

# An employee's duty to take care of himself

Section 7 of the Health and Safety at Work Act:
'It shall be the duty of every employee while at work —
*(a)* To take reasonable care for the health and safety of himself and of persons who may be affected by his acts or omissions at work; and
*(b)* As regards any duty or requirement imposed on his employer or any other person by or under any of the relevant statutory provisions, to co-operate with him so far as is necessary to enable that duty or requirement to be performed or complied with.'

So an employee is criminally liable if he does not 'take reasonable care' for his own health and safety at work and that of his colleagues or workmates. And he must 'co-operate' with his employers, so as to enable or help them to comply with their statutory 'duties or requirements', under the Factories Act, the Offices, Shops and Railway Premises Act, the Health and Safety at Work Act, the Explosives Act, the Alkali and Works Regulations, the Nuclear Installations Act, the Mines and Quarries Acts . . . etc., etc., and all regulations made under them.

In addition, Section 8 reads: 'No person shall intentionally or recklessly interfere with or misuse anything provided in the interests of health, safety or welfare in pursuance of any of the relevant statutory provisions'. Luddites, beware! And note: The Act uses the words 'intentionally or recklessly', rather than the (more difficult to prove) 'wilfully', used in the Factories Act.

These duties are real — but, in practice, unlikely to be enforced through criminal prosecution, other than as a last resort or where there is full union backing. No one wants to turn this Act into a second Industrial Relations Act, regarded as a club to beat the workers. If the Act is to be used to best effect to reduce industrial accidents, then the co-operation of workers and their organisations is essential. Still, it is fair to draw the attention of employees and their representatives to Sections 7 and 8.

It is not wise, though, to threaten prosecutions which will not occur or to cry industrial wolf by warnings to workers of prosecutions which may produce precisely the opposite effect to that intended — to frighten them away from responsibility and to prevent the workforce from regarding health and safety as at least one matter on which they and management can unite their efforts.

The following brief letters are variations of letters in the previous Chapter. They may be used on their own, but they may also be included in warning letters (as in the preceding and next chapters).

\* \* \*

## 330  Employee may be prosecuted

I was sorry to hear that your foreman, Mr Black, had to remind you once again that the law requires the wearing of protective goggles or spectacles, when working at an abrasive wheel/lathe. Please would you ensure that you never again fail to wear your protective gear.

Please bear in mind that the Health and Safety at Work Act places a positive duty on employees themselves to take reasonable care for their own safety. Failure to do so may lead to prosecution — and while we are primarily concerned with the protection of your eyes, we must point out that if the Inspector were to note your breach of the law, you could well be prosecuted.

## 331  Danger to mates

By failing to follow the safety rules — and in particular, by removing the guard from your machine and allowing swarf to accumulate in the gangway — you are causing a danger to your colleagues. You are also in breach of the Health and Safety at Work Act and if this breach is noticed by the Factory Inspector, you would be liable to prosecution.

To protect your colleagues as well as yourself, please do ensure that there is no future breach of the company's safety regulations.

## 332  Simple warning

By your dangerous behaviour in removing the guard from

your machine (*or as the case may be*), you have not only
caused a hazard to yourself/and to your colleagues, but you
have been in clear breach of Section 7 of the Health and
Safety at Work Act. The Act, of course, is a criminal statute
and offenders against its rules may be prosecuted.

Please do not give any further cause for complaint on this
score.

# Chapter 39

# Acknowledgements, receipts and undertakings from erring employees

### 333 Receipt of warning — acknowledged

I agree that I have received, read and understood your letter dated . . . , in which you insist on my keeping the guard on my machine in position.

NOTE:
*If the employee refuses to sign, then make a careful note of that refusal on the document — and file it.*

### 334 Alternative receipt

Thank you for your letter concerning the wearing of safety helmets. This I have read and understood.

### 335 Undertaking for the future

I have read and understood your letter dated . . . , concerning the importance of my wearing my safety mask/using my ear defenders. I appreciate the importance of this rule and undertake that in future I will wear the mask, as required.

### 336 Agreement to guard lathes — danger to others appreciated

I have received your letter dated . . . concerning my failure to keep the guard on my lathe in position, and you have explained to me the danger which may result not only to myself but also to passersby, who may get grit/splinters in their eyes. I will keep the guard in position in future.

(Signed) . . . . . .

## 337   Simple acknowledgement

I have received, read and understood your letter of ... ,
regarding ....

(Signed) ......

## 338   Acknowledged that letter handed over

You [and my shop steward] have handed to me the letter
dated ... concerning my failure to .... You have explained
to me the seriousness of the matter — which I fully understand.

## 339   Acknowledgement to chairman of safety committee

You have explained to me the importance placed by the
Safety Committee of my not .... You have also handed to
me the letter from the Committee — which I have read and
understood.

# Chapter 40

# Contractors and sub-contractors on your premises

As we have seen (in Chapter 35), Section 2 of the Health and Safety at Work Act codifies the civil law on an employer's liability to his employees and transfers it to the law of crime. Section 3 has the same effect on an employer's duty towards visitors, neighbours and the general public.

Thanks to Section 2, you must take all such steps as are 'reasonably practicable' not to submit your employees to risk to their health and safety while they are at work. Thanks to Section 3, you must do all that is 'reasonably practicable' to see that people other than your employees do not suffer risk to their health or safety as a result of work activities under your control.

*The Occupiers' Liability Act, 1957,* imposes a 'common duty of care' on all occupiers towards their lawful visitors. That is a duty to take such care as is reasonable in all the circumstances, to keep those visitors safe while on the premises for the purposes for which they are permitted to be there.

As always, what is or is not 'reasonable' depends on all the circumstances of the particular case. A warning (says the Act), none too helpfully, 'may or may not be sufficient' − everything depends on the nature of the warning and of the person who receives it.

Again: Contractors, sub-contractors and others who visit your premises 'in the exercise of their calling' − that is, while doing the jobs for which they are employed by their employers and engaged by you − may be expected to take all necessary precautions to protect themselves against those risks which are 'ordinarily incidental to their calling'. You must protect them, in so far as you can, against unusual risks − or risks which result from their use of your premises or on equipment supplied by you. But they may be expected to know their job and to guard against the ordinary risks which they would expect to encounter while doing those jobs.

Conversely (says the Act), you must expect child visitors to take less care of themselves than would adults in similar circumstances. This rule has become particularly important since a series of High Court rulings which put most child trespassers in the same legal position as most lawful visitors.

You owe no duty to take care for the safety of trespassers. You must not set traps for them — do not dig a pit at the entrance to your works, not set a spring gun by your stores. But the trespasser — the person who comes onto your premises without your consent, express or implied — visits you at his own risk.

Still, where you know that children are likely to come onto your land, precisely because they are children you must take as much care of them as you would if they were your own. And if there is any 'allurement' — in one important case, an open fire; but it might just as easily have been a trolley on rails, or even a pile of sand or bricks — then you must do what you reasonably can to guard the allurement.

How old is a child? (Or, as one wit put it: When does infancy become adultery?) Unlike the criminal law, which sets the limit at 10 — below which age every child is presumed absolutely to be incapable of crime — there is no such limit in civil law. Nor is there any specific mention of children in the Health and Safety at Work Act.

The new Act awaits interpretation by the Courts. Meanwhile, it is likely that the criteria set up in decisions on the Employer's Liability Act will be looked to, at least as having powerful persuasive effect. Naturally, at civil law you only have to prove your case 'on the balance of probabilities', while those who prosecute under the Health and Safety at Work Act must satisfy the Court of the guilt of the accused 'beyond all reasonable doubt'. However: Once an unsafe practice is proved — whether affecting employees, visitors or strangers — the burden of proving that reasonable steps (or 'reasonably practicable' ones, as the case may be) were taken rests on the accused.

As with Section 2, so with Section 3 — to show that you were not guilty of unsafe or unhealthy practices — or that you took all those steps which would have been taken by a 'reasonable' employer in the circumstances — you will need letters.

Again: While you can pass the buck both upwards and downwards in the case of your own employees because if you can establish that the fault was that of 'some other person', you will be entitled to be acquitted — so, in the case of contractors or sub-contractors — you may well be able to prove that the fault lay with those who employed the people at risk.

The Inspector decides upon whom to serve the improvement or prohibition notice (Chapter 47). He will also decide whom to prosecute, — and when. If your documentation is in order and shows that you are not at fault, then you will have achieved one major victory. It is great to be acquitted if you are prosecuted — but far greater not to be prosecuted in the first place.

## 340 Warning to contractors – dangerous premises

I enclose herewith, as arranged . . . copies of our safety pamphlet, one copy of which must be given to each of your employees before he enters our premises. This important document summarises the main hazards which your employees may face when working in our factory/shop/works. I would, however, especially draw your attention to the following:

1 . . . .
2 . . . .
3 . . . .

Kindly acknowledge receipt of this letter and of the pamphlet and confirm that copies will be given to your men. With best wishes.

NOTES:

*1 In due course, regulations may be made under the Act, requiring information to be given to specified classes of visitors. Meanwhile and in any event, the provision of a safety booklet for visitors is highly advisable – and really well-run businesses already provide this. If you do not, then why not?*

*2 An alternative to sending copies of the pamphlets is to hand one to each visitor, when he first enters your premises. Thus:*

## 341 Contractors' employees handed safety pamphlet

Welcome to the premises of . . . .

In order that you avoid any unnecessary risk on our premises, you will be handed together with this letter a pamphlet, setting out the main hazards. Please read it with care and follow the rules laid down for your safety.

In addition, of course, you will be required to take proper care in connection with your own job – and not to cause danger either to yourself, to your work mates or to employees of our company, as a result of your work here.

You will be required to sign that you have received this letter and the enclosed pamphlet.

With best wishes.

NOTES:

*1   As with your own employees, so with those of others — no signature is required by law, but once the visitor has signed that he has received a document, he will be unable successfully to deny receipt of that document. He will also be presumed to have read and understood its contents.*

*2   If your pamphlet is in any way obscure — or likely to be so to a visitor who does not know the premises and/or who is not particularly intelligent, then by all means add a paragraph to read: 'If you have any queries about the meaning of this pamphlet or regarding safety measures in our premises, please contact [our safety officer, Mr . . . , in room . . . ].*

### 342   One major hazard — be warned

This company takes pride in looking after the health and safety not only of its own employees but also of all visitors to its premises. Please adhere to all safety rules and in particular, note the following:

    1 . . . .
    2 . . . .
    3 . . . .

Because of the nature of our work/the siting of our premises/the nature of the work which you will be doing, the major accident risk is likely to arise from . . . .

In the circumstances, please take special care to . . . .

### 343   Warning to employers — major hazard

I am very pleased that you will be sending in your men on . . . to carry out . . . on/at our premises at . . . .

Please take careful note of one major hazard, caused by the nature/siting or our premises/the work which you will be doing. That is: [Insert particulars of hazard — and of steps necessary to reduce it to a minimum].

### 344   Protest to contractors — danger to your employees

I am extremely concerned at the unsafe manner in which

your employees are carrying out their work on our premises. In particular, I have received serious complaints concerning the following:

1　The leaving of packing cases/wiring/obstructions in gangways.
2　Careless stacking of equipment/supplies.
3　Reckless operation of cranes/hoists/forklift trucks.
4　. . . .
5　. . . .

Please do ensure that immediate measures are taken to rectify these complaints. Apart from the danger caused to employees of this company – and, of course, to your own employees – the enforcement of the rules laid down by the Health and Safety at Work Act could be disastrous – and we would have to hold you fully responsible.

This letter is being delivered by hand. Please would you contact me personally, without delay.

## 345　Danger to own employees

I have noted with anxiety that the scaffolding erected by your employees in our premises is in a dangerous condition/ that your employees are not wearing the safety goggles whicn we have provided for their use while on our premises. I appreciate that the prime responsibility for any resultant accident would rest upon you – both in civil law and under the Health and Safety at Work Act. But for the sake of your employees and also because of the Act, I would be obliged if you would look into the above matters at your earliest possible convenience.

NOTES:

*1　Unless and until a Court rules on the duty of occupiers towards visiting contractors, we shall not know the weight of the burden placed on occupiers by Section 3. If you spot a dangerous practice which does not affect your employees but which could cause injury or even death to employees of your contractors, do you not have in any event a moral duty to speak out?*

*2　Because you do not 'employ' your contractor's workmen – you do not deduct PAYE from their pay nor hold their cards (a good rule of thumb, this, when trying to decide whether or not a person is your 'employee') — you may still have a legal responsibility for their safety. You 'control' your premises? Then you are bound by the Act not to cause danger to others (do you provide them with defective equipment? Are your staircases or gangways defective?).*

*3   Conversely: While your visitors must take care for the safety of those whom they employ — or, for that matter, for those they manage (see Chapter 35 for duties of directors and managers), they must also avoid causing unnecessary risks to your employees. The trouble is, though, that if you do not handle the matter tactfully, your visitors may down tools. Therefore an approach by one of your top men to one of theirs is normally best. If in doubt, try this one — brief but incredibly effective:*

## 346   Warning — the inspector cometh

In view of the current state of your scaffolding/as your employees are not using guards on their machines/as a result of the way in which wiring and boxes are cluttering up the gangways, I thought you might like a tip off: We are expecting a visit from the Inspector any time/day now. And he is busy enforcing the Health and Safety at Work Act.

I have thought it best to contact you direct, rather than to speak to the people on site — which I am sure that you will wish to do yourself.

With best wishes.

## 347   Immediate danger — warning to foreman

I write to you as foreman in charge of the work being carried out by your company on our premises at . . . . We have been most disturbed to note the use of/failure to use . . . /your employees unsafe practices in connection with . . . . As a result, considerable danger is being caused not only to your own people but also to ours — and I must ask that you ensure that the practice concerned is discontinued/that safety rules are immediately complied with.

I am contacting your Head Office, but because we consider that there is an immediate danger here, this note is coming to you by hand.

## 348   Architect — to site occupier

When visiting the site at . . . this morning, I was concerned to note the following dangerous practices:

1    The scaffolding is unsafe.
2    Ladders are not properly footed/lashed.
3    . . . .
4    . . . .

The responsibility — both in civil law and under the Health and Safety at Work Act — rests upon the occupiers of the site and upon the employers of the people concerned. However, we are not only concerned with the safety of our clients and their employees but also with these liabilities — and I am sure that you would want to look into these matters without delay.

With my best wishes.

NOTE:

*There is considerable dispute as to the extent (if any) that architects are liable under the Health and Safety at Work Act, in respect of dangerous practices at sites on which work is being carried on which they are supervising. In my opinion, Section 3 is quite wide enough to cover them. The architects 'undertaking' includes the supervision not only of the structures but of the way they are being erected. In any event: An architect who sees a dangerous practice which is liable to cause death or injury on a construction site should not close his eyes. Construction accidents cause far too high a percentage of industrial disasters.*

## 349   Erectors and installers — take care

I write to you officially because your engineers are in the process of erecting vessels/machinery at our premises at . . . . I am sure that you would wish to know that their methods of work appear to be dangerous in the following respects:

1    . . . .
2    . . . .
3    . . . .

We appreciate that erectors and installers are made personally responsible under Section 6 of the Health and Safety at Work Act — in addition to their normal duties to their employees under Section 2. But as we are also concerned for the safety of our own employees — and as we know of the high repute of your company and your wish to carry out your work in a safe manner — we decided to have this letter delivered to you by hand/sent to you express.

I would respectfully suggest that you arrange to have matters put right without delay. You may also wish to know that we are due for a visit from the Factory Inspector at any time now.

# Chapter 41

# Contractors and sub-contractors— replies to warnings

If you believe that complaints made concerning your health or safety measures or those of your employees are unjustified, then say so — in writing. Just as site occupiers may seek to place the blame on you, so you are entitled to pass it back whence it came. Oral complaints should not be ignored — but written ones should most definitely be replied to — in kind. Thus:

## 350 Contractor denies danger

Thank you for your letter concerning . . . . I respectfully disagree that there has been any breach of building regulations/the Factories Act/the Health and Safety at Work Act — nor any avoidable danger . . . to my employees or yours.

Without prejudice to the foregoing, I am of course concerned to preserve the highest standards and I am immediately arranging for one of my senior managers to visit you, and to discuss the entire matter with you.

NOTES:

*1 The magic words 'without prejudice' keep appearing in this book — and should be used whenever you are prepared to make a concession which you would not wish to have put before a Court.*

*2 Even if you do not agree with the allegations of a dangerous or unhealthy practice, you should still investigate — if only because failure to do so would inevitably be negligent and a subsequent accident may be as disastrous for you personally as it is for your company — and especially for the person injured or killed.*

## 351 Defects remedied

Thank you for your letter dated . . . . I appreciated not only the concern which you have shown for the employees of this company, but especially the trouble you took in bringing to my personal notice the dangerous practice concerned. I took immediate steps to ensure that the defect was remedied/the scaffolding was strengthened/my employees wore their safety helmets/used their protective clothing.

I trust that similar circumstances will not arise in future — but if they do, perhaps you would care to telephone me? My company places paramount importance on health and safety at work and is always pleased to co-operate in the taking of safety precautions — for the benefit not only of its own employees but all others affected.

With kind regards.

## 352   From window cleaners to clients

As a result of the Health and Safety at Work Act, we are reconsidering all measures for the health and safety of our employees at work. Our employees are now required to wear safety harness when working at heights — and I would ask for your kind co-operation in ensuring that adequate hooks or other anchor points are made available to them, so that all unnecessary accidents may be avoided. I look forward to hearing from you.

## 352   Sub-contractor blames head contractor

Thank you for your letter drawing attention to . . . .

The fault (if fault there be) is not ours. The system of work is provided/equipment specified and provided by our head contractors, . . . Ltd of . . . — to whom I have sent a copy of your letter. I hope that you will be hearing from them very swiftly.

NOTE:
*Buck passing is not a routine confined to employers — but it has its dangers. Having been put on notice of the risk concerned, the sub contractors are certainly justified in requesting action from their head contractors, if the fault lay with those head contractors. But equally, they should take immediate steps, in so far as they can, to avoid any further risk to their own employees.*

## 354  Contractor blames site occupier

I acknowledge receipt of your letter dated . . . . I deny that there is any avoidable danger in the system as operated by us. Any danger is caused through defects in the structure of the premises in/upon which we are working. I would draw your attention especially to the following:

    1 . . . .
    2 . . . .
    3 . . . .

No doubt you will arrange for these matters to be looked into without delay — and as our company is, of course, far more concerned with the existence of danger than with the element of blame, please do not hesitate to contact me.

Chapter 42

# Child visitors — wanted and unwanted

The Health and Safety at Work Act makes no specific reference to children — but courts are likely to apply the same principles as those established under the Occupier's Liability Act. You must take special care for child visitors because they are likely to take less care for themselves.

Recent Appeal Court decisions have established that if you know that children (or, indeed, adults) are likely to be on your premises, you may 'owe them a duty of care' — in civil and in criminal law. This is a 'humanitarian' as well as a 'legal' duty.

## 355   Children — banned

Our security men at the gate have instructions to hand a copy of this letter to every driver — our own and those of other companies.

CHILDREN ARE NOT PERMITTED
TO ENTER THESE PREMISES

If you have a child with you in your cab, then he must be left at the gate. These premises are dangerous for children — do not risk disaster for your own child — or anyone else's — by ignoring this warning.

Please sign the duplicate of this letter, to acknowledge that you have received, read and understood it.

NOTES:
*1   There are many establishments which ban children. Leaving in the gatehouse may cause aggravation, but drivers should soon get the message.*
*2   If you believe that drivers do not bring their own children into your premises you could be right! But in case you are wrong (as is, alas, probable), consider having this follow-up letter available:*

## 356   No children — further warning

Once again I remind you that no children are allowed on these premises. In future, please do not bring children with you in your cab — or this could lead to serious consequences.

Please sign the receipt for this letter.

NOTE:

*For rules on acknowledgements, receipts and the signature of documents, see Chapter 39.*

## 357 Children not to leave cab

These premises are dangerous for children. The child with you must not be allowed to leave your cab under any circumstances, once you have passed the gatehouse. If he needs to use the toilet, facilities are available at the gatehouse and you must personally take the child with you and accept full responsibility.

In future, we ask you not to bring children with you when making deliveries to our works/factory/cold store/warehouse.

I hope that you will understand that we have made this rule in order to protect the health and safety of children. We ask for your co-operation, for their sake.

## 358 Children in grounds — parents beware

I was sorry to note that your child has been wandering about our grounds. THIS IS DANGEROUS.

As I expect you know, a child tragically drowned in our quarry last year — it is not possible for us to fence off the entire area and we must ask you to ensure, as best you can, that your child does not again come on to our land.

We would especially draw your attention to the following dangers on our premises:

1   Piles of sand, which are attractive to children but may collapse upon them.
2   Trenches which may seem ideal to explore, but which are not shored up and cannot be made 'child proof'.
3   Trolleys on rails — which are fun to play on — but which may easily crush a child who gets in the way of one when on the move.
4   Roofs — particularly glass ones — which children like to climb on, but through which they may easily fall.

We do, of course, appreciate your difficulties in preventing your child from coming on to our land — but we must warn you that while we will continue to take every reasonably practicable step to protect children who come on to our premises, we regard them as trespassers; we do our best to keep them off; but the ultimate responsibility must rest with parents. So please take this matter very seriously — for the sake of your child.


### 359   Older child trespasser — beware

As I am sure you know, you are not permitted to enter these premises/this land. The reason is that there are dangerous places/processes/machinery which could easily cause you to suffer injury or even death. That is why the rule forbidding young people to come here is very strictly enforced.

You must leave these premises/this land at once — and not return.

Our security guard will ask you for your name and address. Please give them to him — and sign the enclosed sheet to say that you have received this letter and that you have either read it or had it read to you and that you understand it.

NOTES:

*1   Naturally, you have to catch the youngster before you can push a letter in his hand — and he may refuse to give his name and address. If you suspect that he may be coming to steal, then you would in any event be entitled to call in the police and to hold him until they arrive — private individuals may arrest when they reasonably suspect that a theft (or other 'arrestable offence') has been committed and they reasonably suspect the individual held to have been guilty of that offence. If you do keep a youngster until the police arrive, where he is trespassing on your land, the chances of your getting successfully sued for wrongful arrest (or 'false imprisonment') by or on behalf of the individual arrested are almost nil. The same principle, incidentally, applies to adults — including your own employees — whom you wish to arrest — perhaps because they refuse to submit to search.*

*2   As usual, requiring the individual to receive — and, if possible, to sign — a letter will not only emphasise to him the seriousness with which you treat the matter but will help you to prove that you have taken 'reasonably practicable steps' to keep him safe in future.*


### 360   Lawful child visitor — take care

We are very pleased to welcome you to our factory/works/

premises, and hope that you will have an interesting time here.

Please remember, though, that this is a place of work which could cause danger to you, if you are not careful. I remind you especially of the following:

1   Take special care when . . . .
2   Keep away from . . . .
3   At all times wear the safety helmet with which you will be provided . . . .
4   Do not remove the cap/hat with which you will be provided − this is required for reasons of hygiene and health.
5   Under no circumstances leave your guide. If you wish to use the toilet, tell us and you will be taken there.
6   Co-operate with your guide's requests, at all times − for your own safety. You will be safe, if you follow his instructions − but the company can accept no responsibility for your health or safety if you wander off on your own or otherwise fail to keep to the rules and to obey your guide.

Please sign the tear off slip at the foot of this letter, to say that you fully understand what I have written.

With all best wishes to you for a happy and safe visit.

NOTES:

*1   If the party is organised by a school then teachers will always be pleased to co-operate in getting these letters handed out and signed.*

*2   You may like to sugar coat the pill by attaching the letter to your handout or pamphlet or other literature − so that the youngsters receive it as part of a major package. Alternatively, to emphasise the importance of the letter, you may in any event like to deal with it separately.*

### 361   Warning to child of particular danger

Please take special care when you are visiting these premises/on our land. Children/young people have in the past been injured by/when on/as a result of/. . . .

To emphasise the importance of your avoiding risks by . . . , this letter is being handed to you personally. Please sign to show that you have received and understood it.

With best wishes to you.

# Chapter 43

# The executive complains

The executive must communicate with the Company, on his own behalf, in the best possible manner. If he does so within the framework of the Act, then the same rules of good sense apply to him as when he is wearing his Company hat. There is one exception — if he has been shown the door and wishes to obtain compensation for unfair dismissal, then he should note carefully the rules (and the precedents) in this book — and (standing them on their head, where necessary) employ them for his own purposes. (Compare also the executive's own protection against unfair dismissal.)

Here are some other cases in which individual letters may be of help, from the executive's own viewpoint.

## 362 Refusal to superior to contravene Act

I have given very careful consideration to your suggestion that we should . . . .

May I respectfully refer you to Section . . . of the Health and Safety at Work Act? I think that you will agree with me that if we were to take the step proposed by the Board, we would be flying in the teeth of the Act — and while the Union might not wish to invoke the procedures provided by this legislation, I would not count on it.

In the circumstances, I would suggest that this matter deserves careful reconsideration, so as to avoid even worse dislocation in our production.

I will be pleased to call upon you to discuss this matter if you will be good enough to let me know what time would be convenient to you.

Meanwhile, I trust that you will appreciate the reason for my reluctance to carry out the procedure referred to in your letter.

With my best wishes.

## 363   Refusal to dismiss unfairly

I must ask you to reconsider your decision to dismiss Mr Green. I fully appreciate the grounds for that decision — but I fear that we may run into very serious difficulty under the provisions of the Industrial Relations Act which enable an employee, on occasion, to obtain as much as £5200 as compensation for so-called 'unfair dismissal'.

Under the Act, a dismissal which we would regard as fair may nevertheless be 'unfair'. And once an employee has been dismissed, there is a presumption of unfairness — the burden of proving 'fair' dismissal rests upon the employers.

In the circumstances, I think that we would be well advised to exercise further patience with regard to Mr . . . . However, if the Board decides despite my views to proceed with the dismissal, I know that it will take into account the potential financial risks — which I have felt it my duty to draw to your attention.

With best wishes.

# Chapter 44

# Neighbours and nuisances—and pollution of the air

At 'common law' — as a result of the decisions of judges over the centuries — no one may use his land in such a way as unreasonably to interfere with his neighbour's enjoyment of his (the neighbour's) property. We may all have to put up with a certain amount of noise, smoke, fumes, vibration or dust as 'part of the give and take of neighbourly life'. But when the degree of disturbance goes beyond that which a normal, reasonable, healthy person would expect to have to put up with, then it becomes a 'nuisance' in law, as well as in fact. Nor is it any excuse to say that the nuisance has existed for some time and that the complainant 'came to it'.

Still, the neighbourhood is taken into account. Anyone who lives in a factory district cannot expect the same degree of peace as someone else who dwells in a smart residential neighbourhood.

The neighbour disturbed may apply to a Civil Court for an injunction, restraining the continuation of the offence complained of — and for damages. Section 3 would now enable the offender to be prosecuted, if the neighbour's health or safety was at risk — health, probably through disturbance of his sleep patterns; safety, perhaps through projecting buildings, obstruction of pavements, dangerous stacking of goods alongside public footways or overhanging pathways.

Again: Public Health Inspectors* have long had limited powers to curb excessive disturbance through (for example) the pouring of dust or fumes or smoke into the air through factory chimneys. Their hands are now strengthened by Section 5 of the Act, which provides:

1    That everyone must use 'the best practicable means' to avoid polluting the air with noxious or offensive fumes.
2    In so far as the best practicable means cannot prevent the polluting of the air, then all reasonably practicable steps must be taken to render the fumes harmless and inoffensive.

Strictly speaking, Section 3 as it affects neighbours and Section 5 as it covers 'emanations' into the air come outside the scope of employer's liability. Hence the sample letters in this Chapter are few.

Finally, note: Section 5 in any event deals with pollution of the air only and not with the pouring of filth onto the land or into lakes or rivers. That is the subject of other, more precise legislation.

*Prosecutions under Section 5 are rare. The Public Health Acts are more likely weapons — still.

## 364  Noise – kept to minimum

I was sorry to receive your letter and to learn that the noise from our generator is disturbing you. As you know, we do our best to cause the least possible disturbance to our neighbours. I think it fair to point out that yours is the only complaint we have received/it is really not possible for us to avoid a certain amount of noise/the noise is confined to normal working hours. But in any event, *without prejudice* and in view of our wish to maintain the best possible relations with you, we are arranging to insulate the room concerned/take steps to reduce the noise still further. We must ask you to exercise patience for about . . . weeks, while work is being carried out.

NOTES:
*1  Never admit nuisance – and always remember to use the words 'without prejudice'.*

*2  Letters of this sort all too often end up before courts – so maintain a dignified, friendly, courteous attitude – however rude the letter you have received. Thus:*

## 365  Offensive letter – reply to

I was sorry both to receive your letter and to note its very offensive tone. I am sure that on reconsideration you would have wished to phrase it differently – particularly as I could have told you – had you only asked me – that we have already arranged to take still further steps to deal with the matters referred to by you.

I can assure you that we are using the best practicable means to keep the disturbance to our neighbours to an absolute minimum – but I must respectfully point out to you that you live in a manufacturing district and that with the best will in the world, it is simply impossible to avoid the normal effects of manufacturing processes.

## 366  Solicitor's letter – answered

I acknowledge receipt of your letter dated . . . regarding

the alleged nuisance. This is denied. I am referring your letter to the company's solicitors, Messrs . . . , of . . . , to whom any further correspondence should be addressed.

I wish to add that we have always prided ourselves on our good relations with our neighbours and that we regard both the intervention of solicitors and the tone of your letter as totally unwarranted.

## 367 Fumes not 'noxious'

We are sorry that you have received complaints from neighbours regarding fumes from our chimney. Our comments are as follows:

1 We had wished to build the stack up by an additional . . . feet — but these plans were vetoed by the Planning Authority.

2 We are already using the best practicable means to avoid the emission of fumes and to render such fumes as are emitted both harmless and inoffensive — but we are fully prepared to discuss with you any suggestions which you might be able to make in that regard.

3 Both from the viewpoint of Section 5 of the Act — and because of our wish to maintain the highest standards of management — we will continue to do everything in our power to reduce disturbance to our neighbours to a minimum. But I am sure that you will appreciate that we operate in a factory neighbourhood; that if our processes are to continue, a certain amount of disturbance is inevitable; and that we cannot produce . . . without also producing some fumes. In our view, the complaints you have received are unreasonable.

Please do call on me personally when you are next in our neighbourhood, so that I can discuss this whole matter with you.

With best wishes.

NOTE:
*These matters are best discussed — but it is wise to put your case firmly on the written record.*

# Chapter 45

# Designers, manufacturers, importers, suppliers, erectors, installers

Section 6 of the Health and Safety at Work Act imposes totally new duties on those who put industrial plant and components – and 'substances' (liquid or solid, gas or vapour) – into potentially dangerous circulation. Designers, manufacturers and suppliers (cash or credit, hire, lease or sale, it matters not) are all covered – and all come within the jurisdiction of our Courts. But where the manufacture, design and supply are outside the Court's jurisdiction, then the burden rests on the importer – whether acting as principal or agent.

Strictly speaking, the liabilities imposed by this Section rest on the seller (or, with importers, on the buyer) – and on those who design or manufacture – rather than on the employer. Hence they come outside the scope of this book. Nevertheless, employers may wish to pass off liability up the line to those who supplied them – and an employer may in any event also be the designer, manufacturer, importer or manufacturer – so here are a few of those letters which may serve to keep him out of trouble.

In addition, Section 6 covers 'installers and erectors'.

\* \* \*

## 368   Allegation – faulty manufacture

We write to notify you that an accident occurred at our above works on . . . , resulting in personal injuries. An investigation is to be instigated by the Health and Safety Commission. No doubt you will be hearing from them. Meanwhile, we must inform you that suspicion attaches to certain tools which you have supplied to us. If you will contact our works manager, Mr . . . , at the above number, he will be pleased to provide you with details.

### 369    To designer — what testing done?

I have received a complaint about the design of . . . . This comes within the sphere of your responsibility and I would be grateful if you would let me have details of research and testing done to ensure, so far as is reasonably practicable, that the . . . is safe when properly used. Please be especially careful in the preparation of these details because I fear that we may run into difficulty under the Health and Safety at Work Act.

### 370    Designer — fault lies with materials

Thank you for your letter. I enclose a schedule of the research and testing done by us on the items concerned.

I note the alleged difficulties with the . . . . I suspect that these must have been caused by the materials used.

### 371    Research and testing by others

Thank you for your letter. I enclose herewith copies of documents received from our suppliers, Messrs . . . . You will see that they have carried out testing, examination and research as set out therein. Having regard to the high repute of those suppliers, we relied upon the results of their testing, examination and research, as provided for in Section 6(6) of the Health and Safety at Work Act.

As I expect that you will be contacting Messrs . . . , I am sending them copies of our correspondence.

### 372    Customer's written undertaking

I hereby undertake that we shall take the following steps to ensure, so far as is reasonably practicable, that the items supplied by you will be safe and without risk to health when properly used, as provided for by Section 6(8) of the Health and Safety at Work Act:

     1 . . . .
     2 . . . .
     3 . . . .

In the circumstances, there will be no need for you to take

those steps – so kindly supply the plant/machinery/equipment as ordered, as swiftly as possible and in accordance with our specifications.

## 373 Reliance on customer's undertaking

I enclose herewith a copy of the undertaking received from our customers, Messrs . . . . As you will see, we were merely required to supply the plant/equipment/components in accordance with their specification and they undertook in writing to carry out all necessary examination, research and testing to ensure that the items were safe.

As no doubt you will be making further enquiries from them in accordance with Section 6(8) of the Health and Safety at Work Act, I am sending copies of this correspondence to their Sales Director.

## 374 Erectors and installers – reminder of responsibilities

Before you commence installing the vessel/plant/equipment on our premises at . . . , I am instructed to remind you of Section 6(3) of the Health and Safety at Work Act. As the article concerned is to be used by our employees at work, it will be for you to ensure so far as is reasonably practicable that nothing about the way in which it is erected or installed makes it unsafe or a risk to health when properly used.

For our part, we shall be pleased to co-operate with you – and we shall also be providing a copy of our works safety rules to each of your employees who work in our plant.

With best wishes.

## 375 Supplier's alternatives – guarding

All hydraulic guillotines must be fitted with effective operator guards or both the supplier and the customer may be guilty of a serious breach of the law which, as a result of *The Health and Safety at Work, etc. Act, 1974,* may lead to prosecution and to very heavy penalties. Front, side and rear guard must be provided and both front and side guards fitted as standard equipment.

You will note that the rear guarding is offered by us as an extra, which you may consider expensive. It may be that you can make or obtain this guarding more reasonably from a sheet metal works in your area. In addition, there are so many variables affecting the guarding of the rear of the machine — types of handling or lifting equipment; points of access; location in shop; and local factory inspectors' views — that we would not find it possible to make a guard which is universally acceptable.

In the circumstances, there are two alternatives. On the one hand, we would (as indicated) be pleased to supply the rear guarding, after discussions with you and your acceptance of our estimate. Alternatively, if you decide to procure the rear guarding independently of us, then we are only able to supply the machine to you upon receipt of a written undertaking from you that you will do so.

We look forward to hearing from you as to whether you wish us to provide the necessary guarding or whether you will yourselves do so and provide us with the necessary written undertaking.

### 376   Written undertaking — guarding

In the consideration of your supplying to us the equipment set out in Part 1 of the Schedule below, we . . . Ltd of . . . , hereby undertake to carry out the work specified in Part 2 of the Schedule below.

(Signed) . . . . . .                    (Date) . . . . . . .

*Schedule — Part 1 — Parts*
*and/or components to be supplied*

(1) . . .
(2) . . .
(3) . . .

*Schedule — Part 2 — steps to*
*be taken by customer*

(1) . . .
(2) . . .
(3) . . .

# Chapter 46

# Denial of liability

### 377  Manufacturer denies fault

The tools/equipment were in accordance with the contract and it is denied that they were unsafe or dangerous to health, as alleged. I am passing your letter to the company's solicitors for their attention.

NOTE:
*When there is a potential threat of prosecution, call in the lawyers.*

### 378  Research and examination adequate

Thank you for your letter. I note the allegations therein contained and deny that there was any lack of necessary research/or investigation or that the design of the goods was in any way defective, as alleged or at all. All reasonably practicable steps were taken to ensure the article was safe without risk to health when properly used, and under the circumstances liability is denied.

### 379  Sales letter

*The Health and Safety at Work etc. Act, 1974*
*Your Order No. . . . . . . . . . . . . . . . . . . . . . . .*
*Machine No. . . . . . . . . . . . . . . . . . . . . . . . . . . .*

We thank you for your above order and confirm that the machinery concerned has been inspected by you or on your behalf.

For your protection, we must respectfully draw your attention to the Health and Safety at Work Act and in particular to the requirements of Section 2. The above machinery as purchased by you does not conform in all respects to the law. It is therefore necessary for us to obtain from you your written undertaking that you will, as discussed with us, fit all such safety features and interlocks that are necessary to ensure conformity not only with regulations but also with your local factory inspectorate.

It may be helpful to point out that we now fit necessary interlocks and key switches to all our new machinery and that we have found Messrs . . . very helpful in that regard.

We are sending this letter to you in duplicate. Please sign one copy and return it to us, so that we can then effect immediate despatch.

With our renewed thanks for your business.

We hereby undertake to take the steps specified above sufficient to ensure, so far as is reasonably practicable, that the machinery the subject matter of our above order will be safe and without risks to health when properly used.

(Signed) . . . . . . . . . . . . . . . . . . . . . (Date) . . . . . . . . . . . . .

NOTE:

*The Act requires that (to provide protection) a written undertaking must be given in respect of 'specified steps'. If there are specific 'steps' which could and should be 'specified', then these should be incorporated in the body of the letter.*

# Chapter 47

# The almighty inspector

The Health and Safety Executive holds sway over an integrated inspectorate — the factory inspectors, mines and quarries inspectors, alkali inspectors and the rest (including, since the Employment Protection Act, the agricultural inspectors) all come under the same aegis. They have mighty powers.

The inspector may serve a 'prohibition notice', if he considers that a particular practice is likely to cause imminent risk of serious personal injuries. The recipient may appeal to an industrial tribunal, but the notice stays in effect.

The inspector may also serve an 'improvement notice', if he considers that the practice is unsafe but that there is no imminent risk of serious personal injury. Improvement notices generally give time to put matters right — rather than prohibiting the use of the machine, system or as the case may be. An appeal against an improvement notice suspends the operation of that notice until the tribunal has adjudicated on its necessity — or, more likely, in practice, on whether sufficient time has been given to put matters right.

In practice, thousands of these notices have been served, far more than originally expected. Many have been on the direct initiative of managers who could not induce their companies to spend money on putting matters right. Tip-offs are invariably oral and unprovable.

There have been few appeals against these notices and nearly all of those few have been against time given rather than against the notice as such — and most have failed.

The inspector decides whether or not to serve the notice. If he serves a prohibition notice which is not justified and which has been served negligently then — in theory at least — he may be personally sued for damages by the recipient who has suffered damage as a result. He will be indemnified against such claim by the Executive. Anyway, he must be careful before serving such a notice.

Equally, if he only serves an improvement notice and someone is killed or seriously injured while the process continues, then his misjudgement may be blamed for the tragedy. He has a narrow path to tread.

Notices apart, the inspector decides: To prosecute or not to prosecute. If you receive a notice and fail to obey, then prosecution is almost inevitable. Otherwise, the inspector's discretion is fettered only by his good judgement.

There are no private prosecutions under the Act without the consent of the Director of Public Prosecutions – which means that there are none at all. The inspector, then, decides what is or is not 'reasonable' or 'reasonably practicable' . . . whether there is a dangerous practice which warrants bringing you before the court . . . whether a warning or a notice will suffice or a prosecution (with all its potentially horrendous results) is warranted in the public interest.

The inspector also has powers to enter . . . to inspect . . . even to destroy dangerous substances . . . . In practice, these powers are exercised with discretion. But they must be recognised nonetheless.

Should you ask an inspector for advice, if you are doubtful whether a particular practice is justified?

An ancient sage gave this rule for happiness: 'Love work; hate tyranny; live righteously; and do not let your name get too well known to the authorities'.

If you do call in the inspector and get his advice, be prepared to follow it. Moreover: If you bring him into your premises and steer him, around the main hazards, and you are prosecuted for a dangerous practice, do not expect to rely on the inspector having been to your place and having said nothing.

There are now about a thousand inspectors covering the entire country. They cannot conceivably make as many calls as they should, nor supervise as effectively as the Executive would wish. The Act is to a large extent self-policing, relying upon managers, trade union officials and individual employers and employees for information – but, above all, hoping that the penalties provided and the personal liabilities imposed will induce people to give priority to health and safety, of their own accord.

The Act is working. The number of accidents, fatal and non-fatal, is dropping. Companies are giving time and sparing money for safety training. The inspectors are getting co-operation and help from all sides. Prosecutions, too, are multiplying. Adequate paper work is essential when dealing with the inspector.

## 380    Complaint – against contractors/sub-contractors

For . . . weeks/months, we have employed . . . Ltd to carry out contracting/sub-contracting work in our plant/premises at . . . . We are concerned at their failure to comply with what we regard as adequate safety standards and our efforts to induce them to do so have failed. You will appreciate that we have also had to be tactful, because we are anxious to have their work duly completed.

In the circumstances, would you be kind enough to make a call at our premises as soon as you can — preferably without indicating the source of the request. If you agree with us, then no doubt you will be able to induce them to mend their ways.

In our view, there is a danger not only to their own employees but also to ours. So your swift attention to this request would be very much appreciated.

## 381 Complaint against neighbours

We are sorry to trouble you again, but we have failed to induce our neighbours to take such steps as are reasonably practicable to avoid causing danger to our employees, through their undertaking. The matters complained of are as follows:
 1 . . . .
 2 . . . .
 3 . . . .
We would be grateful if you would investigate these complaints and, if you take the same view as ourselves, if you would ensure — doubtless with co-operation of the local authority — that our neighbour's conduct is brought up to the appropriate standard.

With my thanks in anticipation of an early reply.

## 382 Complaint against own company — confidential

I would be obliged if you would treat this letter as entirely confidential. I write only because I can see no other way in which I can induce my company to take steps which are both necessary and reasonably practicable in order to avoid considerable danger to employees/contractors/sub-contractors/visitors (*or as the case may be*). I have also attempted to reach you by telephone, but have failed.

The situation complained of is as follows:
 1 . . . .
 2 . . . .
 3 . . . .
I would be very grateful if you could arrange to look into these matters at an early date — and, of course, it is vital that

this letter be treated as strictly confidential.

NOTES:

*1   This letter should be used only as a last resort – a complaint made orally may be just as devastating to your own position as one in writing, but writing is (as always) so much easier to prove. In general, proof is useful (or vital) – in this case, it could result (directly or indirectly) in the loss of your job.*

*2   Still, it may be necessary to write in order that danger may be dealt with – or even so as to protect your own position, if the danger which you fear gives rise to injury or death and you are blamed and wish to thrust the responsibility back where it belongs – on your superiors who are failing or refusing to carry out the safety measures which you recommend.*

### 383   Complaint against Inspector

I write with regret to complain of harrassment suffered by my company at the hands of your inspector, Mr . . . . The facts are as follows:
    1 . . . .
    2 . . . .
    3 . . . .
I appreciate that the inspector has a job to do; our company prides itself on its health and safety practices and is, has been and always will be pleased to co-operate with your inspectorate; but we consider that on this occasion your inspector's behaviour has far exceeded the bounds of reasonableness or necessity. I am myself available to discuss the matter with you at any time, either at my office or at yours – and I look forward to hearing from you.

NOTES:

*1   This letter may be addressed either to the inspector's immediate superior or to the Chairman of the Health and Safety Executive (Baynards House, Chepstow Place, London W2 4TF).*

*2   The letter should be written by the chairman or managing director – and, of course, care taken to get the facts absolutely right and, where possible, documented. If there has been a letter of complaint to the inspector himself (such as that which now follows) then a copy should be attached.*

## 384 Complaint to inspector

My safety officer, Mr Jones, has referred to me a serious complaint regarding your behaviour when you visited our works on . . . . I appreciate that you have an important job to do, but before deciding what other steps ought to be taken (if any) in this regard, I would be grateful if you would call on me at your early convenience. The nature of the complaint is as follows:

1 . . . .
2 . . . .
3 . . . .

I look forward to an early reply.

NOTE:

*An inspector should carry out his job with firmness and determination – but with courtesy and restraint. Complaints against inspectors are rare – but occasionally serious.*

## 385 Complaint to Health and Safety executive – inconsistent decisions

We operate plants *inter alia* in the following places: (insert addresses and details).

On . . . , we installed machinery, particulars of which are appended hereto, in our . . . Works. This was duly approved by your local inspector, Mr . . . .

On . . . , we installed the identical machinery in our . . . Plant. Your local inspector, Mr . . . , has refused to approve the same, maintaining that it needs additional guarding (*or as the case may be*).

We consider that the machinery as installed at our . . . premises is safe and that the decision of your local inspector was correct in approving the same. We have now been placed in grave difficulty by the inconsistent decision in our other works – and would ask for this decision to be reviewed without delay. Our production is affected most adversely and may well lead to redundancies.

Your earliest attention would be most appreciated.

## 386   Complaint to MP

I enclose herewith correspondence in which complaints are raised against our local factory inspector, Mr . . ./in respect of the non-approval of machinery/systems/methods in our . . . works in your constituency. We consider this failure to be unreasonable, particularly as the same machinery/system/method has already been approved in our works/premises in . . . . Our production has been adversely affected; redundancies are now likely; we cannot get swift action from the inspector's superiors; and we would therefore be grateful if you would take up this matter on our behalf at your earliest convenience.

With my thanks in anticipation of your usual swift and helpful action on our behalf and on behalf of those of your constituents who we employ.

NOTES:

*1   Every MP is concerned with employment in his constituency; whether or not you agree with his political views is irrelevant – it is his job to help you; and most Members are pleased to extend that help to the employers in their constituencies.*

*2   If the matter is sufficiently serious, you should seek an interview with your MP – which could be in his constituency or at Westminster. No MP will refuse to see employers in such circumstances.*

*3   An MP will only see and help his won constituents. He cannot interfere in matters concerning other Members' constituents.*

## 387   Confirmation to inspector

My colleagues and I were grateful to you for sparing us so much of your time when you visited our works at . . . last . . . . We were particularly pleased to have had the opportunity of demonstrating to you our new . . . machine and were glad that you shared our view that it was well and safely guarded.

Do please call in on us whenever you are in our neighbourhood.

NOTE:

*The importance of this letter is not so much to act as evidence or as an aide memoire for this inspector, but in case one of his colleagues comes next time and takes a different view.*

## 388 Request for visit

I know that you are extremely busy, but as Factory Inspector for our neighbourhood, we would be most grateful if you would call and see us at your early convenience. We are especially concerned because:
1 . . . .
2 . . . .
3 . . . .

## 389 Chaser to inspector

I refer to my letter of the . . . in which I asked you to be kind enough to call at our Works at your earliest convenience, because we have a particular safety problem in connection with . . . . We have neither heard from you nor have you been able to visit us. And while we fully appreciate the calls upon your time, we would be most obliged if you would now treat this as a matter of urgency.

With our thanks in anticipation of speedy action.

## 390 To inspector — notice complied with

I refer to the prohibition/improvement notice which you served upon me/my company on the . . . . I am pleased to inform you that the requirements of that notice have now been complied with. I would be obliged if you would return to our works/site at your earliest convenience, so as to confirm your satisfaction with the alterations/work carried out.

NOTES:

*1 You are not bound to inform the inspector of your compliance with his notice; you are entitled to recommence operations or the use of the machine or system (or as the case may be), as soon as you have made the alterations or otherwise carried out the work specified in the notice.*

*2 However: If the inspector is informed and he is satisfied then you are sure of avoiding unwanted trouble with the law.*

### 391   To inspector — thanks for confirmation

We appreciated the way in which you returned to our works/site at our request to inspect the alterations carried out as a result of the improvement/prohibition notice served upon us; and are glad to confirm that you informed us that you were satisfied that the notice had been fully complied with. We appreciated your courtesy.

NOTE:
*This letter has two objects. It confirms your understanding of the inspector's approval; and it is a pleasant courtesy which should help to maintain future good relations with him.*

### 392   To inspector — specifying further work to be done

We thank you for visiting our works/site yesterday and confirm that you consider that the following changes in our system/work/machine are still required to be made in order that we may comply with the improvement/prohibition notice dated the . . . . We estimate that the job will be completed by the . . . , and we will then immediately contact you in the hope that you will be able to return at the earliest possible moment in order to confirm your satisfaction — and so that full production may be resumed. We know that you do understand the importance of time for us — if we cannot get our assembly line/production/work/machine operating again with full efficiency very shortly, the survival of the company may be in jeopardy.

NOTE:
*The final sentence must be adapted with special care to suit your circumstances. There is no reason why you should not emphasise the importance of prompt action, from your company's viewpoint.*

# Chapter 48

# Protective clothing

The art of inducing employees to use protective clothing provided is the subject of Chapter 38. Its provision is dealt with in Section 9 of the Health and Safety at Work Act: 'No employer shall levy or permit to be levied on any employee . . . any charge in respect of anything done, or provided in pursuance of any specific requirement of the relevant statutory provisions'.

In other words: If there is a specific requirement that you provide the clothing or equipment, then you are not entitled to charge for it. Otherwise, a charge is a matter for you — for negotiation with your employees or their representatives.

The Protection of Eyes Regulations, for instance, require the provision of protective goggles or spectacles for certain processes. Even if you have to provide expensive, prescription lenses . . . or to replace spectacles, lost by the wearer . . . you must bear the full cost.

Similarly, specific regulations may force you to provide protective footwear, on pain of prosecution. You may not charge the wearers any part of the cost, even if you suspect that the boots are being used for gardening — or lost, through gross carelessness.

On the other hand, you may think it wise to provide glasses or boots when there is no 'specific requirement' that you do so. Whether or not you charge is a matter for you and not for the law.

\* \* \*

## 393   Protective boots — employees to pay half

I am pleased to tell you that we have arranged for a large selection of protective footwear to be made available to all employees in the . . . workshop/plant. The Board has also agreed that the company will bear the full cost of one pair of footwear for each employee per year, provided that he undertakes to wear it at all times at work/to subsidise this footwear by paying half of the cost of each pair.

Please do encourage all concerned to acquire, use and take
care of this footwear. There has in the past been too many
accidents to people's feet — which have caused unnecessary
suffering. The wearing of these shoes and boots should make
a big difference and we are sure that you and your men will
be pleased that this footwear is available.

If you have any queries about this letter, please do not
hesitate to contact me.

### 394   Charge for replacements only

As you know, the company now provides free protective
footwear for all who work in your department/works. However, I must remind you that we cannot provide free replacements. While employees may certainly take the footwear
home, if they wish, or use it as they see fit, they must then
accept the responsibility of acquiring and paying for all
replacements.

Happily, even replacement footwear is provided by the
company on a subsidised basis. The company urges you to
use the footwear at all times when at work and to take care
of it.

### 395   Catering department — footwear subsidised

We found from our accident book that a number of the
ladies working in our kitchen and canteen have fallen and
hurt themselves. In the circumstances, as the company places
paramount importance on health and safety at work, I am
pleased to tell you that we have decided to get in a large
stock of non-slip footwear and to make this available to all
those who work in our catering department, at half cost price.

Please do come and inspect this footwear which is both
comfortable and as attractive as possible. We hope that you
will take advantage of this arrangement as soon as possible —
and so reduce the chances of your slipping and hurting yourself.

# Chapter 49

# Medical examinations

The Act does not require employers to submit employees to medical examinations. Regulations may in due course be made, requiring medical examinations — but sufficient unto the day are the examinations thereof. Note: this is an 'enabling statute', giving vast powers to make regulations — 'delegated legislation'.)

Meanwhile, though, how can you say that you are taking such steps as are 'reasonably practicable' to care for the health of your employees, if you do not even enquire as to their state of health?

So here is another area in which it is wise to be a step or two ahead of the oncoming law.

How can you achieve medical examinations when you have no doctor in the Works? Some companies have taken on full-time doctors and reckon that they make a profit — employees who previously took days off to visit their own GPs now come to work. Other employers take on part-time GP help in the area.

However: It is essential in any event to set up the arrangements with your employees, by letter.

## 396   Medical examinations now available

As you know, your company has always prided itself on its health and safety practices. But as a result of the Health and Safety at Work Act, it has now taken still additional measures for the welfare of all employees. In particular, it has made arrangements for medical examinations for employees (*or:* for the following categories of employees, in which you are included: . . .).

Please would you ensure that you take advantage of this new facility.

With best wishes.

## 397   Medical examinations — required

Now that medical examinations are available for all employees/for employees in your department/doing your job, we feel it right that full advantage should be taken of these facilities and we ask that you arrange for your examination at an early date. Please contact the nurse so as to fix a mutually convenient appointment.

NOTE:

*You cannot force existing employees to submit to medical examinations – although it may possibly be 'fair' to dismiss an employee, in certain circumstances, if he refuses to be examined when he is at particular risk. New employees, though, may be required to submit to medical examination as a term of service – an example follows. But some trade unions retain archaic rules which forbid the inclusion of such terms in their members' contracts.*

## 398   Term in contract – employee to be medically examined

I confirm that your terms of contract will contain our standard agreement that you will submit to medical examination, as and when required by the company.

# Chapter 50

# Suspension from work on medical grounds

An employee suspended from work by his employer on medical grounds as the result of:

'(a) Any requirement imposed by or under any provision of any enactment or of any instrument made under any enactment, or

(b) Any recommendation in any provision of a Code of Practice issued or approved under Section 16 of *The Health and Safety at Work etc. Act, 1974.*'

will be entitled to be paid for up to 26 weeks, while he is suspended on such medical grounds. The object, of course, is to ensure that where an employer does not follow the Health and Safety Act rules and as a result his employee is left without work, he (the employee) will not suffer financially as a result.

It is not yet clear how wide an area will be covered by this new rule.

To qualify for this right, the employee must have been continuously employed for up to 4 weeks ending with the last complete week before the day on which the suspension begins. He must not be 'incapable of work by reason of disease or bodily or mental disablement'. Like the case of guarantee payments, he must be available for work and must 'comply with reasonable requirements imposed by his employer with a view to ensuring that his services are available'. As usual, complaints of non-compliance go to Industrial Tribunals.

\* \* \*

## 399 Remuneration enclosed — medical suspension agreed

As a result of the prohibition notice served upon the company under the Health and Safety at Work Act, we were forced to close your department for the whole of last week, which resulted in no work being available for you. However, you are entitled to your pay in accordance with the Employment Protection Act, and I enclose your remuneration herewith/ and instructed the accounts department to forward this to

you/to include this money with your next pay cheque.
With best wishes.

## 400    Denial that suspension due to breach of health and safety rules

You have been suspended in accordance with our union agreement, because of your conduct — and not as a result of the alleged or any breach by the company of any Health and Safety rules, as alleged by you or at all.

The circumstances are well known to your union and I propose discussing this matter with the convener. If you wish to discuss the matter further, by all means contact the convener or myself.

## 401    Employee's health caused suspension

You have been suspended as a result of your health and not through any breach by the company of any duties placed upon it by the Health and Safety at Work Act or by any Code of Practice.

In the circumstances, your claim cannot be accepted.

# Chapter 51

# Passing the buck

The Health and Safety at Work Act (like the Trade Descriptions Act before it) seeks to lay the blame on the guilty head — and on none other. Thus:

1   If the company is to blame, it may be fined (up to £400 by the Magistrates, or an unlimited sum by a Crown Court).

2   If the individual manager is guilty, then he may be fined (as above) and/or, in some cases, sent to prison for up to two years by a Crown Court.

3   If either the company or an individual is charged and alleges that the fault lay with some other person, that other person may be charged with the offence, whether or not the charge is dropped against the original defendant.

4   If the buck is passed to the true culprit and the company or the individual is free of guilt, then (unlike the civil law) the criminal law will free the employing company or the managerial superior from blame. Under this Act, you are only held responsible if you were guilty of a crime. The civil rule on 'vicarious liability' of an employer for the misdeeds of his employee does not apply.

It follows that:

1   As an individual, you may need to pass the blame to others. The fearsome penalties under the Act do not encourage a brave acceptance of fault.

2   Conversely, each must watch out for possible attempts to shift the blame for dangers onto him.

Documentation is essential.

\*   \*   \*

## 402   Manager complains to superior*

I am deeply concerned about the following unsafe practices in my department:

    1 . . . .
    2 . . . .
    3 . . . .

I have spoken to you about each of these matters on a

number of occasions and you have assured me that you would
do everything possible to have the complaints rectified – and
I am sure that you will have done so. But nothing has happened and I fear that any or all of these unsafe practices may lead
to accidents and/or prosecutions.

I will be very grateful if you would take urgent steps to put
matters right.

*Compare letters for executives in Chapter 16.

## 403   Manager – to subordinate

I am confirming in writing our numerous conversations
regarding the failure of operatives/men in your section/
workshop/gang to wear their protective spectacles/footwear
(*or as the case may be*).

As I explained to you, apart from the company's urgent
wish to ensure the safety of its employees, there is now a real
risk of a prosecution under the Health and Safety at Work
Act.

In the circumstances, please use your best endeavours to
ensure that the safety rules are complied with, and note that
all infringements of the rules must now be reported to me.

## 404   Note of default – for file

Date: . . . .
Name: . . . .
*Nature of Breach of Health and Safety Rules:* . . . .
I said: . . . .
He/she replied: . . . .
Witness: . . . .

NOTE:
*The above information can be put straight onto an employee's file
without formality in any appropriate case. But the formalising of the
system may make it easier to follow, particularly by line managers. Explain to them that this system is neither bureaucracy nor red tape but:*
(a)   *The knowledge that you are making a note should encourage the
employee concerned to take the complaint seriously.*
(b)   *The existence of the note will enable further disciplinary pro-*

*cedures to be taken, if necessary. And*

(c) *Production of the note will almost certainly free the manager concerned from criminal liability because it will help him show that he 'exercised all reasonable persuasion and propaganda' to avoid committing the offence.*

## 405  Request to Board for action

Please would you put the following matter onto the agenda of the next Board meeting:-

The need for additional guarding of . . . machines (*or as the case may be*).

In my view, it is vital that the above steps be taken, despite the expense. I am sure that if the fierceness of the Health and Safety at Work Act is explained to the Board — along with the personal liability placed on those who do not take such steps as are reasonably practicable to protect employees — they will approve my request for action.

NOTE:
*If you have sought to induce the Board to take action and they (provably) refuse, you should be (criminally, if not morally) in the clear.*

## 406  Instruction to managers

I write to you, along with all other top managers/plant managers (*or as the case may be*), to urge you to ensure that the company's (very carefully worked out and documented) safety measures are fully complied with. As a reminder, I enclose copies of some of those most relevant to you.

I must emphasise the heavy responsibility placed by the Health and Safety at Work Act on all managers at every level to ensure that all employees at every level fully comply with the company's rules. The company itself is taking all reasonably practicable steps to ensure the health and safety at work of its employees; but it must rely on every level of management to ensure enforcement of those rules.

NOTE·
*Since the famous House of Lords' ruling in the Trade Descriptions Act*

*case of* Tesco *v.* Nattrass, *it has been clear that if the company does take proper steps to set up and to implement an adequate system to avoid breach of the law and if that system is ignored or flouted by a manager, it is the manager personally and not the company who will have to bear the criminal blame. The employer, of course, remains vicariously liable to compensate the party who suffers due to the employee's negligence in the course of his employment.*

# Chapter 52

# Consultation and committees

The Health and Safety at Work Act empowers the Secretary for Employment to make regulations requiring employers to consult with appointed representatives of recognised trade unions. The equivalent Section empowering him to make regulations requiring consultation with elected representatives of the workforce was replaced by the Employment Protection Act. The current position is as follows:

1    You must consult with representatives appointed by those independent trade unions which you recognise for bargaining purposes.

2    You may, if you wish (and you probably should, if possible) consult with non union employees or their representatives, on health and safety matters — although you will not be forced by law to do so.

3    The trade unions concerned will select their own representatives, as and when and how they see fit. There is much dispute among trade unions as to whether such representatives should be shop stewards (they usually are) or employees who are particularly interested in health and safety but who have not been elected to office by their fellows. You may be able to exercise behind-the-scenes influence — particularly if you (or your safety officer) are on particularly good terms with the union representatives.

4    As we go to press, the regulations — together with a code and guidance — are still in draft form — but any changes are likely to affect the following precedents marginally, if at all.

The law does not lay down the nature, composition, powers, procedures or number or regularity of the meetings of a safety committee. These should be evolved so as to achieve the best possible results — which means: if possible, the elimination of accidents and otherwise their reduction to the irreducible minimum. It also means: that you will be able to show that safety matters have been properly thrashed out and considered at every level.

However, even the safety committees have their dangers. If your committee recommends a change or an improvement and you turn it down, then you accept a heavy responsibility.

### 407   To convenor — please appoint

In accordance with the Health and Safety at Work Act regulations — and in any event in line with the company's policy — we shall be most pleased to consult with the appointed representative of your union/together with representatives of other recognised unions in our plant/company, on health and safety at work matters. I would be glad if you would appoint your representatives as soon as possible, so that we may establish the best possible arrangement, at the earliest possible date.

### 408   Confirmation — no personal liability on 'watchdogs'

I have consulted the company's lawyers and am pleased to confirm that the law is clear — neither the Health and Safety at Work Act nor the regulations made under it impose any civil or criminal liability whatsoever on your union representative, in connection with their activities in acting as health and safety 'watchdogs', nor in connection with their work on our safety committee. Having made that clear, I trust that you will now find it possible to appoint your representatives without further delay — and that you will have enough people who are not only prepared to do the job but who are genuinely interested in industrial safety matters.

### 409   Request for more frequent meetings

Both due to the absence of the works manager and to difficulties in fixing dates for other reasons, I am told by our safety officer that meetings of the safety committee have not been held on a regular or indeed on a frequent basis. We are sure that you will agree that this is regrettable, and I would appreciate your help in ensuring that a further meeting is held without delay — and that future meetings are held on a far more regular basis.

## 410 Agreement to safety committee recommendation

I am pleased to confirm that the Board has agreed to carry out the changes recommended by the Safety Committee at its meeting on . . . . In particular:

1 . . . .
2 . . . .
3 . . . .

It will take a little while to put these changes into operation, but we expect the work to be carried out by . . . .

With my best wishes and thanks for your co-operation.

## 411 Turning down committee's recommendation

The Board gave very careful consideration to the suggestion made by the safety committee, namely that: . . . .

We have regretfully come to the conclusion that it would not be possible for us at the present time to comply with the suggestion, for the following reasons:

1 . . . .
2 . . . .
3 . . . .

I would emphasise that even though the cost of implementing the suggestion is very high, the Board would nevertheless have carried it into effect if we were satisfied that there would be a substantial improvement in the safety situation were we to do so, or that there was any substantial risk of injury or accident under the present arrangements [by continuing to use the machine as at present (*or as the case may be*)]. But we do not consider this to be the case and we cannot therefore justify the expenditure. Balancing the cost against the risk, we do not feel that — especially in the present economic circumstances — the expenditure would be justified.

I would add that we have also sought the best advice obtainable (give details, if desired), and our view has been confirmed.

We will, however, of course keep the matter strictly under review and please assure your committee that its concern is appreciated.

NOTES:

*1 Cost is a consideration — but not the only one. It is important to get on record the fact that you give primary and paramount importance to life and limb.*

*2   The taking of expert advice is wise – and may enable blame to be passed on or avoided altogether. Do be sure, though, that the advice itself is, if necessary, provable.*

## 412   Partial compliance with recommendation – safety shoes/boots

I am pleased to tell you that the Board has agreed to go a long way towards meeting the wishes of the safety committee/ trade union safety representatives, concerning the provision of safety shoes/boots in the . . . plant/stores/workshop/to engineers (*or as the case may be*). We would not feel justified, having regard to the enormous cost involved (probably exceeding £ . . .), in providing shoes or boots for everyone free of charge. But we are prepared to make a very heavy subsidy, to encourage people to buy their own shoes at a rate which will make them less expensive than the ordinary footwear which so many are wearing at the moment. This will also, of course, avoid the present situation where people who do spend their own money on safety footwear are, in effect, being financially penalised.

We hope that this decision will please you; that the facilities which we will now make available will be fully used; and that we will have your full support in inducing all employees concerned to wear the footwear made available.

I am arranging for the personnel manager/safety officer to obtain samples/catalogues of a wide range of footwear, so that each individual will have the opportunity to choose shoes/boots which are comfortable and which he will be pleased to wear.

With my renewed thanks for your co-operation.

NOTES:
*1   It is wise to emphasise the positive – that you are going some distance towards meeting the recommendation – rather than the negative – namely that you have turned down the suggestion that boots be provided free of charge.*

*2   You should indeed give very careful thought before you turn down the request for safety footwear, fully paid by you. You recognise the danger of crushed or injured feet? Of course – that is why you are spending money on subsidising footwear. You realise that while some employees will take advantage of your offer, some will not because they will not be prepared to meet their share of the cost? Then are you really doing everything that is 'reasonably practicable' to meet the situation? The answer will be a question of degree, as always.*

"WE HAVE A WELL DEVELOPED WRITTEN COMPLAINT PROCEDURE!"

*Part Six*

# CRIME AND SECURITY

*Chapter 53*

# Introduction

## SEARCH

You are entitled to search the person or property of a suspect —
employee, customer or anyone else — with (but only with) his consent.
This may be obtained in two ways:

1    In the case of an employee, by including a term in his contract of
service that he will agree to be searched at the request of the
management.

2    Ask, at the time: 'Will you please empty your handbag/briefcase/
pockets. . .', 'Open the boot of your car . . .', 'Let me see what you
have in that box. . .'.

Even if you get permission from an employee in his contract, you
should still seek consent at the time of the proposed search. To search
without consent is an assault (a 'trespass to the person') or a 'trespass
to goods'.

If the suspect refuses to be searched, then call in the police. If the
suspect refuses to await the police, then arrest him.

## ARREST

The private citizen is entitled to arrest if an arrestable offence, e.g. theft
or other serious crime, has been committed and he reasonably suspects
the person arrested of having committed that offence. If you put a
constraint on a person's freedom to move, that is an arrest. But if a
suspect refuses to submit to search, then you will almost certainly
'reasonably suspect' him of villainy.

## TIME FOR ARREST

Theft is committed where a person dishonestly 'appropriates' someone
else's property with the intention 'permanently to deprive him thereof',
*Note:* borrowing is not criminal — except in the case of motor vehicles
and other conveyances.

A person 'appropriates' property as soon as he takes it into his possession. You do not have to wait until a suspected pilferer leaves your premises before you arrest him. In a recent case, a woman who had taken a bottle of whisky and put it inside her knickers was held to have been correctly convicted of theft even though she had not reached the pay-out counter.

Still: It is wise to wait as long as you reasonably can because the prosecution must prove guilt beyond all reasonable doubt. And where the suspect has left the premises he can hardly say that he was 'Looking for someone to pay'; 'Trying to find the supervisor, to get permission to take it away'; 'Only looking at the items in the light' — or any other spurious excuse.

## DEALING WITH THIEVES

Once you have caught an offender, you may hand him over to the police — or you may exercise mercy, if you see fit. You may also do a deal and say: 'Give back everything that you have stolen and we will not report you'. Provided that you do not blackmail the offender, e.g. by demanding with menaces more than you are lawfully entitled to claim, deals of this sort with criminals are now legal.

## PROSECUTION

If you hand the offender over to the police, they prosecute if — but only if — they wish to do so. They may decline, for one or more reasons:
1    Some police forces as a matter of policy leave prosecution of shoplifting or what they choose to call petty theft to the victims. And in any event
2    The prosecution must prove guilt — and the police will not sign the charge sheet unless they are satisfied that they have a good enough case.

If a citizen is *(a)* acquitted of the charge and *(b)* can show that it was brought out of 'malice', i.e. a desire to harm him rather than a wish to see justice done — then he can claim damages in a civil action for 'malicious prosecution'.

## PRIVATE PROSECUTIONS

If the police invite you to sign the charge sheet, then take care before you agree. You, like the police, may face a malicious prosecution charge if you prosecute both maliciously and unsuccessfully.

You are entitled to hold the offender for a reasonable time while you seek advice on whether or not to hand him over to the police. And if you are in doubt as to whether or not to prosecute, consult your lawyer. Note:

1    While you can withdraw a civil action at any time on payment of the costs of both sides, a prosecution may only be withdrawn with the consent of the court — which will only be given for good reason.

2    Just as you cannot force the police to prosecute, they cannot require you to do so.

If you are to prosecute, make sure that you have sufficient evidence. And if you do suffer from theft, establish a system under which your staff know what steps to take if they spot a crook at work.


## COSTS AND PROCEDURES

How, then, can you prepare for possible legal battle against the crooks? Here are some suggestions:

1    Remember that you will have to prove your case — so try to ensure that any observation is carried out by more than one employee — and that any accusation is made in the presence of a witness. Even if observation and accusation are initially effected by one person, a witness should always be present during any questioning — if only to ensure that the questioner is not accused of either blackmail or twisting the words of the suspect.

2    If you decide to sign the charge sheet — a very simple procedure — you should first call in the police and obtain their guidance. They will help you with your prosecution, even if they decide to leave the charging up to you.

3    An accused person may be convicted on the evidence of one witness and even without corroboration. If, for instance, you testify that you saw the culprit taking the goods from their proper place in a furtive manner and hiding them in his brief case and you are given an unsatisfactory explanation and if the court believes you — then you will win your case. But (as an example) over 60 per cent of women who plead not guilty to shop lifting charges and are tried by jury are acquitted. Corroboration is sensible if not essential.

4    The better prepared your evidence, the swifter and more satisfactory the procedure is likely to be. If you have prepared a case which a court is almost certain to accept, then the accused will probably plead guilty before the Magistrates' Court and not trouble to elect for trial by jury – in which case the entire business may be over very swiftly. If the accused elects for trial by jury, though, it may be many months before the case is heard. If the accused is an employee, then you must also consider whether or not you have enough evidence of misconduct to warrant dismissing the person 'fairly'. If in doubt, discuss proposals with your solicitor.

5    If you do the prosecuting, you may not have to pay the costs. If the prosecution was properly brought, in many cases the costs should be paid out of public funds. Once again: talk to your solicitor.

\*    \*    \*

Security companies and the police often warn that it is cheaper and quicker to prevent theft than to go to law. Unfortunately, though, thieves cannot be banned and the law must frequently be mobilised – if only to discourage other crooks from following the same expensive path. Follow the above rules, though, and you should avoid producing more trouble for yourself than you do for the villain. No one can guarantee that the accused will be convicted – in a recent case, the Court of Appeal emphasised that however common the defence raised, e.g.: 'I wasn't thinking . . . I did not realise what I was doing . . .'), a court must avoid the temptation to treat it with cynicism – the defence must be considered on its merits.

However: A properly prepared case should not produce a civil action for malicious prosecution. Consider the facts, the evidence and the tactics before you launch into any prosecution. You are entitled to make your decision. Do so with your eyes well open.

Chapter 54

# Search and prosecution

### 413 Confirming agreement to search*

I confirm that you — like all other members of our staff — have agreed that the management may search your person or property at any time when you are on the company's premises. Having regard to the recent rash of stealing — and especially to the unfortunate suspicion which this has tended to cast on the innocent, along with the guilty — we are convinced that the spot checks which will be arranged from now on will be of benefit not only to the company but to all concerned — and we are grateful to you for your co-operation.

### 414 To trade union — re search

I must ask you to reconsider your union's decision to refuse to agree to the inclusion of a search clause in the contracts of employment of your members. I would emphasise that there is no intention whatsoever on the part of the management to victimise any individual or group — but only to take such steps as are reasonable to avoid the heavy losses which are at present caused through pilferage. This stealing not only causes vast problems for the company but also suspicion and unnecessary ill-will as between employees.

I shall be pleased to discuss this matter again with you at any mutually convenient time, and look forward to hearing from you.

### 415 Allegation of wrongful search

I protest at the series of searches of my person and property during the past three weeks. I am being victimised in a most unpleasant and improper fashion and hereby give you notice that I shall not in future agree to be searched other than at your personal request.

*More 'search' precedents are in Part 1.

NOTE:

*The employee who refuses to be searched, in breach of a term in his contract of service, may or may not have 'repudiated' the contract. If an employee is being victimised through the use of the search procedures, then it would certainly be 'unfair' to dismiss him as a result.*

## 416   Confirming why police were called

I greatly regret yesterday's incident in which you refused to be searched and we called in the police. Because the company is suffering so greatly from pilferage/theft, these spot checks are vital. You were in breach of your contract of service in refusing to agree to search; and in the circumstances, the security officer followed out normal procedures in calling in the police.

While regretting the unpleasantness caused as a result, this was entirely due to your own breach of contract/refusal to comply with the reasonable request of our security officer, in the exercise of his duty. I trust that in future you will remove the need for such procedures by co-operating with our security measures. And because of their importance, I must warn you that any future refusal may be grounds for dismissal.

## 417   Arrest — unreasonable refusal to be searched

Your refusal to agree to empty your pockets/open the boot of your car was wholly unreasonable. In view of the major losses through theft from which the company is suffering, our security officers had instructions to restrain any employees — from shop floor to board level — who refused to comply with requests to undergo a search of person or property. The resultant unpleasantness in your case was entirely the result of your own behaviour and I must warn you that this procedure will remain unchanged in future and that a most serious view will be taken of any cases in which an employee causes unnecessary difficulty to our security men in their already difficult job.

## 418   Instructions to security officers

Please convey the following instructions to your men, regarding future search and arrest arrangements:-

1   Neither the persons nor the property of employees are to be searched without their permission.

2   Most employees have by now accepted terms of service which include agreement to be searched at the request of the management. However, such request must always be renewed, prior to the carrying out of any search of person or property.

3   If it is not possible to obtain consent — either because the individual has refused or because he is not available or for any other reason, the co-operation of the police must be sought and obtained.

Any employee who refuses to agree to search of his person or property is to be asked to remain in the gatehouse/security room/office while the police are called. If he refuses to remain voluntarily, then the minimum force reasonably necessary to restrain him shall be used. He must not be permitted to leave until the search has been carried out. As all searches will be required because of the commission of theft (which is, of course, an 'arrestable offence') and as any individual who refuses to agree to the search of his person or property would inevitably reasonably be suspected of having committed that offence, the arrest of such person would be lawful.

5   However: I repeat that as any forcible search of person is an assault (a 'trespass to the person') and any laying hold of the property of another without his consent would be a 'trespass' to that property, the police should be called upon to co-operate where consent is unobtainable or unavailable.

6   All steps must be taken promptly. In particular, there should be no delay in contacting the police after an arrest.

7   If a suspected thief (whether or not an employee of the company) is arrested, then the company's procedures on enquiries and prosecution must be carefully followed. I must

emphasise that the law permits a suspect to be held for a reasonable time while instructions are sought or a decision taken as to future action. But this delay should be kept to the unavoidable minimum.

If you have any queries in this regard, please contact me at once.

## 419   Procedures for enquiries and prosecutions

The following are the company's procedures which will in future be followed by all security officers, where a suspect is arrested and a prosecution is contemplated:

1   Wherever possible, the suspect's behaviour should be observed by more than one person — and in the event of the observation producing results, these should be recorded by each such person in his notebook at the earliest opportunity. 'Contemporaneous records' may be referred to by witnesses in court — those that are not 'contemporaneous' will be excluded from the witness box.

2   Wherever possible, all enquiries should be carried out by more than one person. Where an employee is to be questioned as to his behaviour, then such questioning should be carried out, wherever possible, in the presence of a staff/trade union representative. Once again, details of questions and answers should be recorded.

3   Where it is decided that the person concerned may be prosecuted, he should be informed that he is not bound to answer questions and that any answer given will be taken down and may be used in evidence. Note: It should not be stated that such statements 'will' be used in evidence nor that they will be used in evidence 'against' the person concerned.

4   If it is felt that there is enough evidence for a prosecution, in normal circumstances the police should be informed and invited to prosecute. If they refuse so to do, then (and only then) should the question arise of a prosecution by the company.

5   A charge sheet should be only signed on behalf of the company by . . ./with the authority of . . . . Before such signature or authority is given, the company officer must be satisfied as to the following:

*(a)*   That there is sufficient evidence against the accused to warrant a prosecution.

*(b)*   That the prosecution is in the interests both of justice and of the company. And

*(c)*   That a fair and reasonable opportunity has been given to the proposed accused to explain his behaviour — and that the explanation is unacceptable.

Please note the following:-

1   The company is not bound either to hand the suspect over to the police nor (still less) to initiate a prosecution.

2   The prosecution may only be withdrawn with the consent of the court.

3   If a prosecution is both unsuccessful and proved to have been brought out of 'malice' — that is, a desire to harm the person prosecuted, rather than to see justice done — both the company and the individual prosecutor may be faced with a civil claim for damages for 'malicious prosecution'.

4   No criminal prosecution may be dropped without the consent of the court — which will only be given for some very good reason.

If you have any queries regarding the above, please contact me without delay. And please ensure that these instructions are both received and understood by all security men under your control and/or supervision.


## 420   Company policy — prosecute

Having regard to the intolerable level of 'shrinkage' suffered by the company during the past year as a result of thefts by both employees and customers, the Board has decided that all offenders who are apprehended will be prosecuted. Naturally, if there is any reasonable doubt as to the guilt of the person concerned, the company's usual procedures will be followed — including, where necessary, consultation with the company's solicitor. But both employees and customers should be informed that in future security officers have no discretion in matters of prosecution, where a culprit is caught red-handed.

### 421    Without prejudice apology to innocent suspect

I have carefully considered your letter concerning your
recent arrest by the company's security officer. Without
prejudice to my view that this arrest was entirely brought
about by your own behaviour, the incident is of course
greatly regretted. I hope that in future you will agree to be
searched/not take home the company's tools without written
permission from your foreman/supervisor/that you will comply with the company's security procedures, so that no such
action by our security men will be necessary.

### 422    Referral of complaint to solicitors

I am in receipt of your letter complaining about your
detention by the company's security officers/prosecution
for theft. It is denied that the arrest was unlawful, unjustified
or caused otherwise than as a reasonable response to your
own conduct; it is further denied that the prosecution was
malicious or improper in any way; and I am passing your
letter to the company's solicitors, Messrs . . . , to whom all
future correspondence on this matter should be addressed.

### 423    Denial of defamation

Thank you for your letter.
I have consulted the company's solicitors concerning your
allegation that you were defamed through being asked to
empty your pockets/questioned regarding the theft of . . ./
challenged by the company's security officers regarding the
presence of . . . in your car/bag. I am told that the occasion
was privileged — the company's officers were taking proper
steps/making appropriate enquiries/. . . for the protection of
the company. Further and in any event, if (which is denied)
you were defamed, there was no 'publication' of such defamation.
Without prejudice to the foregoing and in any event, the
security officers were carrying out their job in a proper
manner — and their job was not made any easier by your
unreasonable and unwarranted refusal to co-operate with
them.

## 424 Confirming deal with culprit

I confirm our conversation in which you admitted that you had wrongfully appropriated the following items of the company's property, to a total value of £ . . .:
(a) . . . .
(b) . . . .
(c) . . . .

I further confirm that provided you repay to the company by . . . the above full amount [*Note:* do not demand more than was wrongfully appropriated], I shall not inform the police or take any other steps against you. However, as I further informed you, it is not possible for the company to retain you in its service and you will be paid your full remuneration up to the . . . and your cards will be sent to you as soon as possible and in any event not later than . . . .

I greatly regret that our association has to come to an end in such an unhappy manner. I trust, however, that you will repay the company as agreed and so avoid our having to take other steps against you.

## 425 Warning – but no prosecution

I am sure that you will be pleased to learn that the Board has instructed me to inform you that they do not intend to take any further steps regarding your admitted misconduct in connection with . . . . This means that the company will not prosecute; that the police will not be informed; and that the matter is now regarded as closed.

I trust that you will not regard this exceptional clemency as a sign of weakness. If there should be any recurrence, however minor, not only will you be dismissed forthwith from the company's service but a prosecution will almost inevitably result.

The reasons why the Board have decided to take no such steps on the present occasion are the following:
1    Your lengthy and loyal service to the company.
2    The excellence of your work.
3    The exceptional strains which were placed upon you at the time in question by your/your wife's/your child's illness/by the death of . . . (*or as the case may be*).

NOTE:

*The above letter should be marked 'Personal — Private and Confidential' — and should preferably be handed personally to the individual concerned and a receipt or acknowledgement obtained from him. If this is done at the time when the culprit is informed of the company's kindness, there should be no difficulty in obtaining such a signature. This letter, of course, will also serve as a written warning of possible dismissal, in accordance with the Code of Industrial Relations practice.*

# Chapter 55

# Theft

It is a crime wrongfully to appropriate property belonging to another person, with the intent at the time of the taking 'permanently to deprive him thereof'. It is not normally a crime to borrow — anything other than a motor vehicle or other conveyance which must not be taken away without the owner's consent or other lawful excuse. *Exception:* it may be a crime *dishonestly* to borrow your employee's money from the till.

In practice, most large scale employers are plagued by theft, by employees and others. Security arrangements are, of course, essential — but so are letters making the situation and the rules abundantly clear to all. The following letters explain those rules, as well as the law which lies behind them.

## 426   Warning — no 'perks'

I am writing to you and to all other supervisors to ask you to make plain to everyone under your supervision or control that the following conduct is absolutely forbidden:

1   The taking home of tools or equipment, for whatever purposes.
2   The removal from the premises of off-cuts/leftovers/ stationery/office supplies/. . . or any other property belonging to the company, without the prior, express, written consent of . . . or . . . .
3   The borrowing of money from petty cash or till, whether or not an IOU is left.
4   The use of company telephones for private calls.

I understand that some employees have removed company property and when challenged said that they understood that they were entitled to do so as a 'perk'. There are no such 'perks'; breach of these rules will be treated extremely seriously and may lead to dismissal; and employees found with company property in their cars or homes may be prosecuted.

I ask for your co-operation both for the protection of the

company — which has been suffering from theft on an un-
precedented scale — and from that of the employees concerned, who must know the position so as to avoid risk to
their jobs and, potentially, to their freedom.

## 427   When to challenge and arrest

I have been asked to explain when suspected thieves/shop-
lifters should be challenged and/or arrested. The law is that a
person is guilty of theft as soon as he removes an article from
its proper place, with the necessary dishonest intent. So there
is dishonest 'appropriation' the moment that goods are taken
from a shelf/store/counter/display by a person who intends
to steal them.

On the other hand, it is often difficult to prove intent. The
employee may maintain that he was looking for someone from
whom to ask for permission to remove the item/the customer
may allege that he was merely seeking somewhere to look at
the article in the light. It follows that the further away the
article is from its proper place, the less likely these excuses
are to be effective. You are therefore asked to allow the suspect to take the article as far as possible away from its proper
place before you challenge. Naturally, you must not wait so
long that the suspect may escape — but patience is important.

With many thanks for your co-operation.

## 428   Instructions on 'finding'

To avoid misunderstandings about goods found on the company's premises, the position is as follows:

1   All goods found belong to their owners, i.e. to the losers.
Failure to take reasonable steps to trace the owner may lead
to a prosecution for theft.

2   Steps must therefore be taken in all cases to trace the
owner — unless the goods have been obviously abandoned.
All employees who find goods should hand them in to . . . .
A careful note will be taken of the date, time and place of
such finding and of the finder. Equally, any person other

than an employee who finds goods should be asked to hand them in.

3   Where goods are of little value, they will be kept for six months when they will be handed over to the finder. In law, where an employee finds property in the course of his employment, that property belongs — if the true owner does not turn up — to the company. However, as a matter of policy, the company wishes to encourage the handing over of lost property and will not assert its claim as against employees who find and hand in.

4   In the case of valuable property, e.g. rings or other jewellery left in the wash room, such steps will be taken as the personnel manager/ . . . considers reasonable in the circumstances in an attempt to trace the owner.

## 429   Borrowing — and theft

I note your complaint that your . . . was borrowed by a colleague. Borrowing anything other than a motor vehicle or other conveyance is not normally illegal, even if the consent of the owner is not obtained. Nor is it a breach of the employee's contract of service. In the circumstances, I have asked the personnel manager to have a word with Mr . . . , to avoid any recurrence — for the sake of good relations among employees. But it is not proposed to take legal action in this sort of case.

## 430   Warning — motor vehicles

There seems to be a peculiar and incorrect idea in our transport department that the borrowing of the company's motor vehicles without consent is permitted.

1   The borrowing of a motor vehicle without the owner's consent or other lawful excuse is a criminal offence. Please warn employees that no vehicle may be used without the company's consent — so that there can be no question of any employee who is caught borrowing successfully alleging that he thought that the company's permission would have been

available, if sought. The use of company vehicles without prior consent is expressly forbidden.

2   Further, the taking of company vehicles without consent will be regarded in future as a most serious breach of an employee's contract of service, rendering him liable to be dismissed. Please warn all drivers and others employed in your section that the current practice or borrowing company vehicles for private purposes without prior consent must cease forthwith.

### 431   Suspension — suspected of stealing

I confirm that you are suspended (on full pay/without pay) as from today's date, because you have been found with property belonging to the company/another employee in your possession. You told me that you had no intention permanently to deprive the company/your colleague of this property, but whether or not it is decided to report this matter to the police and whether or not they prosecute, you have absolutely no right to behave as you did.

I expect to be in touch with you again within the course of the next few days, after a full inquiry has been made, during which time I suggest that you remain available.

# Chapter 56

# Bribery and corruption

It is a crime to give or to receive, to attempt to give or to seek to obtain any consideration for the giving of a favour. Whether in cash or in kind . . . however small or large the gift . . . if the intent is 'corrupt', the gift is illegal – and could lead to prosecution, conviction and heavy penalties.

Note: The prosecution must normally prove intent. But where the bribe concerns an official of a local or public authority, there is a presumption of guilt which the accused (giver or receiver, as the case may be – or both) must attempt to shift.

The test of 'corruption'? Usually: secrecy. That which is done or given openly and above board is seldom 'corrupt'. That which is given or received under the counter . . . furtively . . . is usually bribery, 'the drop', 'dropsy', 'greasing the palm', 'payola' – in a word: Bribery.

Here are some letters designed to show that honest, business gifts must not and cannot be interpreted as criminal bribes.

\* \* \*

## 432 Christmas gift – to customer

I have today arranged for the despatch to you of a crate of whisky/a crate of wine/a box of cigars – which I hope that you will accept as a small token of our great appreciation for your many kindnesses. It has been a pleasure working with you and we all appreciate that you have gone out of your way on many occasions to be kind and accommodating.

We wish you a most happy Christmas – and health and prosperity in the coming year.

## 433 Commission – consult the boss

I write to confirm that my company will be pleased to pay you commission on any orders placed by your company with mine on the following basis:

    *(a)* . . . .
    *(b)* . . . .
    *(c)* . . . .

I understand that no objection will be taken to this arrangement by your company — and I would be grateful if you would let me have your written confirmation, or that of your managing director, at an early date.

NOTE:
*There is nothing improper in the giving or acceptance of commission — and many people rely upon it for at least a substantial part of their livelihood. It is the dishonest, corrupt, hidden giving or receipt of a pay-off, rake-off or other hand-out which is a criminal offence.*

## 434 Requirement to staff — gifts to be returned

Kindly inform all employees — and in particular, all buyers/ catering managers — that under no circumstances are any gifts to be accepted from suppliers, at any time. Reasonable hospitality may be accepted — but only if the company has full knowledge of that hospitality, so that the person able to place orders on behalf of the company will be under no personal obligation to the giver of the largess.

Kindly confirm that you have received and understood this letter and that all concerned personnel will be duly informed. Any breach of this rule must lead to immediate disciplinary action, its nature and extent depending upon the circumstances.

## 435 Gifts to be reported

The Board has carefully considered the question of gifts to buyers. It has agreed that these need not be returned, provided that full details of each gift are provided to the appropriate manager, without delay. Any failure to report gifts will lead to the immediate dismissal of the buyer concerned.

## 436 Food and drink — for canteen or party

The Board has decided that gifts of drink received at

Christmastime need not be returned, but should be reported. In normal circumstances, these will be put into the pool for the staff party/canteen Christmas celebrations.

Other gifts — whether in cash or in kind — must be returned to the senders, in future as in the past.

## 437 Covering letter with returned gift

It was extremely kind of you to think of me and to send such a generous gift. However, we have an absolute and unshakeable company policy that no gifts must be accepted by staff, however senior, on pain of the most severe penalties! In the circumstances, I hope that you will not be offended that I have arranged for your gift to be returned to you.

Nonetheless, I heartily reciprocate your Christmas greetings.

## 438 To supplier — protest at gifts to buyers

I understand that you have persisted in sending Christmas gifts to buyers, in spite of protests from my company. I hereby warn you that any future gift will lead to the placing of no further orders by my company with yours — a result which both I and my Board would regret but which we would regard as inevitable. It is firm and absolute company policy that no gifts must be accepted by any employee at any level — and I would ask for your co-operation in this regard.

## 439 Dismissal — for gifts

You have been warned — both orally and in my letter to you of . . . — that you are not permitted to accept any gift of any sort, in cash or in kind, from any supplier or his representative. It has now come to my attention that you have once again flouted this rule. In the circumstances, your further presence at the company's premises will not be required; kindly return all samples forthwith — and deliver up the company car to our garage at . . . , without delay. Upon receipt of the samples and of the car, you will be paid all outstanding money due to you.

# Chapter 57

# The rehabilitation of offenders

The purpose of *The Rehabilitation of Offenders Act, 1974,* was to remove some of the disadvantages previously suffered by people convicted of criminal offences — whether in civilian life or in the services — but who have subsequently gone straight. The Act gives no help to persistent offenders or to people sentenced to more than 2½ years imprisonment. For the rest, it offers the prospects of a clean sheet — in a way that every employer ought to understand.

\* \* \*

Anyone who has been convicted of a criminal offence and not sentenced to more than 2½ years in prison, will become a 'rehabilitated person' at the end of a 'rehabilitation period', if he has not been convicted again during that period of an indictable offence. His conviction will be treated as 'spent' after expiry of the rehabilitation period.

For most purposes a spent conviction is treated by the law as if it never happened. In general there is no need to disclose spent convictions and a rehabilitated person cannot later be prejudiced if it is discovered that he failed to disclose a spent conviction. The Act also makes it an offence to disclose information about spent convictions from official records otherwise than in the course of someone's official duties.

The rules relating to the length of time a person has to wait before he can be classed as 'rehabilitated' are complex; in general, the longer the sentence, the longer the rehabilitation period.

Section 4: With exceptions, a person who has become rehabilitated 'shall be treated for all purposes in law as a person who has not committed or been charged with or prosecuted for or convicted of or sentenced for the offence or offences which were the subject of that conviction'.

In general, then, a rehabilitated person can regard himself as a person of good character who has no criminal convictions. When completing a job application form, or answering questions at an interview, he may lawfully answer 'no' to questions like — 'Have you ever been convicted of a criminal offence?' Any failure to disclose a spent conviction or any circumstances ancillary thereto shall not be a proper ground for dismissing or excluding a person from any office, profession or occupation or employment, or for prejudicing him in any way in any occupation or employment. Nor, of course, does his untrue statement make him guilty of committing a fraud.

Major exception — the Act does not apply in the case of later criminal proceedings. But in a Practice Direction, the Lord Chief Justice recommended that reference to spent convictions in such proceedings should not be made if it could reasonably be avoided and only with the consent of the Judge.

There are certain occupations to which these benevolent rules do not apply. The excepted classes of employment include:

Policemen; prison officers; traffic wardens; certain jobs in the Court's service; teachers — and other employees in schools 'which involves access to persons under 18'; social services and national health service employees; employees of youth clubs, local authorities or other bodies concerned with the promotion of leisure or recreational activities for people under 18; certain positions in insurance companies; employees in occupations requiring a licence, certificate or registration from a Gaming Board; and employees in private hospitals and nursing homes.

In addition, a person may be refused entrance to a profession because of a spent conviction and such convictions are admissible evidence in disciplinary proceedings against professionals — including doctors, lawyers, accountants, nurses, opticians, pharmacists and teachers.

Spent convictions may also be taken into account in relation to applications for licences, including licences to employ abroad people under the age of 18 and licences granted by the Gaming Board or to deal in securities.

Police records of convictions, including spent convictions, continue to be kept but it is now an offence for anyone who has official access to criminal records to disclose spent convictions otherwise than in the course of his official duties. Any person guilty of this offence may be fined up to £200 by a Magistrates' Court. Any person who obtains any specified information from any official record by means of fraud, dishonesty or bribe also commits an offence and is liable to a fine of up to £400 or six months in prison or both.

Under the general law on defamation, anyone giving a reference is not liable in damages for libel or slander if he proves that he honestly believed that what was said was true and that he did not abuse the occasion for some extraneous or improper purpose ('malice').

This remains the position under the Act. Referees may disclose spent convictions in honest references, provided there is no 'malice' (and provided they do not make improper use of official records). However, Section 8 of the Act provides that a defendant in a libel action shall not ' . . . be entitled to rely upon the defence of justification if the publication is proved to have been made with malice'. Malice therefore destroys the defence of justification in this class of defamation case only. A referee is therefore at risk if he gives 'malicious' reference which mentions a spent conviction, even if what he says is true.

There is no obligation on referees to disclose spent convictions; and it is good and compassionate practice for employers not to disclose discreditable episodes in a man's past, which he has lived down through his good behaviour over a prolonged period.

Finally, anyone applying for a visa or work permit abroad should disclose all convictions (if asked), whether spent or not, since such visas or permits are granted or refused on the basis of the laws of the particular foreign country and not on English law.

\* \* \*

## 440   Instructions to staff − re spent convictions

I enclose herewith an explanation of the Rehabilitation of Offenders Act and would be grateful if you would read it − and ensure that our firm's practices in general and yours in particular (in particular when dealing with the giving of references) comply with the law.

## 441   Spent convictions − ground for refusal of professional employment

We regret that it is not possible after all for us to offer you the position of . . . , as we had hoped. We appreciate that your conviction is 'spent', but our profession is covered by *The Rehabilitation of Offenders Act, 1974 (Exceptions) Order, 1975.*

We are sorry to disappoint you.

## 442   Failure to disclose − application for professional post

When you were interviewed for the position of . . . , you were specifically asked whether you had been convicted of a criminal offence. You failed to disclose an offence involving dishonesty. We appreciate that this is a 'spent' offence which, in the case of most jobs would not have to be revealed. But ours is a profession covered by *The Rehabilitation of Offenders Act, 1974 (Exceptions) Order, 1975.* You were told at the time of the interview that because of this Order you were required to disclose your convictions. And in the circumstances, your employment is terminated herewith and you will not be required to attend further at our office/premises.

I have instructed our accounts department to despatch not only your pay to date but also your full pay in lieu of notice, without prejudice to the advice that we have received that in view of the foregoing you are not strictly speaking entitled to such pay in lieu.

NOTE:

*If the job is sufficiently sensitive, non-disclosure may be a ground for summary dismissal. However, it is invariably wiser and kinder to give pay in lieu of notice. To do so 'without prejudice' provides an added protection. And anyway, provided that the conviction came to light within six months of the start of the employment, the employee will be outside the protection of the unfair dismissal rules.*

## 443 Justification for reference including spent conviction

I note that Messrs . . . have shown you a reference which I gave to them and which included a note of your conviction for . . . . The note was accurate; in view of the nature of the business in which you were seeking a position, we felt obliged to state the facts; and in the circumstances, we are advised that there has been no breach of the Rehabilitation of Offenders Act.

## 444 Malice alleged

I am in receipt of your letter in which you allege justification for dredging up my conviction in 19.., which was long ago 'spent'. There could be no justification for this obviously malicious behaviour; and having regard to my previous treatment by and on behalf of the company, I am advised by my solicitors that I would have every prospect of proving 'malice' in law, as well as in fact.

In the circumstances, I am passing the correspondence to

my solicitors, Messrs . . . and . . . , and you will no doubt be
hearing from them shortly.

## 445   Malice denied

Thank you for your letter dated . . . . I deny that the company or anyone acting for the company or on its behalf has
been guilty of malice, as alleged in your letter or at all.

If you see fit to place the matter in the hands of your
solicitors, you do so at your own risk in costs. And if you
carry out your implied threat to issue proceedings against the
company, those proceedings will be most vigorously defended.

We regret that we found it necessary to reopen old wounds;
if you are so unwise as to choose to keep them open, that will
be a matter for you.

"IT WAS THE <u>PERFECT</u> BLACKMAIL LETTER — TROUBLE WAS,
I INCLUDED A STAMPED ADDRESSED ENVELOPE FOR THE REPLY!"

# Part Seven

# DISPUTES AND DISAGREEMENTS

# Chapter 58

# Disputes and strikes

Disputes are inevitable — with the best will in the world, perpetual industrial harmony is either a dream of Utopia or a nightmare of dictatorship. Disagreements, though, should not needlessly turn into strikes — stoppages and industrial disruption are a last resort.

To prevent an industrial disaster, the old saying, 'Least said, soonest mended', has much to recommend it. And while careful documentation is vital to deal successfully with (for example) allegations of unfair dismissal, careless words on paper cost valuable days lost in disputes.

On the other hand, accurate and conciliatory letters may avoid misunderstandings.

\* \* \*

### 446   Employer to unions — trouble protest

I was pleased to meet your colleagues and yourself regarding your dispute over . . . . At the very least, our discussion cleared the air and I will now discuss your proposals with my colleagues and I know that you will put ours to your committee. I hope that as a result we shall reach some amicable conclusion. I am sure that you all appreciate that any break in production could prove disastrous to the company — and hence, of course, to employment prospects.

With best wishes.

NOTE:

*Unions must do the best they can for their members — and must strike a balance between obtaining top terms and not killing the goose that lays the wage packet. If the company is having troubled times and if redundancies are a real possibility if production is interrupted, then reference to this misery is fair and sensible. Stronger terms, even, may be necessary — thus:*

### 447    Beware of redundancies

When we met, I made a full disclosure to you of the current situation in the company. You now know just how important it is to keep production moving. For our part, we will make every effort to settle the current dispute in an amicable fashion — and I do hope that you and your colleagues will do the same. The Board is most anxious to avoid any unnecessary redundancies — but a stoppage would certainly mean a permanent reduction in our work force.

When you and your colleagues have had time to consider the management's latest — and, I am afraid, final — offer, please do not hesitate to contact me personally.

With my best wishes.

### 448    Offer accepted

My Board has carefully considered the proposition which you have put forward on behalf of the Union and on the whole it is considered fair. So I am pleased to tell you that it is accepted — and I confirm its terms as follows:

> 1 . . . .
> 2 . . . .
> 3 . . . .

### 449    Acceptance — with reservations

Your offer is accepted — but I must point out that under no circumstances can the company consider any further improvement in pay until productivity substantially improves. We are now stretched to the absolute limit — certainly with our present work force.

### 450    Terms agreed — as in letter

Thank you for your letter dated . . . . I confirm that the terms agreed between your Union and the Company are correctly set out. I hope that this agreement signals a permanent end to the unfortunate animosity between your Union and the Company — and the start of happy co-operation

between us, both individually and on behalf of the management and the Union respectively.
   With kind regards.

## 451   Counter-offer — all terms not agreed

   Thank you for your letter, setting out proposed terms of
agreement. These are accepted, with the exception of paragraph . . . . The company cannot agree for the following
reasons:
   1 . . . .
   2 . . . .
   3 . . . .
   Instead, we propose that . . . .
   I look forward to hearing from you.

## 452   Agreement not correctly set out

   Thank you for your letter in which you refer to the agreement which we arrived at in my office this morning. There
appears to be a misunderstanding on two points:-
   1 . . . .
   2 . . . .
   I have a clear recollection — and also, incidentally, a note
— that as to (1), we agreed . . . , and as to (2), we agreed . . . .
   I am sorry that I cannot accept the terms as set out in your
letter — and I hope that on reflection, you will agree that my
recollection and note are correct. I look forward to hearing
from you, so that the new arrangement can be put into immediate effect — for the benefit of your members, and, I
hope, for that of our company.
   With best wishes.

NOTE:
*If terms of agreement are set out in a letter, it is vital that you check
these through with the greatest of care. If you do not agree with any
term as specified, you must say so — otherwise you are asking for
trouble. If there is a dispute and a letter has been written setting out
the terms and you have failed to challenge any which are in dispute, you
are unlikely to be believed. The union representatives will be fully
entitled to say: 'If you did not agree with the terms as I set them out,*

*then obviously you would have said so. You are now — a long time afterwards — trying to pull a fast one.' Maybe you are not — but appearances are against you.*

## 453    Let us meet again

I am sure that since our meeting on Monday we must both have had second thoughts. Rather than allow the situation to cascade into chaos, causing infinite harm both to the company and to your members — why do we not meet again?

Perhaps you would telephone me to arrange a mutually convenient appointment?

With best wishes.

## 454    The ever-open door

Our efforts seem doomed to failure, but my door is always open to you if you have second thoughts. It would be a great pity if we cannot reach an agreement — for the benefit of your members, as well as that of the company.

## 455    Must you strike?

I was perturbed to learn that you feel that the circumstances are now so serious that you propose taking industrial action. Naturally, this would cause grave harm to the company — but I am sure that you will appreciate that it will prevent our retaining the present high level of employment — and make eventual short time working absolutely inevitable. If you would care to discuss the matter with me, even at this eleventh hour, please do not hesitate to contact me.

## 456    Complaint at vituperation

I am surprised at the way in which you have seen fit to write to me. I hope that, on reflection, you will regret the intemperate language you have used — and the accusations which you have seen fit to make against my company and myself. These are totally without foundation.

I appreciate that you are working under considerable stress at the moment and in the circumstances, I shall not reply in kind. However, I wish to deal with certain specific allegations of fact:-

(a) . . . .

(b) . . . .

(c) . . . .

Despite the nature of your letter, we are still prepared to meet with you and your colleagues — and to attempt to re-establish the sort of atmosphere within which good industrial relations may prevail, to the benefit of your members as well as that of the company.

## 457  Negotiations at an end

I have read your letter with care. I have already dealt with your allegations, many times — I would refer you in particular to my letters of the . . . , the . . . and the . . . .

No useful purpose would be served by prolonging this correspondence. It is simply impossible for the company to improve its offer — which I hope that you and your colleagues will, on reflection, appreciate goes a very long way to meeting your wishes, and if accepted, would provide considerable benefits for your members.

## 458  The door re-opened

My door will always be open to you — and you will be welcome to come in for a chat — in the future, as in the past. There must be some way out of this horrible mess — for the sake of your people, as well as mine.

## 459  Why strike must end

As a result of the current industrial dispute, the company has lost . . . days production and your members . . . days pay. This situation suits no one — and I cannot believe that — with goodwill and the understanding of the damage caused to all concerned, on both sides — we cannot find an answer.

If you agree that our talks resume, then please let me know.

## 460   Company in trouble through strike — notices given

We have struggled to keep the company afloat and the workforce intact — but this strike has meant the downfall of our efforts. If it continues beyond . . . , we shall have no alternative other than to terminate the contract of employment of our entire workforce/all those employees engaged in . . ./all those employees still on strike.

My colleagues and I would deeply regret having to take this step, but we do hope that you will not leave us with no other alternative.

## 461   Dispute at an end

Just a note — to express the pleasure of my colleagues and myself that the dispute between your union and our company has now come to an end. I hope that in future we shall manage to resolve our differences in amicable fashion. And I look forward to seeing you, with a view to seeing how we can make up some of the lost production — and pay — resulting from the strike.

# Chapter 59

# Replies to threats of legal action

Once a dispute — whether with an individual employer or employee, union, firm or anyone else — has reached the stage when the contestants are threatening court proceedings, letters must be written with consummate care. They may well be placed before a Court — unless they contain 'without prejudice' negotiations.

When replying to threats of litigation, the following drafts should be useful.

\* \* \*

## 462 Employers to unions — troubled protest

Thank you for your letter. I was extremely perturbed to learn that you feel that the circumstances are now so serious that you wish to take the dispute over the meaning of our agreement, to a court of law for interpretation. Surely we can sort matters out between ourselves, with a little more patience and goodwill? I would be pleased to see you, if you would like to contact me.

## 463 Management to union — calling the bluff

If you wish to go to court, we cannot stop you.

## 464 Management to union — please think again

Before you plunge into litigation, may I respectfully suggest that you and your colleagues might reconsider the following points?
(a) . . .
(b) . . .
(c) . . .

### 465    Suggested meeting outside door of Court

The only people who are absolutely certain to emerge victorious from our current battle are the lawyers. We are bound to meet inside the Court tomorrow morning. I shall be there half an hour early, just in case you might care to meet me outside.

I assure you that in spite of what has happened — and without prejudice to our views as to the merits — there is a fund of goodwill in the company, for your union in general and for yourself in particular.

NOTES:

*1    Few laymen really approve of lawyers — until they need them. So if you cannot join with your opposition in mutual love, perhaps mutual dislike of lawyers might do the trick! Even if you are fond of men of law, no one enjoys paying legal costs.*

*2    Even the most unreasonable of men sometimes turn friendly, when they are actually within sight of the witness box. Only a few exhibitionists really enjoy being cross-examined. And anyway, there is something salutory about hanging around in draughty court corridors — with the prospects of useless, aggravating, boring, protracted further hours of (extremely expensive) misery, in precisely the same place.*

*3    Even if you decide not to write a letter of this sort, you might bear in mind that a vast majority of cases which actually reach the door of the court are settled without adjudication by the judge.*

### 466    Denial of justification for complaint

There is a misunderstanding. Your complaint is unjustified, for the following reasons:
>    *(a)* . . .
>    *(b)* . . .
>    *(c)* . . .

If you see fit to proceed with your case, then it will be most strenuously opposed.

Without prejudice to our views, we are perfectly prepared to meet you to see whether some compromise arrangement can be arrived at. We maintain our view that this form of litigation is of no use to anyone — except, perhaps, to the lawyers.

I shall telephone your office, tomorrow morning, to see whether you and I cannot hammer out some sensible arrangement.

With my best wishes to you personally.

NOTES:

*1  Litigants are always afraid of 'showing weakness' by apparently seeking a settlement. So olive branches are usually waved rather gently.*

*2  On the other hand, hostility and aggression tend to breed a like response. So moderate letters are normally sensible, when industrial relations are concerned — even in reply to thoroughly aggressive outbursts. Such letters show maturity as well as restraint — and are far more likely to lead to satisfactory results than the venting of steam. This may make you feel better to 'get it off your chest', but aggressive responses are bad medicine, in almost every case.*

*3  Letters like the above — which make it plain that there is no ill-will between the writer of the letter and its recipient — may pave the way to future good relations. It is important, where possible, to distinguish between a man's views and his personality. One of the joys of both Parliament and the Courts, from the viewpoint of Parliamentarians and lawyers, is the comradeship and friendliness which exist outside political or legal battle (as the case may be). Life is sufficiently short and unpleasant without forming personal animosities against opponents. And the same should also apply in the world of industrial relations.*

*If you say something unkind, stupid, aggressive or hurtful, then it may be forgotten — or, perhaps, explained away as a misunderstanding. Or the hearer may even convince himself that he has misheard. Not so if you put your remark into writing. It is then available to be mulled over — not only by the recipient but also by others.*

*4  There are colleagues who have to see the letter — and if you humble the recipient, you will do so in the eyes of others — and make it harder for him to lift his head and hence to compromise. And you will also do so in the eyes of the Court — unless the letter is marked 'without prejudice'. When dealing with complaints made to an Industrial Tribunal, precisely the same principles apply when you put pen to paper as they do when you are coping with ordinary litigation. The effect which your letter has on its immediate reader is doubtless important — but you should have your sights fixed on the future — and in particular on the effect which the letter is likely to have on the Court, i.e. on the individual or people who will eventually decide your case, one way or the other. Thus:*

## 467   Letter will be referred to the Court

I really am surprised at the way in which you have seen fit to write to me. I hope that on reflection, you will regret the intemperate language you have used — and the accusations which you have seen fit to make against my company and myself. These are completely without foundation.

Your letter, of course, will be brought to the attention of the Court, in due course. I am sure that it will make as bad an impression upon the judge as it has done upon me and my colleagues.

I do appreciate, though, that you are working under considerable stress at the moment. In the circumstances, I shall not reply in kind. However, I wish to deal with certain specific allegations of fact:

   *(a)* . . . .
   *(b)* . . . .
   *(c)* . . . .

Despite the nature of your letter, we are still prepared to meet with you and your colleagues — and to attempt to re-establish the sort of atmosphere within which good industrial relations may prevail, to the benefit of your members as well as that of the company.

## 468   When negotiations are at an end

I have read your letter with care. I have already dealt with your allegations, many times — I would refer you in particular to my letters of the . . . , the . . . and the . . . .

No useful purpose would be served by prolonging this correspondence. Unfortunately, it appears that this matter will now have to be decided by the Court.

# Chapter 60

# Misunderstandings and apologies

If only people knew how to say 'Sorry' — how many disputes would never occur? Some battles are necessary. Many could be avoided, were it not for pride, feasting upon misunderstandings.

To apologise, though, is not easy. The following letters are designed to make the written apology less hurtful, more dignified — and even, on occasion, to turn it to good account.

\* \* \*

### 469   Misunderstanding — on your part

I have heard that you believe that the management will . . . .
I cannot conceive where this idea came from. It is totally without foundation.

If the fault was mine because I failed to express myself sufficiently clearly — or if I said something which could have been misinterpreted in that way — then I apologise.

The management's position is in fact as follows: . . .

With that misunderstanding out of the way, I hope that we can now get together and see whether we cannot sort out our disagreements. Do please contact me.

### 470   Misunderstanding — your fault

Forgive me if I have misunderstood — but I have been told that you have informed your members that we agreed that they would be paid at the rate of . . . .

There is clearly a misunderstanding here — and the sooner we meet and talk about it, the better. I repeat: Whatever the basis of that misunderstanding, it is very real and if I caused it by anything that I said, I am sorry.

However, I suspect that someone has simply given you incorrect information which you have passed on and I am now anxious that we should meet so as to prevent the

situation from getting out of hand. I look forward to hearing
from you.

With best wishes.

## 471   Agreement — misunderstood

I expect it was because we did not finish arguing until the
early hours of the morning — but I have now seen a copy of
the Minute which you have sent round your members regarding our agreement. Unfortunately, there are several matters
contained in it which differ totally from my note and also
from my recollection.

It is therefore essential that we meet again so as to sort out
this misunderstanding — can you please contact me immediate
ly?

I think that we will both have to learn a lesson from this —
that however late at night we finish our labours, it would be
worth staying on just a little longer so as to put our agreement onto paper — together!

With best wishes.

## 472   Apology — without frills

The fault is entirely mine — and I apologise. I should not
have lost my temper — and I did not mean what I said.

There are, I am afraid, times when one is under great
strain — this was just such a time. I was also extremely tired.
My apologies to you. I understand that you were insulted —
that was not my intention.

I trust that you will accept this apology in the spirit in
which it is offered — and that you will join me for a drink
this evening at . . . . For the sake of your members as well as
that of the management, it is obviously disastrous that you
and I should fall out — and I am very sorry that my words
should have caused the unnecessary breach.

Looking forward to seeing you and with all best wishes.

"HOW DO YOU SPELL 'DEAR SIR'... ?"

"WHAT DO YOU MEAN COMMA MY MIND IS ALWAYS ON MY WORK QUESTION MARK "

*Part Eight*

# APPENDICES

# The new law—summarised

Employers and personnel managers are sometimes so overwhelmed by the flood of new legislation that they panic. There is no need for alarm. Those whose standards are already high are little affected; and even those who are not proud of their employment or safety practices can avoid trouble if they recognise the main features of the new laws and change their practices now.

The following is a summary of the legislation. This is the law – the rest is largely commentary.

\* \* \*

### The Industrial Relations Act

This Act was repealed by *The Trade Union and Labour Relations Act, 1974.* The unfair dismissal rules were re-enacted (strengthened); and the Code of Industrial Relations Practice (main feature: at least one written notice of dismissal required, wherever possible) is retained, save insofar as superseded by Codes produced by the Advisory, Conciliation and Arbitration Service.

### Unfair dismissal

The Employment Protection Act has again strengthened the unfair dismissal rules – through powers of tribunals to *order* reinstatement; through 'basic' and 'additional' awards of compensation – which take the potential penalty of one unfair dismissal into five figures; and by the removal or reduction of certain exclusions (part-timers, small business and close relatives. The consolidated protection is not as follows:

1     All employees are covered *except* the following:
a     Those employed for less than six months – other than people dismissed because of discrimination on grounds of trade union membership or activities, sex or race discrimination (for whom there is no minimum).

*b*    Men above 65, women above 60 (or above the normal retirement age).

*c*    Those who normally work less than 16 hours a week (or 8 hours after 5 years' service) from 1 February 1977.

*d*    Husbands and wives.

*e*    Those who 'ordinarily work' outside the UK, even if they also ordinarily work inside the UK.

*f*    Those with fixed-term contracts of two years or more who have effectively contracted out of their rights under the Act.

2    Any employee who is not excluded must prove that he was 'dismissed' in order to obtain any rights. Dismissal may be effected in one of three ways:

*a*    *Actual* dismissal — where a person is 'fired', or where he is demoted or his hours or place of work changed, or suspended without pay and without his consent, so that the employer is refusing to keep him on, on the same terms as before.

*b*    *Constructive* — where the employee is forced out of his job. He may be asked to resign, with the alternative of dismissal; or anyone at any level (including charge-hand, foreman, supervisor or other line manager) may 'wear him down' — making his life a misery so that when he leaves he is entitled to do so as a result of the employers conduct.

*c*    *Fixed-term* contract expires without being renewed (see above exclusion, where employee contracts out).

3    Employee must be careful not to jump the gun — leave before he is actually dismissed, even where he is warned that a dismissal (perhaps for redundancy) is inevitable. He should ask for his marching orders. No 'dismissal' means no right to compensation for unfair dismissal; to damages for wrongful dismissal (see later); or to redundancy pay.

4    Once an employee has shown that he was dismissed, the burden of proof shifts onto the employer to show the *reason* for the dismissal and that he acted reasonably in treating that reason as sufficient to warrant depriving the employee of his livelihood. There are many statutory reasons for dismissal, including: lack of capability, e.g. health or ability; lack of technical qualification (perhaps because the job itself has changed); redundancy; conduct (including failure to follow safety rules); illegality, e.g. foreigner whose work permit has expired; or redundancy.

It will be fair to treat the reason as sufficient to warrant dismissal if the correct procedure has been followed (including, where possible, at least one written warning; explanation to employee of circumstances; employee given opportunity to explain his case and to appeal); and if the measure taken bears reasonable relationship to the circumstances and is reasonable and just. Take particular care when selecting people for redundancy — many claimants have obtained both redundancy pay and compensation for unfair dismissal.

5 Maximum compensation for successful claimant: £5200 or £50 a week for two years — but an employer must prove loss. Plus a 'basic award' — two weeks' pay at up to £80 a week and/or a sum equivalent to the redundancy money which he would have received, had he been made redundant — even if he has suffered no actual loss. Also he may get an 'additional award' if a tribunal orders 'reinstatement' (which may only be done at the employee's request) and the employer fails to obey this order — maximum £4160, or one year's pay at up to £80 a week if dismissal for discrimination — otherwise 3 to 6 months' pay at up to £80 a week.

## Wrongful dismissal

A dismissal is 'wrongful' if the employee is entitled to notice or pay in lieu which he does not receive. Measure of damage: what he has lost.

An employee is entitled to agreed notice; in the absence of agreement to reasonable notice; and in any event to not less than the statutory minimum — which went up (from 1 June 1976) to: 7 days after 4 weeks' service; 2 weeks after 2 years; and an additional week per year up to a maximum of 12 weeks after 12 years.

*Note:* these are minimum periods only. There is no 'statutory period of notice'.

## Reasons for dismissal

Since 1 June 1976 an employee of 6 months' standing has been entitled to request that his employer gives reasons for the dismissal — in writing and within 14 days of the request. Failure to supply adequate written reasons may cost him £160 (2 weeks × £80).

## Contracts of Employment

'Dismissal' is the termination of a contract of employment. The contract may be made orally or in writing. Either way the employer must provide written particulars of the main terms of service, within 13 weeks of the commencement of the employment; and of any variation, within 4 weeks of that.

Written particulars (since 1 June 1976) must include not only the date of commencement of service; name of employer; place and hours of work; holiday entitlement and how this is arrived at; grievance procedures; and details of any pension or sick pay schemes — but also 'job title' (which should be stated clearly but flexibly, e.g. 'and all other work normally incidental thereto'); whether present job is or is not continuous with previous employment and if it is, then when the previous employment began; and the employer's disciplinary procedures or where these are easily accessible to the employee.

**Pay statements**

Pay statements must be itemised, setting out not only the total of pay but how this total is arrived at. Again, probably from the end of 1976.

**Redundancy**

The basic redundancy rules remain unchanged. An employee who is 'dismissed as redundant'; who is not a pensioner or a part-timer (working 16 to 8 hours minimum, as above) is entitled to redundancy pay. The maximum (after 20 years' service at appropriate ages and ranks), £2400, 40 per cent of which is recoverable from the Redundancy Fund.

As from 8 March 1976 every employer must inform any relevant, independent, recognised trade union of the intended redundancy of any of its members, however few. In addition, where the employer intends to dismiss 10 or more people at one establishment within 60 days, he must consult with the trade union and notify the Department of Employment at least 60 days before the first dismissal takes effect; and where he intends to dismiss a hundred or more at one establishment within 90 days, then the warning period is 90 days.

Failure to consult trade unions could lead to a 'protective award', equal to the pay which the employee would have received during the period when consultation should have taken place; and a fine of up to £400 plus loss of up to 10 per cent of redundancy rebate, if inadequate notification to the Department.

Insolvency

If an employer becomes insolvent, his employees have new rights — as from 20 April 1976. These include preferential treatment for various debts and (much more important) the right to claim up to 8 weeks arrears of pay; pay in lieu of notice, up to 6 weeks' holiday pay, etc. (with limits of £80 per week) from Redundancy Fund.

Guarantee payments

Companies that go onto short time may be required (starting 6 April 1977) to provide a maximum of £30 (5 days at £6 per day) during each three-month period (beginning 1 February, May, August and November), to employees. Main exception: where 'workless days' are caused through trade dispute involving employee in employing (or associated) company.

Time off work

Since 1 June 1976, employees have been entitled to time off when made redundant, to seek other work and/or training for it; for public service (JPs, councillors, school governors, etc.). By about Spring 1977 trade union officials will be entitled to time off for industrial relations and similar duties. Code of Practice to be produced by Advisory, Conciliation and Arbitration Service will provide guidance.

Disclosure of information

Probably from Spring 1977 (when ACAS Code of Practice is in final form and approved by Parliament), employers will be required to disclose to independent, recognised trade unions information during the course of collective bargaining. Exceptions include: where disclosure would cause substantial harm to the business; and where the information is confidential to others. Disputes go to ACAS — and, where necessary, on to Central Arbitration Committee (which has now replaced Industrial Arbitration Board).

## Advisory, Conciliation and Arbitration Service

ACAS is now on statutory basis. Its officers provide free (and extremely useful) advice; they conciliate, and they set up arbitrations. They also prepare Codes of Practice (see above). And they deal with disputes over the recognition of trade unions. Do not hesitate to contact ACAS — direct or via local Department of Employment.

## Women's rights

1   On 29 December 1975 the Equal Pay Act (as amended by the Sex Discrimination Act) and the Sex Discrimination Act came into full force. Women are now entitled to equal pay for like work or for work assessed in like manner. It is unlawful to discriminate on grounds of sex or marital status in connection, for example, with appointment, promotion, transfer, training or dismissal.

2   As from 1 June 1976 it has been unlawful to dismiss a woman because of pregnancy or confinement. She is also entitled to be reinstated in her job, at any time within 29 weeks of her confinement (plus 4 weeks, if unfit), provided that by 11 weeks before the expected date of her confinement she has worked for the employer for at least 2 years; that she stays on until the beginning of the 11th week (unless she is dismissed earlier because of her condition); and that the cause of her absence is her pregnancy or confinement. She must also (where reasonably practicable) state her intention to return at least 3 weeks before she leaves.

Wise employers now request notice of her intention to be given in writing — so stating in the original terms of service and in a form given to the mother before she leaves to have her baby.

3   As from 6 April 1976 a mother who has been employed for 2 years by the beginning of the 11th week before her expected confinement and stays on until that date (unless she is dismissed earlier because her condition makes this impossible) will be entitled to up to 6 weeks Maternity Pay. Rate: 9/10ths of her normal pay minus maximum current Maternity Allowance. Source: new 'Maternity Fund' to which all employers will pay expected 0.05 per cent of their pay roll (£1 in £2000).
*Note:* right to Maternity Pay does not depend upon intention to return to work.

**Health and Safety**

*The Health and Safety at Work Act, 1974,* revolutionised the approach
to industrial safety. Its main features are as follows:

1 All employees 'at work' are now covered — in farms, parks, hotels,
places of entertainment, roads, hospitals, schools, research laboratories —
everywhere. About 5 million workers brought under the protection of
industrial safety law.

2 Personal liability imposed on everyone from chairman to foreman —
all 'directors, managers and secretaries' with whose consent or connivance or with a result of whose 'neglect' an unsafe practice takes place.

3 The old legislation (Factories Act; Offices Shops and Railway
Premises Act, etc., and regulations made under them) remain in force —
but subject to new penalties and procedures.

4 New penalties; conviction before Magistrates Court — maximum
fine, £400; or on indictment (before Crown Court), no limit on fine
plus possible imprisonment of up to 2 years.

5 New procedures: 'Prohibition notice' prohibiting dangerous activity,
with imminent risk of serious personal injury; 'improvement notices' —
requiring improvement within a specified time. Thousands already
served. These must be complied with.

6 Individual workers also covered by Act — and by notices. But they
must take reasonably good care of themselves and of their colleagues
and obey safety rules. But their failure to do so is usually blamed on
Management, for failing to convince them of necessity to follow the
rules — prosecution of individual workers is very rare.

7 Supervision of Health and Safety measures now under control of
Health and Safety Commission; and enforcement (through integrated
inspectorate — now including agriculture) through Health and Safety
Executive.

8 Employers must now take such steps as are reasonably practicable
to protect their own employees at work; and to protect others affected
by their 'undertaking' including contractors, sub-contractors, visitors
and the general public. (*Note:* common law on negligence and occupiers
liability remains in force. But recent decisions show that where you

ought reasonably to expect a person – child or adult – to be visiting your premises, he will not be classed as a 'trespasser'. You 'owe a humanitarian and legal duty' to take reasonable steps for his safety).

## Industrial tribunals

Industrial tribunals now have immense power, including disputes over unfair dismissal; redundancy pay; most employment protection rules; sex and race discrimination; and appeal against prohibition and improvement notices.

## Race discrimination

Legislation currently before Parliament will strengthen rules – and set up procedures (roughly and generally) equivalent to those provided for women for Sex Discrimination Act.

## Worker participation

The Bullock Committee is sitting; legislation requiring worker participation is unlikely in the 1976/77 Parliamentary Session; meanwhile note:

1   Implementation of the disclosure of information rules will remove major barrier against worker participation in all businesses with trade unions recognised for bargaining purposes.
2   Under the Health and Safety at Work Act, consultation with safety representatives is now mandatory.
3   Required redundancy notification has been operative since March 1976.

# Forms

This appendix contains reproductions of several forms that you may be called upon to complete so as to comply with recent legislation:

1 Originating Application to an Industrial Tribunal.
2 Application for reference of a recognition issue to ACAS.
3 Notice of intention to claim rebate from the Redundancy Fund.
4 Application to the Secretary of State for Employment for a payment under *The Redundancy Payments Act, 1965.*
5 Employer's Calculation of Redundancy Payment and Employee's Receipt.
6 Notification of intention to reduce a redundancy payment on account of pension or lump sum superannuation payment.
7 *The Sex Discrimination Act, 1975* — the questions procedure.
8 Complaint of unlawful discrimination.
9 Health and Safety Executive: Improvement Notice.
10 Health and Safety Executive: Prohibition Notice.

# Originating Application to an Industrial Tribunal

NOTES FOR GUIDANCE

Before completing the application form please read —

THESE NOTES for guidance

LEAFLET ITL I which you were given along with this form

THE APPROPRIATE BOOKLET referred to under the relevant acts below

(Copies of these booklets are obtainable FREE from any local employment office, Jobcentre or unemployment enefit office)

I  **RELEVANT ACT(S)** — You can ask the tribunal to decide under the —

TRADE UNION AND LABOUR RELATIONS ACT 1974
— on whether you were unfairly dismissed.
You can find further information about your rights in the booklet "Unfair dismissal".

REDUNDANCY PAYMENTS ACT 1965
— questions about entitlement to or amount of a redundancy payment or rebate.
Further information is available in the leaflet RPL 6 or the booklet "The Redundancy Payments Scheme".

CONTRACTS OF EMPLOYMENT ACT 1972
— on the terms of your employment because you have not received a written statement of them or of any alterations to them OR because your written statement does not give sufficient information to meet the requirements of the Act.
For details see the booklet "Guide to the Contracts of Employment Act".

EQUAL PAY ACT 1970
— on a question about entitlement to or on a claim for the same pay or other term of a contract of employment as a person of the opposite sex in the same employment.
For details see the "Guide to the Equal Pay Act 1970".

SEX DISCRIMINATION ACT 1975
— on whether in the employment training and related fields, you have been discriminated against as defined in the Act, ie sex discrimination, discrimination against married persons or discrimination by way of victimisation for pursuing your rights under this Act or the Equal Pay Act 1970.
For further information see the booklet "A Guide to the Sex Discrimination Act 1975".
See chapter 8 of this booklet regarding the means of questioning the respondent in writing about the alleged discriminatory act.

EMPLOYMENT PROTECTION ACT 1975
— on a question about entitlement to payment by the Secretary of State for Employment of certain debts owed to you by an insolvent employer — for details see the leaflet "Employees' Rights on Insolvency of Employer".

**PTO**

ITI (Revised March 1976)

— on a question about the entitlement to payment by the Secretary of State to occupational pension schemes in respect of contributions owing on behalf of employees of insolvent employers — for details see leaflet "Insolvency of Employers, Safeguard of Occupational Pension Scheme Contributions" available from insolvent employers' representatives.

— (in the case of a recognised independent trade union) on whether an employer has complied with the requirements to consult recognised trade unions about proposed redundancies.

— (in the case of an employee) about entitlement to or amount due under a protective award made by an Industrial Tribunal.

— (in the case of an employer) on an appeal against reduction of redundancy payment rebate for failure to notify proposed redundancies.

For details see the booklet "Employment Protection Act — Procedure for Handling Redundancies"

— on a claim that a woman has been unfairly dismissed because she was pregnant or for reasons connected with pregnancy or that she has not been permitted by her employer to return to work following absence because of maternity — see booklet "Employment Protection Act — New Rights for the Expectant Mother".

— on a question about entitlement to reasonable time off in order to look for work or make arrangements for training or about entitlement to payment in respect of such time off — see booklet "Employment Protection Act — Time Off to Look for Work or Make Arrangements for Training".

— on a claim that an employer has failed to pay all or part of an amount of medical suspension pay to which an employee is entitled — see booklet "Employment Protection Act — Suspension from Work on Medical Grounds".

— (in the case of an employee) on whether an employer has taken action short of dismissal because of trade union membership or activities; or, if the person objects to union membership on religious grounds, because they refuse to join a union.

— on a question about a written statement of reasons for dismissal — see the booklet "Dismissal Employees' Rights".

— if the Tribunal decide that you were unfairly dismissed they will ask you to state which remedy you would prefer. The remedies which a Tribunal can order are:
Re-instatement ie a return to your old job as though you had never been dismissed.
Re-engagement ie a return to work for your old employer but not necessarily in the same job as before or on the same terms and conditions
Compensation — see booklets "Unfair Dismissal" or "Dismissal-Employees' Rights".

## 2 REPRESENTATION AT HEARING

At the hearing you may state your own case or be represented by anyone who has agreed to act for you in this case. In applications under the Equal Pay Act 1970 or the Sex Discrimination Act 1975 see the appropriate booklet regarding possible assistance by the Equal Opportunities Commission. If you name a representative all further communications regarding your application will be sent to him and not to you; you should arrange to be kept informed by him of the progress of your case and of the hearing date.

## 3 RESPONDENT(S)

If you are in any doubt as to the respondent(s) to name in item 4 of your application you should seek advice from any local employment office, Jobcentre or unemployment benefit office.

## 4 GROUNDS OF APPLICATION

You will be able to amplify the grounds of your application at the hearing.
THIS APPLICATION MUST BE MADE WITHIN THE APPROPRIATE TIME LIMIT (See note overleaf)

Do not forget to sign the form

It is advisable to retain a copy of entries in paragraphs 14 and 15.

PLEASE DETACH THESE NOTES AND RETAIN before sending the application form opposite to the Central Office of the Industrial Tribunals.

CENTRAL OFFICE OF THE INDUSTRIAL TRIBUNALS

*347*

# ORIGINATING APPLICATION TO AN INDUSTRIAL TRIBUNAL

**UNDER ONE OR MORE OF THE FOLLOWING ACTS:—**

TRADE UNION AND LABOUR RELATIONS ACT 1974
REDUNDANCY PAYMENTS ACT 1965
CONTRACTS OF EMPLOYMENT ACT 1972
EQUAL PAY ACT 1970
SEX DISCRIMINATION ACT 1975
EMPLOYMENT PROTECTION ACT 1975

| For Official Use | |
|---|---|
| Case Number | |

**IMPORTANT:** DO NOT FILL IN THIS FORM UNTIL YOU HAVE READ THE NOTES FOR GUIDANCE. THEN COMPLETE ITEMS 2, 4, 5 AND 14, AND ALL OTHER ITEMS RELEVANT TO YOUR CASE

To:— The Secretary of the Tribunals
   Central Office of the Industrial Tribunals (England and Wales)
   93, Ebury Bridge Road, London SW1W 8RE          Telephone: 01–730–9161

1   I hereby apply for a decision of a tribunal on the following question (*State here question to be decided by the Tribunal and explain the grounds overleaf*)

2   My name (*Surname in block capitals first*) is Mr/Mrs/Miss

   OR title (*if company or organisation*) is

   Address and telephone no.

3   If a representative has agreed to act for you in this case please give his name and address below and note that further communications will be sent to him and not to you ( *See Note 2*)

   Name

   Address and telephone no.

4   (a)   Name of respondent(s) (*in block capitals*) ie the employer, person or body against whom a decision is sought (See Note 3)

      Address(es) and telephone no.(s)

   (b)   Respondent's relationship to you for the purpose of the application (eg employer, trade union, employment agency, employer recognising the union making application, etc.)

5   Date of birth ........................................

6   Place of employment to which this application relates,
   or place where act complained about took place.

7   Occupation or position held 'applied for, or other relationship to
   the respondent named above (eg user of a service supplied by him)

8   Employment began on ..................................................and (*if appropriate*) ended on ...........................................

9   Basic wages 'salary ........................................................................................

10  Other pay or remuneration ...............................................................................

11  Normal basic weekly hours of work ................................................................

12  (In an application under the Sex Discrimination Act)
   Date on which action complained of took place or first came to my knowledge ...................................................

IT 1 (Revised March 1976 )                    *Please continue overleaf*

13   The grounds of this application are as follows: (See Note 4)

14   (If dismissed) If you wish to state what in your opinion was the reason for your dismissal, please do so here.

15   If the Tribunal decides that you were unfairly dismissed, what remedy would you prefer? (Before answering this question please consult the Notes for Guidance for the remedies available and then write one only of the following in answer to this question: reinstatement, re-engagement or compensation)

Signature ................................................................................   Date ...................................................................

**FOR OFFICIAL USE**

| Issuing office code no. | Received at COIT | Code | ROIT | RO | Inits |
|---|---|---|---|---|---|
|  |  |  |  |  |  |

*349*

## EMPLOYMENT PROTECTION ACT 1975

APPLICATION FOR THE REFERENCE OF A RECOGNITION ISSUE TO THE ADVISORY, CONCILIATION AND ARBITRATION SERVICE UNDER SECTION 11 OF THE ACT

Note:  Only an independent trade union may make an application on this form (see definitions overleaf).

1. Name of the independent trade union making the application:

2. Address for correspondence about this application, and telephone number:

3. Name and address of the employer from whom recognition is sought: (If recognition is sought from two or more associated employers please give all their names and addresses).

4. The trade, industry, eto. in which the employer is engaged:

5. The description of the workers covered by the application (stating where appropriate the part of the undertaking in which they work):

6. Does the employer already recognise the trade union to any extent?

SIGNATURE:                          NAME IN BLOCK CAPITALS:

DATE:                               POSITION HELD IN TRADE UNION:

(This form may be signed only by an official of the trade union who is duly authorised to make such an application on behalf of the union.)

## Definitions

For the purposes of the Employment Protection Act 1975:

(1) "**Trade union**" means except so far as the context otherwise requires, an organisation (whether permanent or temporary) which either —

    (a) consists wholly or mainly of workers of one or more descriptions and is an organisation whose principal purposes include the regulation of relations between workers of that description or those descriptions and employers or employers' associations; or

    (b) consists wholly or mainly of —

        (i) constituent or affiliated organisations which fulfil the conditions specified in paragraph (a) above (or themselves consist wholly or mainly of constituent or affiliated organisations which fulfil those conditions), or

        (ii) representatives of such constituent or affiliated organisations;

    and in either case is an organisation whose principal purposes include the regulation of relations between workers and employers or between workers and employers' associations, or include the regulation of relations between its constituent or affiliated organisations.

    (Trade Union and Labour Relations Act 1974, Section 28(1)).

(2) "**Independent trade union**" means a trade union which —

    (a) is not under the domination or control of an employer or a group of employers or of one or more employers associations; and

    (b) is not liable to interference by an employer or any such group or association (arising out of the provision of financial or material support or by any other means whatsoever) tending towards such control;

    (Trade Union and Labour Relations Act 1974, Section 30(1)).

# Notice of intention to claim rebate from
# THE REDUNDANCY FUND

RP I

## NOTES

See also booklet "The Redundancy Payments Scheme", particularly sections headed:

1 Please detach and complete the attached tear-off form and send to the address shown above item 1 not less than 14 days before the expected date of the first dismissals (not less than 21 days if 10 or more employees qualifying for payment are expected to terminate within 6 days of each other). Please explain at item 5 of the form the reason for any delay; failure to give the required notice without good reason may result in the imposition of a penalty up to 10% of the rebate claimed.

The Redundancy Fund.

Rebate from the Fund

How an employer claims rebate

2 Item 1 of the form — for the purposes of the Redundancy Payments Act an employee is taken to be dismissed if his contract of employment is terminated by the employer, with or without notice, or a fixed term of employment expires without renewal of the contract, or the employee terminates the contract without notice as justified by the employer's conduct. There is no dismissal when an employee accepts a properly made offer of alternative employment with the same employer, or with an associated or subsidiary company (where the employer is a company), or with a new owner of the business (or separate and identifiable part thereof).

Conditions relating to redundancy payments

What is meant by "dismissal"?

Is there any entitlement if further employment is offered?

3 Item 1 of the form — Weeks count for payment under the Act in which an employee is employed for 21 hours or more or in which any part is covered by a contract with the employer which normally involves employment for 21 hours or more weekly. If a week does not count, normally it breaks the record of continuous employment and no period of employment before a break can be counted.

Appendix B Rules for calculating continuous employment

4 Item 2 of the form (and if necessary item 3) — please indicate the reason for the anticipated dismissal of the employees. An employee is dismissed by reason of redundancy if the whole or main reason is that the employer is closing down altogether or at a particular place, or for some other reason the employer's needs for employees to do work of a particular kind at the place in question have diminished or ceased or are expected to diminish or cease.

Conditions relating to redundancy payments.

What is redundancy?

What dismissals are due to redundancy?

5 Item 3 of the form — please use this space for any additional information. If you wish correspondence or enquiries about these redundancy dismissals to be addressed to a particular individual, please give his name, telephone number and extension. Please show the place of work if different from your main address.

6 Item 4 of the form — please enter your tax office and reference number.

7 If you are in doubt on any point, please consult the office shown below the spaces for entry of your firm's name and address.

**PENALTIES** — Any person who makes a statement which he knows to be false or recklessly makes a statement which is false, or produces a document which to his knowledge has been wilfully falsified, is liable on summary conviction on indictment to a fine or imprisonment for a term not exceeding 2 years or both.

*353*

Department of Employment
Redundancy Payments Acts 1965 and 1969

**NOTICE OF INTENTION TO CLAIM REBATE FROM THE REDUNDANCY FUND**

Full title of firm ................................................................................................................................................................
*(in block capitals)*
Address ..........................................................................................................................................................................

.......................................................................................................... Telephone No. ................................................

To: ..........................................................................................................

..........................................................................................................

1     I declare that the employees whose names are listed overleaf (and on the continuation sheets numbered ..............
    to .............. ) are expected to be dismissed, as defined in Note 2 on the tear-off page retained by me, on the
    dates shown in column 6 on each sheet. Each has been employed throughout the stated period for at least
    21 hours weekly or under a contract normally involving employment for 21 hours or more weekly (see Note 3 on
    tear-off page).

2     The reason for the anticipated dismissal (see *Note 4 on tear-off page*) has been ticked in the appropriate box
    below:—

          (1) Closure of the establishment    ☐

          (2) Removal of the establishment to another area    ☐

          (3) Reduction in labour force at the establishment due to
              (a) general reduction in level of activities    ☐

              (b) reduction in activities on which the employees engaged    ☐

              (c) changes in methods of work eg mechanisation, automation    ☐

              (d) elimination of slack in workloads    ☐

          (4) Other reasons (specified at item 3 below)    ☐

3     Additional information (see Notes 4–5 on tear-off page).



    Address at which the employees work if different from above .........................................................................

......................................................................................................................................................................................

4     I understand that to establish my right to any rebate it may be necessary for you to refer to information given by
    me to the Inland Revenue and other Government departments and I hereby give my consent to the disclosure of
    such information for this purpose.

    Tax district office/computer centre ................................................ Tax ref No. ..............................................

5     *The reason for the delay in submitting this notification is (see Note 1 on tear-off portion)



Signature of employer ...................................................................................... Date ........................................

Position in firm (eg director, company secretary) .................................................................................................

*Delete if inapplicable

RP 1

**List of employees who are expected to become redundant and be entitled to statutory redundancy payments.**

**IMPORTANT**  MEN and WOMEN should be listed separately

| | Name and Initials of employee (state whether Mr Mrs or Miss) (See Note (a)) 1 | Occupation 2 | National insurance number 3 | Date of birth 4 | Date employment began (See Note (b)) 5 | Date of termination 6 | Amount of week's pay (See Note (c)) 7 | FOR OFFICIAL USE 8 |
|---|---|---|---|---|---|---|---|---|
| 1 | | | | | | | £ | |
| 2 | | | | | | | | |
| 3 | | | | | | | | |
| 4 | | | | | | | | |
| 5 | | | | | | | | |
| 6 | | | | | | | | |
| 7 | | | | | | | | |
| 8 | | | | | | | | |
| 9 | | | | | | | | |
| 10 | | | | | | | | |
| 11 | | | | | | | | |
| 12 | | | | | | | | |
| 13 | | | | | | | | |
| 14 | | | | | | | | |
| 15 | | | | | | | | |

**NOTES**  (a) Entries in columns 1 to 7 may be carbon copied to form RP 2.  (b) The date sought is that of the employee's first engagement by the dismissing employer or by a previous owner of the business or, if the dismissing employer is a company, by a previous company associated with the present company at the time of his transfer between the companies.

(c) The amount of a week's pay should be calculated according to the rules explained in Appendix D of the booklet "The Redundancy Payments Scheme". If it is not possible at this stage to calculate the amount in any case, please leave the relevant col 7 space blank and forward the information as soon as possible. Please seek early advice, from the office shown above Item 1 overleaf, about calculations involving piece workers or shift or rota workers.

**FOR OFFICIAL USE**

| | INITIALS | DATE | | INITIALS | DATE |
|---|---|---|---|---|---|
| RP 1 received | | | RP 2/3 to RFO | | |
| RP 5 sent | | | RP 2/3 to RFO | | |
| RP 2/3 received | | | RP 2/3 to RFO | | |
| RP 2/3 received | | | RP 2/3 to RFO | | |
| RP 2/3 received | | | RP 2/3 to RFO | | |
| RP 2/3 received | | | RP 2/3 to RFO | | |
| RP 2/3 received | | | RP 2/3 to RFO | | |
| RP 2/3 received | | | RP 2/3 to RFO | | |

1852 2/76 GBR LTD

355

| MLH. No. | Office of issue |
|----------|-----------------|

DEPARTMENT OF EMPLOYMENT

### REDUNDANCY PAYMENTS ACT 1965

# APPLICATION TO THE SECRETARY OF STATE FOR EMPLOYMENT FOR A PAYMENT

This form should be completed only if you have been dismissed because of redundancy and your employer has told you that he is unable to make a payment to you or to make the full payment, or he cannot be traced or is deceased.

If he disputes your right to a redundancy payment or has failed to give you a definite answer to a written application for payment, you should not complete this form but seek advice from your local employment exchange.

**NOTE :** You will not be entitled to a payment if—

You are under 20 or over 65 years of age (60 for women).

You have less than 104 weeks continuous employment with your employer after the week in which you attained the age of 18.

You worked less than 21 hours a week.

**WARNING**

Legal proceedings may be taken against you if you knowingly make a false statement on this form.

I (full name) (state whether Mr/Mrs/Miss) ...................................................................................

of (full address) .......................................................................................................................

.................................................................................................................................................

National Insurance No. ...................................... Income Tax Ref No. .......................................
apply to the Secretary of State for Employment for a payment under Section 32 of the Redundancy Payments Act 1965.

I made a written application to my employer for a redundancy payment on .....................................

.................................................................................

I have been unable to obtain full redundancy payment because .....................................................

.................................................................................................................................................

**RP 21**

Continued overleaf

The reason for my dismissal was ............................................................................................................................................

............................................................................................................................................................................................

The following details are given to help in calculating the amount which may be due to me.

Name of employer ...........................................................................................................................................

Employer's address ..........................................................................................................................................

............................................................................................................................................................................................

Place of employment if different from above ............................................................................................................

Employer's telephone number ...........................................................................................

Date my employment began ..............................................................................................................................

Date my employment ended ..............................................................................................................................

Dates of any breaks in this period ....................................................................................................................

Date of my birth ..............................................................................................................................................

Wages (if not in receipt of regular agreed wages give details of any special arrangements, *eg.* piece work,

bonuses, etc) ..................................................................................................................................................

............................................................................................................................................................................................

............................................................................................................................................................................................

I hereby declare that the information I have given in this application is correct and may be used in any communication with the employer named (or his representatives). I understand that in order to establish my right to any redundancy payment it may be necessary for you to refer to information given to the Inland Revenue and other government departments as to my remuneration and period of service and I hereby give my consent to the disclosure of such information for this purpose only.

Date.................................................................          Signature....................................................

To be completed if in new employment.

Name and address of employer ................................................................................................................

............................................................................................................................................................................................

**RP 21**                    382 893987 110M 12/72 HGW 752

357

Department of Employment
REDUNDANCY PAYMENTS ACT 1965

## EMPLOYER'S CALCULATION OF REDUNDANCY PAYMENT AND EMPLOYEE'S RECEIPT

**NOTES**
1. *If redundancy payment is being reduced because of pension DO NOT USE THIS FORM. Please ask the office which issued this form for the pensions form RP 3(Pen).*
2. *The calculation of payments not arising under the Redundancy Payments Act should be excluded from this form.*

Name of employer ................................................................................................................................

...........................................................................................................................................................

...........................................................................................................................................................

Employee's surname .................................................................................... Initials ..............................

Employee's address ............................................................................................................................

Employee's date of birth .......................................................................................

Employee's employment began on ................................ and terminated during the week ending Saturday ............... 19......

Non-reckonable periods (employment abroad, on strike, service with the Armed Forces—*see guidance in the booklet "The Redundancy Payments Scheme"*)

from.......................... to ...................... reason .........................................................................................

---

### PART I — CALCULATION OF REDUNDANCY PAYMENT
(See guidance in the booklet "The Redundancy Payments Scheme")

1   Total reckonable employment (*exclude employment before age 18. If more than 20 years' employment,*
enter "20") .................... years

2   Number of weeks' pay due
.................... weeks

3   Amount of a week's pay (*see booklet*)
   (1) before applying £80 limit  £.........................................
   (2) after applying £80 limit
£..............................................

4   Amount of redundancy payment (item 2 x item 3(2))
£..............................................
   **NOTE:-** If the employee was aged at least 64 years and one month (man)/59 years and
one month (woman) on the Saturday in the week in which the employment terminated,
items 5, 6 and 7 below should be completed.

5   Number of complete months by which employee's age exceeds 64 (man)/59 (woman)
on the Saturday in the week in which the employment terminated
........................................months

   Amount by which redundancy payment is to be reduced (item 4 x item 5)
£..............................................
               12

7   Adjusted amount of redundancy payment (item 4 minus item 6)
£..............................................

---

### PART II — EMPLOYEE'S RECEIPT FOR REDUNDANCY PAYMENT

**Warning—Do not sign this receipt until you have actually received the full amount stated or you may be penalised.**

I acknowledge that the redundancy payment amounting to £.........................................

was made to me on (date)................................................ Signature ..............................................

Date................................................

---

**NOTE:** If more than one copy of this form is prepared for payment, the top copy receipted by the employee
should accompany the claim for rebate on form RP2

**RP 3**

TS&Co.Ltd. 52-9358 11/75

**Department of Employment**

REDUNDANCY PAYMENTS ACT 1965

## NOTIFICATION OF INTENTION TO REDUCE A REDUNDANCY PAYMENT ON ACCOUNT OF PENSION OR LUMP SUM SUPERANNUATION PAYMENT

**Notes**   *1*  *Before rebate can be approved in respect of any redundancy payment reduced on account of pension, the Secretary of State must be satisfied that the pension scheme satisfies the provisions of the Redundancy Payments Pensions Regulations 1965 — see leaflet RPL 1, paragraph 2.*

      *2*  *Please complete and forward this form according to the scheme which is relevant (see part 1):—*

      *SCHEME 1 — with forms RP2 and RP3 (Pen) when claiming rebate*

      *SCHEMES 2 and 3 — with form RP1 when giving advance notice of the expected redundancies*

      *SCHEME 4 — (a)  with forms RP2 and RP3 (Pen) if the scheme has not altered since the reduction of redundancy payments on account of pension payments was last approved by the Department of Employment, OR*

               *(b)  to the Department of Employment at the address shown on form RP2, at least 21 days BEFORE the date of the first expected redundancy if the reduction of redundancy has not been previously approved by this Department or the rules have been altered since approval was last given.*

      *3*  *If Scheme 3 or 4 is applicable, PART 11A and B overleaf should be completed and certified by the employer and responsible paying authority respectively*

## PART 1 — STATEMENT BY EMPLOYER OF DETAILS OF SCHEME UNDER WHICH THE PENSION AND/OR LUMP SUM IS PAYABLE

**\* Scheme 1**  Superannuation benefits under the scheme consist of lump sums only. Payment has been made in full to the redundant employee(s) and receipt(s) is/are attached

**\* Scheme 2**  Prior to April 1975, the scheme was contracted out of the National Insurance Graduated Pension Scheme. The number of the certificate of non-participation was...................................................................................... and since April 1975 there has been no change affecting either the basis on which the scheme was established or the basis on which pensions are awarded and paid

**\* Scheme 3**  Benefits are secured by a contract of assurance of annuity contract with *(please insert name and address of insurance company, friendly society or provident society whose representative has signed the certificate of assurance at PART 11B):-*

**\* Scheme 4**  Benefits are secured under an irrevocable trust

         \*(a)  The trust deed and rules of the scheme have not been altered since a copy of each was sent to the

             Department of Employment on ................................................................................................................... OR

         \*(b)  A copy of the trust deed and of the rules of the scheme are enclosed (copy of the trust deed(s) and rules must be certified as a true copy by a responsible person eg solicitor, accountant, etc)

             AND

         (c)  A copy of the latest accounts and balance sheet of the Pension Fund is enclosed.

Signature of employer .......................................................................................................... Date ...........................................

Status of signatory ......................................................................................................................................................................

*\* Please delete inappropriate items*

**RP 9**

*Please continue overleaf*

**PART II – CERTIFICATE OF ASSURANCE OF PENSION BENEFITS** *(Complete ONLY in respect of Scheme 3 or 4)*

**A   To be completed by the employer**

I   Name of superannuation scheme ...........................................................................................................................................................................

...........................................................................................................................................................................

2   Name and address of responsible paying authority *(ie the insurance company, friendly society or provident society or, where there is an irrevocable trust, the trustees):—*

...........................................................................................................................................................................

...........................................................................................................................................................................

3   Particulars of employees affected:

| Surname and initials (1) | National Insurance No (2) | Annual value of pension £ (3) | Date payable (4) | Lump sum £ (5) | Date payable (6) |
|---|---|---|---|---|---|
| | | | | | |
| | | | | | |
| | | | | | |
| | | | | | |
| | | | | | |
| | | | | | |
| | | | | | |
| | | | | | |

4   Declaration by or on behalf of employer

I declare that the particulars in columns (3)–(6) of item 3 above have been notified to the employees concerned

Signature of employer .........................................................................................................................................................

Status of signatory .........................................................................................................................................................

**B   To be completed by the responsible paying authority**

This is to certify that the person(s) named in column (I) of item 3 of Part IIA is/are absolutely and indefeasibly entitled to the benefits shown in columns (3) and/or (5) under or by virtue of the recognised superannuation scheme named at item I (or would be so entitled but for their being capable, in accordance with the rules of that scheme, of being terminated or suspended for any cause prescribed under the Redundancy Payments Pensions Regulations 1965) and that the benefits are secured in such a manner and such provision is made for their payment as to make the person(s) named at item 3 assured of them for the purpose of the said Regulations.

Signed for and on behalf of the responsible paying authority .........................................................................................................................

Status of signatory ................................................................................................. Date .......................................................

NOTE – *If the responsible paying authority is not an insurance company or a provident or friendly society, but benefits are secured by contract of assurance or annuity contract, the name and address of the insurance company or society with which that contract is made should be entered here.*

...........................................................................................................................................................................

925 411799 25M 2/76 HGW 752

SEX DISCRIMINATION ACT 1975

## THE QUESTIONS PROCEDURE

CONTENTS

A complainant should obtain TWO copies of this booklet, one to send to the respondent and the other to keep.
Before completing the questionnaire or the reply form (as appropriate), the complainant and the respondent should read Part I of the guidance and (again as appropriate) Part II or III.

Issued by    The Home Office and
            The Department of Employment

1/76

## SEX DISCRIMINATION ACT 1975 –
## GUIDANCE ON THE QUESTIONS PROCEDURE

### PART I – INTRODUCTION

1 The purpose of this guidance is to explain the questions procedure under section 74 of the Sex Discrimination Act 1975*. The procedure is intended to help a person (referred to in this guidance as the **complainant**) who thinks she (or he) has been discriminated against by another (the **respondent**) to obtain information from that person about the treatment in question in order to –
(a)   decide whether or not to bring legal proceedings, and
(b)   if proceedings are brought, to present her complaint in the most effective way.

A questionnaire has been devised which the complainant can send to the respondent and there is also a matching reply form for use by the respondent (both are included in this booklet). The questionnaire and the reply form have been designed to assist the complainant and respondent to identify information which is relevant to the complaint. It is not, however, obligatory for the questionnaire or the reply form to be used: the exchange of questions and replies may be conducted, for example, by letter.

2 This guidance is intended to assist both the complainant and the respondent. Guidance for the complainant on the preparation of the questionnaire is set out in Part II; and guidance for the respondent on the use of the reply form is set out in Part III. The main provisions of the Sex Discrimination Act are referred to in the appendix to this guidance. Further information about the Act will be found in the various leaflets published by the Equal Opportunities Commission and also in the detailed **Guide to the Sex Discrimination Act 1975**. The leaflets and the **Guide** may be obtained, free of charge, from the Equal Opportunities Commission at –

Overseas House
Quay Street
Manchester M3 3HN
Telephone: 061–833 9244

The **Guide** and the EOC's leaflets on the employment provisions of the Act may also be obtained, free of charge, from any employment office or jobcentre of the Employment Service Agency or from any unemployment benefit office of the Department of Employment. The EOC's leaflets may also be obtained from Citizens Advice Bureaux.

**How the questions procedure can benefit both parties**
3 The procedure can benefit both the complainant and the respondent in the following ways:–
  (1)  If the respondent's answers satisfy the complainant that the treatment was not unlawful discrimination, there will be no need for legal proceedings.

---

\* *The prescribed forms, time limits for serving questions and manner of service of questions and replies under section 74 are specified in The Sex Discrimination (Questions and Replies) Order 1975 (SI 1975 No. 2048).*

---

  (2)  Even if the respondent's answers do not satisfy the complainant, they should help to identify what is agreed and what is in dispute between the parties. For example, the answers should reveal whether the parties disagree on the facts of the case, or, if they agree on the facts, whether they disagree on how the Act applies. In some cases, this may lead to a settlement of the grievance, again making legal proceedings unnecessary.
  (3)  If it turns out that the complainant institutes proceedings against the respondent, the proceedings should be that much simpler because the matters in dispute will have been identified in advance.

**What happens if the respondent does not reply or replies evasively**
4 The respondent cannot be compelled to reply to the complainant's questions. However, if the respondent deliberately, and without reasonable excuse, does not reply within a reasonable period, or replies in an evasive or ambiguous way, his position may be adversely affected should the complainant bring proceedings against him. The respondent's attention is drawn to these pos 'e consequences in the note at the end of the questionnaire.

**Period within which questionnaire must be served on the respondent**
5 There are different time limits within which a questionnaire must be served in order to be admissible under the questions procedure in any ensuing legal proceedings. Which time limit applies depends on whether the complaint would be under the employment, training and related provisions of the Act (in which case the proceedings would be before an industrial tribunal) or whether it would be under the education, goods, facilities and services or premises provisions (in which case proceedings would be before a county court or, in Scotland, a sheriff court).

**Industrial tribunal cases**
6 In order to be admissible under the questions procedure in any ensuing industrial tribunal proceedings, the complainant's questionnaire must be served on the respondent either:
  (a)  before a complaint about the treatment concern 's made to an industrial tribunal, but not more than 3 months after the treatment in question; or
  (b)  if a complaint has already been made to a tribunal, within 21 days beginning when the complaint was received by the tribunal.

However, where the complainant has made a complaint to a tribunal and the period of 21 days has expired, a questionnaire may still be served provided the leave of the tribunal is obtained. This may be done by sending to the Secretary of the Tribunals a written application, which must state the names of the complainant and the respondent and set out the grounds of the application. However, every effort should be made to serve the questionnaire within the period of 21 days as the leave of the tribunal to serve the questionnaire after the expiry of that period will not necessarily be obtained.

**Court cases**
7 In order to be admissible under the questions procedure in any ensuing county or sheriff court proceedings, the complainant's questionnaire must be served on the respondent before proceedings in respect of the treatment concerned

are brought, but not more than 6 months after the treatment*. However, where proceedings have been brought, a questionnaire may still be served provided the leave of the court has been obtained. In the case of county court proceedings, this may be done by obtaining form Ex 23 from the county court office, and completing it and sending it to the Registrar and the respondent, or by applying to the Registrar at the pre-trial review. In the case of sheriff court proceedings, this may be done by making an application to a sheriff.

## PART II—GUIDANCE FOR THE COMPLAINANT
### NOTES ON PREPARING THE QUESTIONNAIRE
8 Before filling in the questionnaire, you are advised to prepare what you want to say on a separate piece of paper. If you have insufficient room on the questionnaire for what you want to say, you should continue on an additional piece of paper, which should be sent with the questionnaire to the respondent.

**Paragraph 2**
9 You should give, in the space provided in paragraph 2, as much relevant factual information as you can about the treatment you think may have been unlawful discrimination, and about the circumstances leading up to that treatment. You should also give the date, and if possible and if relevant, the place and approximate time of the treatment. You should bear in mind that in paragraph 4 of the questionnaire you will be asking the respondent whether he agrees with what you say in paragraph 2.

**Paragraph 3**
10 In paragraph 3 you are telling the respondent that you think the treatment you have described in paragraph 2 may have been unlawful discrimination by him against you. It will help to identify whether there are any legal issues between you and the respondent if you explain in the space provided why you think the treatment may have been unlawful discrimination. However, you do not have to complete paragraph 3; if you do not wish or are unable to do so, you should delete the word "because". If you wish to complete the paragraph, but feel you need more information about the Sex Discrimination Act before doing so, you should look to the appendix to this guidance.

11 If you decide to complete paragraph 3, you may find it useful to indicate-
  (a) what kind of discrimination you think the treatment
       may have been ie whether it was
       direct sex discrimination,
       indirect sex discrimination,
       direct discrimination against a married person,
       indirect discrimination against a married
       person,or
       victimisation.
(For further information about the different kinds of discrimination see paragraph 1 of the appendix)

*Where the respondent is a body in charge of a public sector educational establishment, the six month period begins when the complaint has been referred to the appropriate Education Minister and 2 months have elapsed or, if this is earlier, the Minister has informed the complainant that he requires no more time to consider the matter.*

(b) which provision of the Act you think may make unlawful the kind of discrimination you think you may have suffered. (For an indication of the provisions of the Act which make the various kinds of discrimination unlawful, see paragraph 2 of the appendix.)

**Paragraph 6**
12 You should insert here any other question which you think may help you to obtain relevant information.(For example, if you think you have been discriminated against by having been refused a job, you may want to know what were the qualifications of the person who did get the job and why that person got the job.)

13 Paragraph 5 contains questions which are especially important if you think you may have suffered direct sex discrimination, or direct discrimination against a married person,because they ask the respondent whether your sex or marital status had anything to do with your treatment. Paragraph 5 does not, however, ask specific questions relating to indirect sex discrimination,indirect discrimination against a married person or victimisation. If you think you may have suffered indirect sex discrimination (or indirect discrimination against a married person) you may find it helpful to include the following question in the space provided in paragraph 6:
  "Was the reason for my treatment the fact that I could not comply with a condition or requirement which is applied equally to men and women (married and unmarried persons)?
  If so —
    (a) what was the condition or requirement?
    (b) why was it applied?"

14 If you think you may have been victimised you may find it helpful to include the following question in the space provided in paragraph 6:
  "Was the reason for my treatment the fact that I had done, or intended to do,or that you suspected I had done or intended to do,any of the following:
    (a) brought proceedings under the Sex Discrimination Act or the Equal Pay Act; or
    (b) gave evidence or information in connection with proceedings under either Act; or
    (c) did something else under or by reference to either Act; or
    (d) made an allegation that someone acted unlawfully under either Act?"

**Signature**
15 The questionnaire must be signed and dated. If it is to be signed on behalf of (rather than by) the complainant, the person signing should —
    (a) describe himself (eg "solicitor acting for (name of complainant))", and
    (b) give his business (or home, if appropriate) address.

## WHAT PAPERS TO SERVE ON THE PERSON TO BE QUESTIONED
16 You should send the person to be questioned the whole of this document (ie the guidance, the questionnaire and the reply forms), with the questionnaire completed by you. You are strongly advised to retain, and keep in a safe place, a copy of the completed questionnaire (and you might also find it useful to retain a copy of the guidance and the uncompleted reply form).

## HOW TO SERVE THE PAPERS
17 You can either deliver the papers in person or send them by post. If you decide to send them by post you are advised to use the recorded delivery service, so that, if necessary, you can produce evidence that they were delivered.

## WHERE TO SEND THE PAPERS
18 You can send the papers to the person to be questioned at his usual or last known residence or place of business. If you know he is acting through a solicitor you should send them to him at his solicitor's address. If you wish to question a limited company or other corporate body or a trade union or employers' association, you should send the papers to the secretary or clerk at the registered or principal office of the company, etc. You should be able to find out where its registered or principal office is by enquiring at a public library. If you are unable to do so, however, you will have to send the papers to the place where you think it is most likely they will reach the secretary or clerk (eg at, or c/o, the company's local office). It is your responsibility, however, to see that the secretary or clerk receives the papers.

## USE OF THE QUESTIONS AND REPLIES IN INDUSTRIAL TRIBUNAL PROCEEDINGS
19 If you decide to make (or already have made) a complaint to an industrial tribunal about the treatment concerned and if you intend to use your questions and the reply (if any) as evidence in the proceedings, you are advised to send copies of your questions and any reply to the Secretary of the Tribunals before the date of the hearing. This should be done as soon as the documents are available; if they are available at the time you submit your complaint to a tribunal, you should send the copies with your complaint to the Secretary of the Tribunals.

## PART III – GUIDANCE FOR THE RESPONDENT

### NOTES ON COMPLETING THE REPLY FORM
20 Before completing the reply form, you are advised to prepare what you want to say on a separate piece of paper. If you have insufficient room on the reply form for what you want to say, you should continue on an additional piece of paper, which should be attached to the reply form sent to the complainant.

### Paragraph 2
21 Here you are answering the question in paragraph 4 of the questionnaire. If you **agree** that the complainant's statement in paragraph 2 of the questionnaire is an accurate **description** of what happened, you should delete the second sentence.
22 If you **disagree** in any way that the statement is an accurate description of what happened, you should explain in the space provided in what respects you disagree, or your version of what happened, or both.

### Paragraph 3
23 Here you are answering the question in paragraph 5 of the questionnaire. If, in answer to paragraph 4 of the questionnaire, you have agreed with the complainant's description of her treatment, you will be answering paragraph 5 on the basis of the facts in her description. If, however, you have disagreed with that description, you should answer paragraph 5 on the basis of your version of the facts. To answer paragraph 5, you are advised to look at the appendix to this guidance and also the relevant parts of the **Guide to the Sex Discrimination Act 1975.** You need to know:—
   (a) how the Act defines discrimination — see paragraph 1 of the appendix;
   (b) in what situations the Act makes discrimination unlawful — see paragraph 2 of the appendix; and
   (c) what exceptions the Act provides — see paragraph 3 of the appendix.

24 If you think that an exception (eg the exception for employment where a person's sex is a genuine occupational qualification) applies to the treatment described in paragraph 2 of the complainant's questionnaire, you should mention this in paragraph 3a of the reply form and explain why you think the exception applies.

### Signature
25 The reply form should be signed and dated. If it is to be signed on behalf of (rather than by) the respondent, the person signing should —
   (a) describe himself (eg "solicitor acting for (name of respondent)" or "personnel manager of (name of firm)"), and
   (b) give his business (or home, if appropriate) address.

### SERVING THE REPLY FORM ON THE COMPLAINANT
26 If you wish to reply to the questionnaire you are strongly advised to do so without delay. **You should retain, and keep in a safe place, the questionnaire sent to you and a copy of your reply.**

27 You can serve the reply either by delivering it in person to the complainant or by sending it by post. If you decide to send it by post you are advised to use the recorded delivery service, so that, if necessary, you can produce evidence that it was delivered.

28 You should send the reply form to the address indicated in paragraph 7 of the complainant's questionnaire.

# THE SEX DISCRIMINATION ACT 1975 SECTION 74 (1)(a)

## QUESTIONNAIRE OF PERSON AGGRIEVED (THE COMPLAINANT)

Name of person to be
questioned (the
respondent )

To .................................................................................................................................................

Address

of ..................................................................................................................................................

.......................................................................................................................................................

Name of complainant

1. I ..........................................................................................................................................

Address

of .................................................................................................................................................

..........................................................................................................................................................
consider that you may have discriminated against me contrary to the Sex
Discrimination Act 1975.

Give date, approximate
time, place and factual
description of the treat-
ment received and of
the circumstances
leading up to the treat-
ment (see paragraph 9
of the guidance)

2. On

Complete if you wish
to give reasons,
otherwise delete the
word "because" (see
paragraphs 10 and 11
of the guidance)

3. I consider that this treatment may have been unlawful because

SD 74(a)

365

This is the first of
your questions to the
respondent. You are
advised not to alter it

4. Do you agree that the statement in paragraph 2 is an accurate description of what happened? If not in what respect do you disagree or what is your version of what happened?

This is the second of
your questions to the
respondent. You are
advised not to alter it

5. Do you accept that your treatment of me was unlawful discrimination by you against me?
   If not
   
   a   why not?
   
   b   for what reason did I receive the treatment accorded to me?
   
   c   how far did my sex or marital status affect your treatment of me?

Enter here any other
questions you wish to
ask (see paragraphs
12–14 of the guidance)

6.

* Delete as appropriate
If you delete the first
alternative, insert the
address to which you
want the reply to be
sent

7. My address for any reply you may wish to give to the questions raised above is
   * that set out in paragraph I above /the following address

See paragraph 15
of the guidance

Signature of complainant ........................................................................................................................

Date ........................................................................

NB *By virtue of section 74 of the Act, this questionnaire and any reply are (subject to the provisions of the section) admissible in proceedings under the Act and a court or tribunal may draw any such inference as is just and equitable from a failure without reasonable excuse to reply within a reasonable period, or from an evasive or equivocal reply, including an inference that the person questioned has discriminated unlawfully.*

# THE SEX DISCRIMINATION ACT 1975 SECTION 74 (1)(b)

## REPLY BY RESPONDENT

| | |
|---|---|
| Name of complainant | To ............................................................................................................................. |
| Address | of ............................................................................................................................. |
| | ............................................................................................................................. |
| Name of respondent | 1.   I ........................................................................................................................... |
| Address | of ........................................................................................................................ |
| | ............................................................................................................................. |
| Complete as appropriate | hereby acknowledge receipt   of the questionnaire signed by you and dated |
| | ....................................... which was served on me on (date) ..................................... |
| *Delete as appropriate | 2.   I *agree/disagree that the statement in paragraph 2 of the questionnaire is an accurate description of what happened. |
| If you agree that the statement in paragraph 2 of the questionnaire is accurate, delete this sentence. If you disagree complete this sentence (see paragraphs 21 and 22 of the guidance) | I disagree with the statement in paragraph 2 of the questionnaire in that |
| *Delete as appropriate | 3.   I *accept/dispute that my treatment of you was unlawful discrimination by me against you. |
| If you accept the complainant's assertion of unlawful discrimination in paragraph 3 of the questionnaire delete the sentences at a, b and c. Unless completed a sentence should be deleted (see paragraphs 23 and 24 of the guidance) | a   My reasons for so disputing are |

SD 74(b)

1/76

367

b   The reason why you received the treatment accorded to you is

c   Your sex or marital status affected my treatment of you to the following extent:—

**Replies to questions in
paragraph 6 of the
questionnaire should be
entered here**

4.

**Delete the whole of
this sentence if you
have answered all the
questions in the
questionnaire. If you
have not answered all
the questions, delete
"unable" or "unwilling"
as appropriate and
give your reasons for
not answering.**

5.   I have deleted (in whole or in part) the paragraph(s) numbered .......................................
above, since I am   unable/unwilling to reply to the relevant questions of the
questionnaire for the following reasons:—

**See paragraph 25 of
the guidance**

Signature of respondent ...........................................................................................................................

Date ............................................................................................

# THE SEX DISCRIMINATION ACT 1975 SECTION 74 (1)(b)

## REPLY BY RESPONDENT

| | |
|---|---|
| Name of complainant | To ................................................................................................ |
| Address | of ................................................................................................ |
| | ................................................................................................ |
| Name of respondent | 1.  I ................................................................................................ |
| Address | of ................................................................................................ |
| | ................................................................................................ |
| Complete as appropriate | hereby acknowledge receipt of the questionnaire signed by you and dated |
| | ...................................... which was served on me on (date) ...................................... |
| *Delete as appropriate | 2.  I *agree/disagree that the statement in paragraph 2 of the questionnaire is an accurate description of what happened. |
| If you agree that the statement in paragraph 2 of the questionnaire is accurate, delete this sentence. If you disagree complete this sentence (see paragraphs 21 and 22 of the guidance) | I disagree with the statement in paragraph 2 of the questionnaire in that |
| *Delete as appropriate | 3.  I *accept/dispute that my treatment of you was unlawful discrimination by me against you. |
| If you accept the complainant's assertion of unlawful discrimination in paragraph 3 of the questionnaire delete the sentences at a, b and c. Unless completed a sentence should be deleted (see paragraphs 23 and 24 of the guidance) | a    My reasons for so disputing are |

**SD 74(b)**

1/76

b   The reason why you received the treatment accorded to you is

c   Your sex or marital status affected my treatment of you to the following extent:—

**Replies to questions in paragraph 6 of the questionnaire should be entered here**

4.

**Delete the whole of this sentence if you have answered all the questions in the questionnaire. If you have not answered all the questions, delete "unable" or "unwilling" as appropriate and give your reasons for not answering.**

5.   I have deleted (in whole or in part) the paragraph(s) numbered ......................................
above, since I am   **unable/unwilling** to reply to the relevant questions of the
questionnaire for the following reasons:—

**See paragraph 25 of the guidance**

Signature of respondent ...........................................................................................................

Date ..............................................................................

## APPENDIX

### NOTES ON THE SCOPE OF THE SEX DISCRIMINATION ACT 1975

#### Definitions of discrimination

1 The different kinds of discrimination covered by the Act are summarised below (the references in the margin are to the relevant paragraphs in the **Guide to the Sex Discrimination Act 1975**). Some of the explanations have been written in terms of discrimination against a woman, but the Act applies equally to discrimination against men.

2.4 to 2.8    **Direct sex discrimination** arises where a woman is treated less favourably than a man is (or would be) treated **because of her sex.**

**Indirect sex discrimination** arises where a woman is treated unfavourably because she cannot comply with a condition or requirement which

(a) is (or would be) applied to men and women equally, **and**

(b) is such that the proportion of women who can comply with it is considerably smaller than the proportion of men who can comply with it, **and**

(c) is to the detriment of the woman in question because she cannot comply with it, **and**

(d) is such that the person applying it cannot show that it is justifiable regardless of the sex of the person to whom it is applied.

2.9 to 2.12    **Direct discrimination against married persons in the employment field** arises where a married person is treated, in a situation covered by the employment provisions of the Act (ie those summarised under Group A in the table on the next page), less favourably than an unmarried person of the same sex is (or would be) treated **because she or he is married.**

**Indirect discrimination against married persons in the employment field** arises where a married person is treated, in a situation covered by the employment provisions of the Act, unfavourably because she or he cannot comply with a condition or requirement which

(a) is (or would be) applied to married and unmarried persons equally, **and**

(b) is such that the proportion of married persons who can comply with it is considerably smaller than the proportion of unmarried persons of the same sex who can comply with it, **and**

(c) is to the detriment of the unmarried person in question because she or he cannot comply with it, **and**

(d) is such that the person applying it cannot show it to be justifiable irrespective of the marital status of the person to whom it is applied.

2.13 and 2.14    **Victimisation** arises where a person is treated less favourably than other persons (of either sex) are (or would be) treated because that person has done (or intends to do or is suspected of having done or intending to do) any of the following:—

(a) brought proceedings under the Act or the Equal Pay Act; or

(b) given evidence or information in connection with proceedings brought under either Act; or

(c) done anything else by reference to either Act (eg given information to the Equal Opportunities Commission); or

(d) made an allegation that someone acted unlawfully under either Act.

Victimisation does **not**, however, occur where the reason for the less favourable treatment is an allegation which was false and not made in good faith.

#### Unlawful discrimination

2 The provisions of the Act which make discrimination unlawful are indicated in the table on the next page. Those in Group A are the employment provisions, for the purposes of which discrimination means direct sex discrimination, indirect sex discrimination, direct discrimination against married persons, indirect discrimination against married persons, and victimisation. Complaints about discrimination which is unlawful under these provisions must be made to an industrial tribunal. For detailed information about these provisions see chapter 3 of the Guide. For the purposes of the provisions in Group B, discrimination means direct sex discrimination, indirect sex discrimination and victimisation, but not direct or indirect discrimination against married persons. Complaints about discrimination which is unlawful under these provisions must be made to a county court or, in Scotland, a sheriff court. For detailed information about these provisions see chapters 4 and 5 of the **Guide.**

#### Exceptions

3 Details of exceptions to the requirements of the Act not to discriminate may be found in the **Guide.** The exceptions applying only to the employment field are described in chapter 3; those applying only to the educational field, in chapter 4; and those applying only to the provision of goods, facilities and services and premises, in chapter 5. General exceptions are described in chapter 7.

| | Section of Act | Paragraphs of Guide |
|---|---|---|
| **GROUP A** | | |
| Discrimination by employers of six or more employees in recruitment and treatment of employees | 6 | 3.3–3.18 |
| Discrimination against contract workers | 9 | 3.19 |
| Discrimination against partners | 11 | 3.20 |
| Discrimination by trade unions, employers' associations etc | 12 | 3.21, 3.22 |
| Discrimination by bodies which confer qualifications or authorisations needed for particular kinds of jobs | 13 | 3.23–3.25 |
| Discrimination in the provision of training by industrial training boards, the Manpower Services Commission, the Employment Service Agency, the Training Services Agency and certain other vocational training bodies | 14 | 3.27, 3.28 |
| Discrimination by employment agencies | 15 | 3.29–3.31 |
| Discrimination by the Manpower Services Commission, the Employment Service Agency and the Training Services Agency other than in vocational training or employment agency services | 16 | 3.32 |
| **GROUP B** | | |
| Discrimination by bodies in charge of educational establishments | 22 | 4.2–4.6, 4.11–4.15 |
| Discrimination (other than that covered by section 22) by local education authorities | 23 | 4.7, 4.8, 4.14, 4.15 |
| Discrimination in the provision of goods, facilities or services to the public or a section of the public | 29 | 5.2–5.9, 5.13–5.16 |
| Discrimination in the disposal of premises | 30 | 5.10–5.16 |
| Discrimination by landlords against prospective assignees or sublessees | 31 | 5.17 |

# COMPLAINT OF UNLAWFUL DISCRIMINATION

(IF YOU ARE COMPLAINING ON BEHALF OF ANOTHER PERSON, PLEASE ANSWER THE QUESTIONS AS IF YOU WERE THAT PERSON)

**ALL COMPLAINTS**

1. What is your surname or family name? ..................................................................................

2. What are your other names? .............................................. Mr./Mrs./Miss ......................

3. Address: ...................................................................................................................................

   ...................................................................................................................................

4. If you have a telephone at home, what is the number? ..................................................

5. Age:...................   6. In which country were you born? ..................................................

7. If not born in Britain, when did you come to live here? ..................................................

**EMPLOYMENT COMPLAINTS**—*please answer these questions ONLY if your complaint is about EMPLOYMENT*

1. Whom are you complaining about?

   Name: ............................................................ Official position (if known):............ ............

   Address (if known) .......................................................................................................

   .......................................................................................................

2. If the answer to 1 is not the employer himself, who is the employer?..................................

   Name: .......................................................................................................

   Address: .......................................................................................................

   .......................................................................................................

3. State nature of employer's business or industry:..................................................................

4. When did the alleged discrimination occur? ..................................................................

5. If you were refused employment, for what job or post did you apply? ..................................

6. If you are a member of a trade union, give its name?..........................................................

7. Please give full details of your complaint over the page

**OTHER COMPLAINTS**—*to be completed for cases OTHER THAN EMPLOYMENT*

1. Name and address of person or body against whom complaint is made:..................................

   .......................................................................................................

   .......................................................................................................

2. Date and time of alleged discrimination: ..................................................................

3. Place where discrimination is alleged to have taken place (give full postal address):

   .......................................................................................................

   .......................................................................................................

4. Give details of complaint over the page.

# HEALTH AND SAFETY EXECUTIVE
## Health and Safety at Work etc. Act 1974, Sections 21, 23, and 24

# IMPROVEMENT NOTICE

Serial No. I

| | |
|---|---|
| Name and address (See Section 46) | To .......................................................... |
| (a) Delete as necessary | (a) Trading as ................................................ |
| (b) Inspector's full name | I (b) ........................................................ |
| (c) Inspector's official designation | one of (c) ................................................... |
| (d) Official address | of (d) ....................................... Tel no. ........ |

hereby give you notice that at

| | |
|---|---|
| (e) Location of premises or place and activity | (e) ....................................................... |

you, as (a) an employee/a self employed person/a person wholly or partly in control of the premises,

(f) ...........................................................

| | |
|---|---|
| (f) Other specified capacity | (a) ........ are contravening/have contravened in circumstances that make it likely that the contravention will continue or be repeated |

| | |
|---|---|
| (g) Provisions contravened | (g) ....................................................... |

The reasons for my said opinion are:—

..............................................................

..............................................................

and I hereby require you to remedy the said contraventions or, as the case may be, the matters occasioning them by

..............................................................

..............................................................

| | |
|---|---|
| (h) Date | (h) ....... in the manner stated in the attached schedule which forms part of the notice. |

Signature .................... Date ....................

Being an inspector appointed by an instrument in writing made pursuant to Section 19 of the said Act and entitled to issue this notice.

(a) An improvement notice is also being served on

..............................................................

of ...........................................................
related to the matters contained in this notice.

LP 1

## NOTES

1 Failure to comply with an Improvement Notice is an offence as provided by Section 33 of this Act and renders the offender liable to a fine not exceeding £400 on summary conviction or to an unlimited fine on conviction on indictment and a further fine of not exceeding £50 per day if the offence is continued.

2 An inspector has power to withdraw a notice or to extend the period specified in the notice, before the end of the period specified in it. You should apply to the inspector who has issued the notice if you wish him to consider this, but you must do so before the end of the period given in it. *(Such an application is not an appeal against this notice.)*

3 The issue of this notice does not relieve you of any legal liability resting upon you for failure to comply with any provision of this or any other enactment, before or after the issue of this notice.

4 Your attention is drawn to the provision for appeal against this notice to an Industrial Tribunal. Details of the method of making an appeal are given below *(see also Section 24 of the Health and Safety at Work etc. Act 1974).*

(a) Appeal can be entered against this notice to an Industrial Tribunal. The appeal should be sent to:—

(for England and Wales)    The Secretary of the Tribunals
Central Office of the Industrial Tribunals
93 Ebury Bridge Road LONDON SW1W 8RE

(for Scotland)    The Secretary of the Tribunals
Central Office of the Industrial Tribunals
Saint Andrew House
141 West Nile Street GLASGOW G1 2RU

(b) The appeal must be commenced by sending in writing to the Secretary of the Tribunals a notice containing the following particulars:—

(1) The name of the appellant and his address for the service of documents;

(2) The date of the notice or notices appealed against and the address of the premises or place concerned;

(3) The name and address *(as shown on the notice)* of the respondent;

(4) Particulars of the requirements or directions appealed against;

and (5) The grounds of the appeal.

A form which may be used for appeal is attached.

(c) Time limit for appeal

A notice of appeal must be sent to the Secretary of the Tribunals within 21 days from the date of service on the appellant of the notice or notices appealed against, or within such further period as the tribunal considers reasonable in a case where it is satisfied that it was not reasonably practicable for the notice of appeal to be presented within the period of 21 days. If posted, the appeal should be sent by recorded delivery.

(d) The entering of an appeal suspends the Improvement Notice until the appeal has been determined, but does not automatically alter the date given in this notice by which the matters contained in it must be remedied.

(e) The rules for the hearing of an appeal are given in:

The Industrial Tribunals (Improvement and Prohibition Notices Appeals) (S1 1974 No. 1925) for England and Wales.

and The Industrial Tribunals (Improvement and Prohibition Notices Appeals) (S1 1974 No. 1926) for Scotland.

**HEALTH AND SAFETY EXECUTIVE**
Health and Safety at Work etc. Act 1974, Sections 22—24

# PROHIBITION NOTICE

Serial No. P

*Name and address (See Section 46)*

To ...........................................................................

*(a) Delete as necessary*

(a) Trading as ...........................................................

**I** (b)

*(b) Inspector's full name*

one of (c) ................................................................

*(c) Inspector's official designation*

of (d) .....................................................................

*(d) Official address*

.......................................... tel no. ...................

hereby give you notice that I am of the opinion that the following activities,

namely:—

...........................................................................

...........................................................................

which are (a) being carried on by you/about to be carried on by you/under your control

*(e) Location of activity*

at (e) .....................................................................

involve, or will involve (a) a risk/an imminent risk, of serious personal injury.
I am further of the opinion that the said matters involve contraventions of the following statutory provisions:—

...........................................................................

...........................................................................

...........................................................................

...........................................................................

because ...................................................................

...........................................................................

...........................................................................

and I hereby direct that the said activities shall not be carried on by you or under your control (a) immediately/after

*(f) Date*

(f) ........................................................................

unless the said contraventions and matters included in the schedule, which forms part of this notice, have been remedied.

Signature ............................................ Date .................

being an inspector appointed by an instrument in writing made pursuant to Section 19 of the said Act and entitled to issue this notice.

**LP 2**

---

**NOTES**

1 Failure to comply with a Prohibition Notice is an offence as provided by Section 33 of this Act and renders the offender liable to a fine not exceeding £400 on summary conviction or to an unlimited fine or to imprisonment for a term not exceeding two years or both on conviction on indictment and a further fine of not exceeding £50 per day if the offence is continued.

2 An Inspector has power to withdraw a notice or to extend the period specified in the notice, before the end of the period specified in it. You should apply to the Inspector who has issued the notice if you wish him to consider this, but you must do so before the end of the period given in it. *(Such an application is not an appeal against this notice.)*

3 The issue of this Notice does not relieve you of any legal liability resting upon you for failure to comply with any provision of this or any other enactment, before or after the issue of this notice.

4 Your attention is drawn to the provision for appeal against the notice to an Industrial Tribunal. Details of the method of making an appeal are given below *(see also Section 24 of the Health and Safety at Work etc. Act 1974).*

(a) Appeal can be entered against this notice to an Industrial Tribunal. The appeal should be sent to:—

(for England and Wales)    The Secretary of the Tribunals
Central Office of the Industrial Tribunals
93 Ebury Bridge Road LONDON SW1W 8RE

(for Scotland)    The Secretary of the Tribunals
Central Office of the Industrial Tribunals
Saint Andrew House,
141 West Nile Street GLASGOW G1 2RU

(b) The appeal must be commenced by sending in writing to the Secretary of the Tribunals a notice containing the following particulars:—
(1) The name of the appellant and his address for the service of documents;
(2) The date of the notice or notices appealed against and the address of the premises or place contained;
(3) The name and address *(as shown on the notice)* of the respondent;
(4) Particulars of the requirements or directions appealed against;
(5) The grounds of the appeal.
A form which may be used for appeal is attached.

(c) **Time limit for appeal**

A notice of appeal must be sent to the Secretary of the Tribunals within 21 days from the date of service on the appellant of the notice or notices appealed against, or within such further period as the tribunal considers reasonable in a case where it is satisfied that it was not reasonably practicable for the notice of appeal to be presented within the period of 21 days. If posted the appeal should be sent by recorded delivery.

(d) The entering of an appeal does not have the effect of suspending this notice. Application can be made for the suspension of the notice to the Secretary of the Tribunals, but the notice continues in force until a Tribunal otherwise directs. An application for suspension of the notice must be in writing and must set out:—

(a) The case number of the appeal, if known, or particulars sufficient to identify it and

(b) The grounds on which the application is made. It may accompany the appeal.

(e) The rules for the hearing of an appeal are given in:—

The Industrial Tribunals (Improvement and Prohibition Notices Appeals) Regulations 1974 (SI 1974 No. 1925) for England and Wales.

The Industrial Tribunals (Improvement and Prohibition Notices Appeals) (Scotland) Regulations 1974 (SI 1974 No. 1926) for Scotland.

# Codes, guidance—and written statements

Parliament has provided many ways to skin the employer who does not protect his employees. There are laws, laying down rules which range from the general to the specific. Compare: Section 2 of the Health and Safety at Work Act, which requires all employers to take such steps as are 'reasonably practicable' to protect all their employees at work — with Section 14 of the Factories Act, which lays down precise provisions as to the guarding of machinery and dangerous parts. Most general Acts of this sort are 'enabling statutes'. They enable the Government (or the Secretary of State concerned) to make regulations, in cases which lend themselves to precise definition.

When preparing *The Employers' Guide to the Law on Health and Safety at Work* (Business Books) I spoke to an official of the Health and Safety Commission and asked for a list of regulations under the Factories Act and the Offices Shops and Railway Premises Act and the new Act, to include their titles in an appendix. 'Certainly, sir', came the reply. 'It will take us a few weeks to prepare and is likely to be about book length.'

'No, no,' I said. 'I am not wanting the text of the regulations — only their titles.'

'That's right. Their titles . . . book length. . . .'

The Protection of Eyes Regulations . . . the Abrasive Wheels Regulations . . . you name it, they regulate it. And the regulations which were in force under the old laws remain so unless and until they are modified or repealed under the new Act. Note: the Third Schedule to the Health and Safety at Work Act gives the Government powers to make regulations within almost any area of industrial health and safety, and there is little that Parliament can do about it. Delegated legislation is as inevitable and (in the main) beneficial as it may be overpowering and dangerous.

Third: where the subject matter of the rules is too imprecise for regulations, the Government (in the case of the Health and Safety at Work Act, through the Health and Safety Commission) may issue *Codes of Conduct*. Noise, lead, vinyl chloride . . . guidance rules are contained in Codes. Like the Code of Industrial Relations Conduct —

and, indeed, the Highway Code – the Health and Safety Codes must be observed.

A breach of any of the Codes will not of itself constitute either a criminal or a civil offence. But in any civil or criminal proceedings in which that breach is relevant, it may be drawn to the attention of the Court – and will certainly do the offender's case no good at all.

Finally: 'Guidance'. Originally, the Commission intended to produce a Code regarding written statements required under Section 3 of the Act. It later decided that guidance was more appropriate (this is reproduced below). You do not have to follow that guidance – but you would be unwise to ignore it.

\*   \*   \*

**Health and Safety Commission: Guidance notes on employers' policy statements for Health and Safety at Work.**

*These preliminary guidance notes are given in two parts: Part 1 answers some basic questions on the statutory duty of employers under Section 2(3) of* The Health and Safety at Work etc. Act, 1974, *which came into operation on 1 April 1975; Part 2 gives general guidelines to the preparation of a written statement.*

*The written policy statement – blueprint for greater safety and better health at work.*

The Health and Safety Commission attaches the greatest importance to this requirement of the Act. For each employer it is the blueprint on which his entire health and safety at work policy, organisation and activity are based. It should therefore be drafted clearly so that the entire labour force, management and employed, understands it and knows what its responsibilities are.

The Commission issues this pamphlet to give employers preliminary guidance on the preparation of their written policy statements. In the light of experience the Commission will decide what additional guidance is necessary, and whether at any time codes of practice on written policy statements should be prepared to cover particular industries or circumstances.

**Part 1    Some basic questions**

*What is the law?*

Section 2(3) of *The Health and Safety at Work etc. Act, 1974,* says:
> 'Except in such cases as may be prescribed, it shall be the duty of every employer to prepare and as often as may be appropriate revise a written statement of his general policy with respect to the health and safety at work of his employees and the organisation and arrangements for the time being in force for carrying out that policy, and to bring that statement and any revision of it to the notice of all his employees.'

The Act places on employers the statutory duty to ensure so far as is reasonably practicable the safety and health and welfare of their employees at work. Section 2(3) of the Act requires every employer (except those prescribed in regulations) to prepare, revise and bring to the notice of his employees, a written statement covering two distinct aspects: (1) his general policy with respect to the health and safety at work of his employees; (2) the organisation and arrangements for carrying out that policy.

Note: In the larger companies or undertakings it might be necessary to deal separately with matters of organisation and with the arrangements for carrying out the general policy.

*What is meant by 'employee' and 'employer'?*

The Act defines 'employee' as an individual who works under a contract of employment and adds that related expressions shall be construed accordingly. Although the Act does not specifically define an 'employer' it can be taken to mean that an employer is any person, partnership, corporate body or unincorporated association which employs one or more individuals under a contract of employment. All such employers (with the exception of those prescribed in regulations) are to have written policy statements. Where the structure of an enterprise or service is such that a number of subsidiaries (e.g. in a local authority) under its overall policy or financial control are themselves employers, it may be possible for a common policy statement to be applied, but in such cases each individual employer would need to promulgate it under his own authority as part of his written statement.

*Can the employer pass on his responsibility to employees, their appointed/elected safety representatives or to safety committees?*

No. The employer cannot pass on his responsibility to his employees or their representatives. It will be sensible for an employer to consult his employees, through their safety representatives and to heed to the advice of the safety committees, where these exist, in order to ensure that the best arrangements and organisations for safety and health are evolved and maintained. Such consultation does not diminish his responsibility; it is clearly part of his greater responsibility under the Health and Safety at Work etc Act. The Commission will issue separate guidance and draw up the necessary codes of practice concerning safety representatives and safety committees.

## Will all written policy statements look alike?

No. The length and content of each written policy statement, like any blueprint, must be specifically prepared to meet the situation of the particular employer. He must thoroughly assess the possible hazards to the health and safety of his employees which might arise in connection with the activities on which they are employed and in the premises or other working area in which they are required to work.

## Cannot the Health and Safety Commission draw up a model policy statement?

Although it might be possible to produce some sample statements, it is unlikely that these would suit any individual employer. To provide a model might cause some employers to overlook important health and safety measures which their particular activities and premises demanded. Nevertheless, the Commission feel that certain general guidelines might be helpful and these are set out and discussed in Part 2 of this leaflet. In addition, the Executive and its staff will be prepared to advise individual employers on the compilation of written policy statements. Some employers' organisations, industry associations, professional bodies and similar groupings have already issued their own guidance directly related to the activities with which they are concerned, and others may wish to do so.

## What needs to be done about existing written policy statements?

They should be examined against the requirements of Section 2(3) of the Act and considered in the light of the advice given in this leaflet as well as that issued by the employer organisations, etc. Some existing written policy statements might be found to meet all these requirements, others might need some adjustment. The re-writing of policy statements should do nothing to disturb satisfactory arrangements already existing between the employer and employees.

*Will the written policy statement be all that is required to be communicated to employees?*

No. Under Section 2(2)(c) of the Act there is an obligation on every employer to provide such information, instruction, training and supervision as is necessary to ensure, so far as is reasonably practicable, the health and safety at work of his employees. This means, particularly where there are large labour forces and the more complex and potentially dangerous industrial processes, that there is an additional need to publish detailed rules and regulations for particular activities. The written policy statement is not, for instance, the appropriate way of covering detailed rules for the handling of toxic substances, although it would be appropriate for it to refer to the fact that such additional detailed rules were to be maintained and followed. The Commission will issue separate guidance or codes of practice on these additional responsibilities.

*How should the written policy statement be brought to the notice of employees?*

There may already be adequate methods of written communication between the employer and all individual employees. Otherwise the way in which the statement is brought to their notice might be a suitable point for discussion with workers' representatives. A suitable channel for ensuring adequate communication might be the joint safety committee or any other existing joint consultative arrangement in the firm. Nevertheless the employer must ensure that it is brought to the notice of every employee.

*How should the statement be kept up-to-date?*

Every employer must recognise his statutory obligation for keeping up-to-date both parts of the written statement. Where, for instance, those named in the second part as responsible for the various aspects of health and safety are replaced, amendments must be published without delay and brought to the notice of all employees. Then as joint safety committees are developed, these should provide the impetus for improving the existing arrangements and such improvements must then be incorporated into the written policy statements. Other improvements will stem from new regulations, codes of practice, guidance issued by the Commission, research into health and safety at work, from accident analysis and investigation, and from developments in the design and safeguarding of machinery. Wherever such improvements or changes affect the written policy of an employer, they should be reflected in its periodic revision.

## Part 2   Guidelines to drafting

### Structure of written statement

1   Although no model layout could possibly suit all situations, all written policy statements should cover both the essential parts referred to in Section 2(3) of the Act, i.e.

*a*   the general policy

*b*   the organisation and arrangements for carrying it out. (In larger undertakings these two subjects may best be dealt with in separate sections.)

In some larger or more complex undertakings it may also be better to produce the policy statement in the form of two documents:

*a*   a concise statement of the general policy, organisation and arrangements in a single document which could be distributed to all employees and which would make reference to;

*b*   a more detailed document or collection of documents (e.g. including manuals of rules and procedures) which could be held in a central position in each location for all to see on request, or posted where it could be seen by all employees.

### Detailing the levels of responsibility

2   The general policy statement should be a declaration of the employer's intent to seek to provide the safest and healthiest working conditions possible and to enlist the support of his employees towards achieving these ends.

3   In the case of employers engaged in a number of different activities

or where the operations are geographically widespread, the policy may require formulation at more than one level. The highest management level should lay down in writing the principles of the policy whilst the sub-groups or operational units interpret that policy in a realistic written form to suit the identified needs at the lower levels.

4   The policy statement should give the name and where necessary business address of the Director, Secretary, Manager or Senior Executive who is responsible for fulfilling the policy, or designate the appointment wherein that responsibility lies. In the case of mines and quarries, reference should be made to the holders of statutory appointments.

5   Whilst the overall policy responsibility for health and safety rests at the highest management level, all individuals at every level will have to accept degrees of responsibility for carrying out that policy. Wherever appropriate key individuals or their appointments should be named and their responsibilities defined. In addition there should be adequate arrangements to cover the absence of personnel with key safety functions.

6   Where functional expertise exists to advise line management, then the relationship of these functions, e.g. safety adviser, chemist, etc. should be made clear and the extent of their functions defined in relation to safety and health.

7   The policy statement should make it clear that the final level of responsibility is that of each and every individual employee.

*Safety representatives and joint safety committees*

8   Where appropriate, the organisation for joint consultation on health and safety (e.g. joint safety committees) should be described and should be accompanied by a list of persons responsible within the safety organisation, including employees' safety representatives or inspectors (which must be kept up-to-date).

*The employer's policy on training and supervision*

9   The written statement should ensure that all who are at risk are well aware of the hazards, the reasons for control in working practices and the part they as individuals have to play in maintaining a safe and healthy

working environment.

10 However adequate these written statements, etc. are in themselves the aim will not be achieved without good training and thorough supervision. Employers' policy statements should reflect their determination in these areas. It is, for instance, vital to spell out the supervisor's key role as he is the person on the spot who knows how the job is done. It is equally important for management to consider, and then set down, the positive steps which are to be taken to train and equip supervisors for this responsibility.

*Detailing the hazards*

11 Many accidents occur because workpeople do not understand the hazards involved and the precautions that have to be taken. The main hazards should be identified and reference made in the statement to additional rules and regulations which must be observed. It should be quite specific about the employer's policy in respect of certain fairly common hazards, such as the dangers of untidy working areas, the failure to use guards or to wear protective clothing, the introduction of new machinery or substances, maintenance work, etc.

12 Procedures should be laid down for accidents, particularly those involving any personal injury, to be systematically recorded by an employer. Also any information, based on expert analyses of accidents or dangerous occurrences, published by employers' federations, safety organisations of the HSC itself, should be monitored by the employer and relevant extracts made pertaining to his particular activity. The employer should regularly present such records and information to all management levels and his safety committee with a view to identifying and providing against new, or hitherto unidentified, hazards and checking on the frequency of occurrence of known hazards.

*Further information*

13 Additional copies of this leaflet and further information on specific queries are available from local offices of the Health and Safety Executive, or from the Health and Safety Executive, Baynards House, 1 Chepstow Place, London W2 4TF Tel: 01-229 3456 Ext. 688.

\*　　\*　　\*

**Model policies**

The Health and Safety Commission Executive do not favour 'model' or 'specimen' policies — and they do not intend to produce any such publication. However, employers get benefit from seeing the sort of statements which have been produced by others — so I am grateful to those who have prepared the statements which now follow for permission to reproduce them.

\*     \*     \*

## MARKS AND SPENCER LTD: GUIDE TO HEALTH AND SAFETY (March 1975)

**Introduction**

It is the company's policy to provide conditions which ensure the health, safety and well-being of the staff at work. The Health and Safety at Work Act, 1974 has given us the opportunity of re-stating this policy.

Although the final responsibility for the implementation of Company policy rests with the manager, every member of staff must be aware of their individual responsibility for health and safety.

This guide has been prepared to help management check the health and safety arrangements in the store. It is also designed as an aid in training staff to develop an increasing awareness of the health and safety aspects of their work in relation to both themselves and our customers.

Special instructions covering fire precautions are already given in the following documents:

(i)    Fire Precautions
(ii)   Fire Precautions During Building Operations
(iii)  Fire Precautions In Kitchens.

**All staff must:**

- Be constantly aware of any safety hazards and be alert to the possible causes of accidents.

- Appreciate the importance of reporting any faults in machinery or equipment immediately.

- Handle electrical equipment carefully and report any faults in wiring or plugs.

- Understand that any accidents (however minor) must be reported to Staff Management immediately.

- Be aware of the location of First Aid equipment and know the members of staff who hold a First Aid certificate.

- Be encouraged to wear sensible and appropriate footwear.

- Understand the correct methods of lifting and handling.

**These general points must be followed at all times:**

- Staff under 18 years of age must not clean or operate dangerous machines. All staff who do so must be adequately trained and have an entry to that effect on their record card.

- Staff must not attempt to effect any repairs to machinery or equipment unless they have special permission to do so.

- All broken or jagged equipment must be discarded, e.g. chipped glass on frozen and provisions units; snagged metal work on cabinets.

- All maintenance visits must be made at the correct intervals and strictly supervised.

- All Sales Floor cleaning (except sweeping) should be carried out when the store is closed as wet floors can be a hazard.

## SALES FLOOR

### General points

*ALL STAFF MUST APPRECIATE THAT THE SAFETY OF THE PUBLIC AS WELL AS STAFF IS OF PARAMOUNT IMPORTANCE ON THE SALES FLOOR.*

- Doorways must be clear of any obstructions.

- Door equipment must be in perfect working order.

- All gangways and adjacent areas must be kept clean, dry and clear of equipment and stock.

- All countering and sales floor equipment must be correctly assembled and properly maintained. No unauthorised equipment is to be used or modifications made.

- Footwear platforms must be carefully sited. Regular checks must be made to ensure that platforms are securely fixed where necessary.

- Mobile equipment must not be loaded above eye level.

- All mobile equipment, for example wheeled racks, mobile benches, baskets etc. must be taken off the sales floor if they are empty.

- Staff must never attempt to lift or move heavy equipment without adequate help.

- Any maintenance work in progress on the sales floor must be clearly marked, e.g. 'Door not in use'.

- <u>Stowa trolleys on the Food Section must not be left empty and unattended.</u>

- The positioning of wheel stands for wire baskets and the system for collecting and emptying must be strictly controlled.

- All shopping trolleys must be returned to the collection point when not in use. They must be stacked together neatly.


## Movement of counters on sales floors

- Movement of counters and other display equipment on the sales floor must only be carried out if the operation is carefully supervised.

- A member of male management or a Warehouse Foreman must supervise any work which involves counter or equipment movement, except the routine movement of stock on mobile benches or on racks.

- The person supervising the operation must not assist in the physical movement of the equipment but must concentrate entirely on safety.


## Cash registers

- Cash registers must always be moved on a mobile bench with two shelves placed at the middle level.

- All food tills must have a grapple plate underneath them to prevent till movement.

- All textile till stands must have till retaining blocks to prevent the till moving or falling off.

*(Also see section on Batteries)*

### Escalators and passenger conveyors

*Children should be prevented from playing on or near these machines.*

- The yellow lines at the side and along the leading edge of each step must be clearly visible — Building Group must be informed when these lines require re-painting.

- Staff must not use the escalators when carrying bulky equipment or merchandise.

- Flashing lights

  - Any member of staff seeing these lights should immediately go over to the machine to investigate the stoppage. A Warehouseman should be called to assist.

  - If there are no apparent reasons for the stoppage the Warehouseman should attempt to re-start the machine.

  - If the machine will not re-start the barrier chain must be placed immediately at the top and bottom of the stairs.

  - Dress rack barriers with warning cards must be placed at the top and bottom of the escalator as soon as possible, and the maintenance engineers called in.

### Goods lifts

- Any customer using the goods lifts must be accompanied by a member of staff.

- There must be no merchandise or equipment in a goods lift if it is used by a customer.

## GOODS RECEPTION

### Arrival of vehicles in streets/yards where public or staff have access

- Lighting must be adequate to allow safe operating.

- Warning triangles must be anchored and displayed at both ends of the vehicle.

- Wherever possible two male members of staff must be present.

### Positioning of vehicle in yard

- Lighting must be adequate to allow the safe positioning of the vehicle.

- The Warehouseman directing the driver must stand on the offside, at a safe distance and with a clear view of the whole reception area.

- All euqipment and returnable empties must be clear of the vehicle.

- Ramp chocks etc. must never be used under vehicles.

### Unloading of palletised deliveries — including stock vehicles

- Only the driver is allowed to:
  - open the vehicle doors and lock them against the vehicle side (after checking there is enough room).
  - enter the vehicle.
  - operate the tail lift.
  - place pallets on tail lifts and apply brakes.

*NOTE: Only stores with written permission may allow staff to enter the vehicle and assist the driver with pallet handling.*

### Tail guard

- The tail guard must be in position whenever the tail lift is being operated. Stores are responsible for routine maintenance of this equipment and should inform the B.O.C. Transhield Depot Manager if it becomes inoperative.

- The Warehouseman must stand well clear during tail lift operations.
- No more than two pallets to be unloaded at any one time.

**Side plate**

- The side plate must be attached to the tail lift when it is at rest at ground level.
- The side plate must not remain attached to the tail lift while it is in operation.
- Staff must be aware that this equipment can be DANGEROUS if it is not in the correct position.

**Tail lift**

- Pallets must not be removed until the tail lift has come to rest at ground level. The following procedures should then be adopted:
  - (i)   open the tail guard gate
  - (ii)  lower the movable flat (where applicable)
  - (iii) check the pallet straps and tighten if necessary
  - (iv)  release the pallet brake
  - (v)   remove the pallet from the tail lift.

*The operational instructions shown above for unloading pallets also apply when handling and loading empties, except that Warehousemen load empties onto the tail lift.*

**Unloading of non-palletised deliveries — foods, textiles, equipment etc.**

- Only the driver is allowed to:
  - open the vehicle doors and lock them against the vehicle side (after checking there is enough room).
  - enter the vehicle.
- Adequate and suitable equipment must be available e.g. tug bar platforms (rather than mobile benches) should be used for bulky/ heavy items.

### Winni-bridges

- The platform must not be used to carry loads unless it is supported by a vehicle.

- The hydraulic system must only be used to lift/lower the weight of the platform.

- The platform should be parked as upright as possible so that it does not present a hazard to persons in the reception yard.

- Warehousemen should guide vehicles as they reverse back to the loading dock.

- Oil leaks must be reported and any accumulation of oil on the floor must be covered with sand.

- Warehousemen must check that the bolts fitted at the end of the tracks to prevent the 'Winni' over-travelling are in place and secure.

- 'Winni' in open yards without gates are fitted with a steel cover and two padlocks. The cover and padlocks must be secured whenever the area or equipment are left unattended.

### Turntables

*ON NO ACCOUNT SHOULD STORE STAFF ATTEMPT TO AFFECT ANY REPAIRS TO THE TURNTABLE OR ITS CONTROL EQUIPMENT. THE ENGINEERS MUST BE CALLED AS SOON AS A BREAKDOWN OCCURS.*

- The pit area beneath all turntables must only be cleaned out by the nominated contractor and should be cleaned on each routine maintenance visit.

- Power Operated Type

  - Warehousemen must ensure that there is ample clearance around the vehicle so that when it is rotated on the turntable no equipment or persons could become trapped.

- Manually Operated Type

  - Warehousemen must understand that the vehicle and turntable can travel some distance before being stopped. The faster the turntable is moved, the greater the stopping distance.

  - Once the turntable is in the required position, the shoot bolts must be applied so that it will not move when the vehicle drives on or off.

## Lifting and handling

*Staff must be trained on the correct method of lifting and handling as shown in T.D.450A.*

- Correct equipment must be used.

- Where possible pallets should be pushed not pulled to avoid the pallet base injuring feet and ankles.

- If a pallet is difficult to move an additional man must be available to assist.

- Two Warehousemen must be available to move pallets up or down a ramp.

- Female staff must not handle heavy loads or unload trays from fully laden pallets.

## STOCKROOM

### General points

- Lighting must be adequate for safe operating.

- Gangways, doors and exits must be kept clear.

- Floor loading restrictions must be observed.

- Heavy or awkward merchandise must not be stored on shelves above shoulder height.

- Cash registers must be stored on the lowest shelf on bins and never on Wilkins racking.

- Step ladders must never be 'shunted' with a person standing on the ladder.

- Staff must not climb on the stockroom bins or shelves.

- Staff must not climb on any mobile equipment.

- Merchandise on trolleys must not be stacked above eye-level.

- Merchandise on mobile equipment must be stacked carefully and the equipment never over-loaded.

- Brakes must be on when pallets are stationary.

### Display

- Only staff trained in display techniques should be allowed to dress windows or put up wall decor.

- Steel dressmaking pins must never be used as they are liable to splinter when bent. Display staff must use the recommended mild steel plated pins e.g. Short Whites or Lills.

- Pin heads must not be cut off.

- Pins or needles must not be put in the mouth or jacket.

- Nylon thread must not be pulled from the ceiling as this could cause the ceiling clip to catapult.

- Display staff must not suspend anything from electric light fittings.

- Window shoes must always be worn when constructing window displays.

- Window steps must be locked into position before use.

- The Stanley Knife and the Straight Edge must only be used as demonstrated by the Area Sales Promotion Supervisor.

- All pins must be removed from showcards and panels after use.

### Rodenticides

- Pest control notice Z60/326 must be displayed in the stockroom and on the main staff notice board.

- The procedure for pest control as shown on Z60/326 must be followed.

### PLANT AND EQUIPMENT

*NOMINATED CONTRACTORS MUST BE CALLED IN FOR ANY REPAIRS OR SERVICING TO PLANT OR EQUIPMENT. STORE*

*STAFF MUST NOT ATTEMPT TO SERVICE OR REPAIR PLANT OR EQUIPMENT. ANY UNSERVICEABLE OR DAMAGED EQUIPMENT MUST BE WITHDRAWN FROM USE IMMEDIATELY AND REPLACED. ON NO ACCOUNT MAY STAFF REMOVE SAFETY GUARDS.*

## Electrical general

*(Refer to 'Fire Precautions' booklet for instructions on replacing fuses.)*

- All plugs on flexible leads must be fitted by a nominated electrical contractor and checked periodically by the contractor.

- Mains till wiring must be regularly inspected.

- Switchboards must be kept clear of obstructions and rubber mats must be kept in position.

- Stores must ensure that contractors only use 110 volt power tools in accordance with the British Standards Code of Practice.

- Lighting sockets must not be left empty, a bulb or fluorescent tube must be in place.

- All electrical equipment and machinery must be unplugged when not in use or during any maintenance work.

## Sub-stations

- Only authorised persons are allowed in electricity sub-stations.

- $CO_2$ fire protection equipment must be switched off if it is necessary to enter a sub-station.

## Standby generators

- Engine must not be running when cleaning, inspecting and topping up engine sumps or radiators. The set must always be allowed to cool down before operations commence.

- Automatic sets must have the control switch set to the 'off' position during these operations.

- Ear muffs must be worn when working near a running generator.

- Care must be taken to avoid spillage when handling diesel oil for generators.

- Any spillage must be covered with sand and swept up immediately.

## Air conditioning and ventilation

- Fan belts must only be changed by the nominated contractor.

- Building Group must be informed of any difficulties in access to plant areas for transporting filters, salt for water softeners, etc.

- Stores must obtain the authorisation of Building Group before storing any materials in the fan chambers or plant room areas.

- All floor grids must be securely fixed.

## Central heating

- The relevant boiler lighting instructions must be displayed in the boiler room together with the booklet 'Operating Instructions for Heating and Ventilation and Hot Water Plants'. All these instructions must be strictly followed.

- Fans must be switched off and isolated when cleaning heater batteries or removing filters on unit heaters or fan convectors.

## Batteries

- Emergency Lighting and Security Batteries
  - The insulating cover plates must be in place over the large open type emergency lighting batteries.
  - Gauntlet rubber gloves must be worn when topping up emergency lighting batteries.

- Cash Registers
  - The instructions Z60/344 must be followed when topping up and charging batteries.
  - Batteries must always be handled in the upright position to avoid acid spillage.

**Baler**

- Only staff aged 18 and over who have been fully trained and have an entry to that effect on their record card may operate the baler.

- Baling machines must be operated in accordance with H.O. Notice Z60/334.

- Operators must stand clear when releasing pressure on completed bales.

- H.O. Notice Z60/356 must be affixed to all machines.

- Objects must not be placed on the platform.

**Conveyors/tray elevators/escaveyors**

*STAFF MUST NEVER CLIMB, WALK OR RIDE ON THIS EQUIP-MENT.*

- The following items must be checked each day to establish that they are operating correctly:

  - all operating buttons, photo-electric cells, warning lights and buttons.

  - 'pop-up' rollers adjacent to drive drums and fixed rollers (these rollers should fit easily into their slots — any missing ones must be replaced immediately).

  - guardrails and guards.

- Overalls must be kept buttoned so that they do not flap on to the belt or rollers when loading/off loading.

- Operators must not lean across the conveyor, or any other moving part of the machine to reach the controls. The machine must be operated from the correct side.

- Parcels bound with plastic strapping or banding must never be put onto tray elevators.

- Damaged parcels or those with unsealed flaps or sides should not be used on these machines.

- Advices/Delivery notes must not be sent up or down on these machines. Paper can easily become caught in the belt or driving equipment.

**Lifts**

- The instructions for 'Lift Stoppages and Hand Winding Procedures' (Z60/353) must be followed.

- The instructions must be displayed in each lift motor room.

- A summary of the main points is as follows:
  - If there has been an accident or if a person is trapped by the equipment staff must switch off the lift at the main switch and call the Fire Brigade immediately. Staff must not attempt to move the equipment themselves.

  - Staff must only use a lift gate release key where a power operated gate is fitted and only when the lift has been brought to that level.

  - Night security staff must not use lifts outside normal store hours.

  - Lift gate lock release keys must be kept under the control of the Warehouse Manager or Foreman. They must not be displayed.

  - Staff must switch off the lift main isolator switch before beginning to hand wind a lift.

  - When hand winding a lift if the man at the winding wheel stops winding for any reason he must tell the brake man to let the brake grip the coupling and so hold the lift.

  - Staff must not enter Lift Pits under any circumstances.

  - Cleaning out of Lift Pits must only be carried out by Maintenance Engineers during their routine visits.

**Platform Lifts**

- All operating buttons must be checked daily.

- Staff must not ride on the platform unless specially authorised to do so.

- Barrier arms must be in place before the platform is operated.

- Operators must stand clear of equipment whilst it is moving.

- The safe working load indicated on each machine must not be exceeded.

- The load must be placed centrally on the platform so that it is not likely to roll to the edge — brakes must be applied on pallets.

- If the platform does not stop level with the floor the maintenance engineer must be called in.

## Power-operated gates and doors

- The following must be checked daily:
    - Operating buttons
    - Safety edges
    - Floor mats
    - Photo-electric cells.

## Folding leaf doors

- The doors must not be operated if there is any likelihood of personnel or equipment becoming trapped when the leaves bunch together.

## Step ladders and zip-up staging

*ONLY EQUIPMENT ISSUED OR APPROVED BY THE EQUIPMENT GROUP MAY BE USED*

- Step Ladders:
    - Step ladders must not be used on stairs.
    - Both hands must be used when climbing vertical cat ladders.
- Zip-up Staging:
    - When this equipment is used on the sales floor during operating hours a person must be stationed beside it at all times.
    - Store staff must not use zip-up staging over stairs and escalators.
    - Wheels must be locked and safety rails fitted when zip-up staging equipment is in use.
    - The equipment must always be fully erected while in use.

**Floor cleaning equipment**

- Cables and plugs must be checked regularly by the Warehouse Manager/Foreman.

- The correct procedure, as demonstrated by the manufacturer, must always be followed.

- The mains switch must be turned off and the plug removed:

  - when emptying vacuum cleaners and cleaning brushes.

  - when cleaning/changing brushes on floor scrubbing/polishing machines.

- Scrubbing machines must never be over-filled with water.

- Marcaddy reels must only be used with floor cleaning machines.

**Spotting machines**

- The notice OP.1505 and the Instructions for the use of the Spotting machines must be displayed adjacent to the machine. All these instructions must be strictly followed.

**Refrigeration equipment**

- Display Units:

  - Refrigerated units must be turned off before cleaning starts.

  - Fans must be switched off and isolated when cleaning condenser vanes.

  - After maintenance visits the Warehouse Foreman/Manager must check that the nominated contractor has re-fixed all the fan guards properly.

  - Lighting sockets on refrigeration equipment must never be left empty, a bulb or fluorescent tube must be in place.

- Frozen Food and Cold Rooms:

  - Internal handles and lights must be checked daily.

  - Cold Room ramps must be securely fixed to the room.

  - Protective clothing provided must be worn when handling Frozen Foods.

– Ice which forms on the floor in Frozen Food rooms must be cleared, and any regular build up of ice must be reported.

- Dry Ice

*DRY ICE MUST NOT BE USED IN SWEDISH ROYAL UNITS OR BE USED IN "WALK-IN" COLD ROOMS.*

– Only members of staff nominated by store management may handle dry ice.

– Persons handling dry ice must always wear insulated gloves.

– Dry ice must never be allowed to come into contact with the skin.

– Whole blocks of dry ice must be used – no attempt must be made to break blocks into pieces.

## CATERING UNIT

### General points

- Staff must not climb onto equipment to open and close windows.

- Dirty crockery must not be stacked so high on the trolley that it may fall off.

- Broken china and glass must be wrapped in paper before disposal.

- Staff must form an orderly queue at the counter, and unnecessary congestion should be avoided.

- A tray or trolley must be used to carry several items or one heavy item.

- Pans must be stacked singly and upside down on the racks.

- Heavy and bulky foods must not be stored on top shelves of the food cupboard.

- Staff working in the Catering Unit must wear low-heeled shoes, with adequate support all round the foot.

- Vegetables must be cooked in the minimum amount of water necessary.

- Where practical a stainless steel wire skimmer should be used for straining, alternatively vegetables should be strained into a collander placed in the sink unit. The lid of the saucepan must not be used for straining.

## Cleaning

- Any spillage on the floor must be mopped up immediately and dried thoroughly.

- Catering staff must only clean walls to a height which can be reached without climbing onto step ladders or equipment.

- Rubber gloves must be worn when using C and CSR powder and oven cleaners and when using any cleaning material regularly.

- Quitacide solid detergent must only be used in the dispenser provided.

- Only trained staff are allowed to clean and operate Dishwashing Machines, Cookers, Service Counters, Steamers, Boilers and Brat Pans.

- Kitchen floors must not be washed until lunches are over.

## Dangerous machines
## (Refer to 'Office, Shops and Railway Premises Act')

*Refer to the Recipe Book for full instructions on the operating and cleaning of these machines. Only staff aged 18 years or over, who have been fully trained (and have an entry to that effect on their record card) may operate and clean the following machines:*

- Waste Disposal Unit

  - staff must **never** place their hands down the grinding chamber.

  - the correct pusher must always be used.

  - if the machine breaks down it must be switched off immediately and reported to the Warehouse Manager/Foreman.

- Slicing Machine

  - the machine must never be cleaned or left unattended without setting the index to zero, switching off and removing the plug from the socket.

- Mixing Machine and attachments

  - staff must never put their hands into the bowl while mixing is in progress.

— the machine must be switched off when fitting or removing attachments.

— when using the vegetable attachment staff must not use their hands to feed vegetables against the cutter.

— the hopper front must not be opened while the machine is running.

- Dishwashing Machines with Continuous Conveyor

  — Staff must **never** put their hands into or under the conveyor while it is moving.

  — the machine must be switched off before cleaning.

  — the inspection door must **never** be opened when the machine is switched on.

  — the machine must not be left unattended while in use.

### Cookers

- Doors must be opened carefully so that they do not swing back and burn the arms.

- Doors must not be left open once the oven is lit.

- Burners must be turned off when not in use.

- Saucepan handles must not protrude over the edge of the cooker or over an open flame.

- Baking dishes must be removed from the oven and placed on a table to stir or adjust contents.

### Boiler units

- A safety guard must be fitted if the boiling water font is exposed to 'customers' queuing.

- Water from the boiler unit may only be used for making beverages. Draining off excessive amounts of water for any other purpose can be dangerous.

## Portable steamers

- These must only be filled with cold water.
- The water must be allowed to cool before lifting the steamer off the cooker to empty it.

## Knives

- Worn and misshapen knives must be replaced.
- A suitable size and type of knife must be selected for each job and must be held and used correctly.
- Sharp knives must never be left in the water in the wash-up sink but placed on the draining board for the person washing up to see.
- Knives must be laid flat when not in use.

## Oven cloths

- These must be used in accordance with the instructions given in 'A Guide for Catering Staff'.
- Damp or damaged oven cloths must not be used.

## Other equipment

- A fork with a guard must always be used when hand carving meat.
- Only the approved can opener may be used.
- Wheels on the slicer trolley and refrigerator must be locked when the equipment is stationary.

# HEALTH SERVICES

*The Staff Manageress is responsible for implementing Health Services policy in the store.*

### Pre-employment medicals

- All staff except Temporary Seasonal and Saturday-only staff must have a medical examination before being offered employment.

- Temporary Seasonal staff must be medically examined if their employment lasts more than six weeks.

- Temporary Seasonal and Saturday-only staff must be medically examined before they are allowed to work on the Food Section or in the Store Kitchen.

### Medical gradings and reviews

- All staff must be given a medical grading at their pre-employment medical. The grades are as follows:

  Grade A – Fit for all work.
  Grade B – Fit for work but suffering from a minor disability.
  Grade C – Registered Disabled Person.

- The following members of staff must be re-examined every six months:

  – All juveniles (staff under 18 years of age)

  – Staff in medical grades B and C

  – Security staff

  – Staff over retirement age

  – Staff working in Cold Rooms

  – Staff working on Spotting Machines.

### Medical sessions

- Regular medical sessions are arranged in the store.

- All members of staff must be aware that they can attend the Doctor's session for advice if they so wish. Requests for an appointment can be made to the Staff Manageress. The Doctor will see cases referred for advice by the Staff Manageress or at his/her own request.

- The Sessional Doctor will also carry out the following duties:

  - Check absences and follow up any cases or long-term absence with medical reports to the Chief Medical Officer.

  - Check the Accident Book, review all accidents and see staff where appropriate.

  - Carry out a monthly inspection of the store and complete the Store Inspection Card.

### Chest X-ray

- All staff should be encouraged to attend the X-Ray Survey which is arranged for each store every three years. Each person will receive the result of the x-ray individually.

### Cases of vomiting and diarrhoea amongst food handlers

- The Chief Medical Officer must be telephoned at Head Office to report a case affecting any member of staff.

- All staff complaining of diarrhoea and/or vomiting must stay off work until they are free of symptoms and the store has received one negative stool check. Food Handlers must not return to their normal duties until three consecutive negative reports have been obtained.

- Any cases which occur amongst full-time and part-time members of staff who work in the Catering Unit or on the Food Section (including Warehousemen handling foods) must be reported to the Local Health Authority after consultation with Health Services.

- All Food Handlers must have routine medical checks if they have any form of sickness and/or diarrhoea while on holiday. Special instructions have been issued for Catering Staff returning from holiday abroad.

**Dental inspections**

- All staff should be encouraged to attend the store dental inspections which are arranged every six months.

- All Food Handlers must attend the store dental inspections and have any necessary treatment.

**Cervical cytology**

- Cervical cytology sessions are arranged every two years or more frequently if there is a special need.

**Medical room**

- *First Aid Cabinet*

  This cabinet contains basic first aid equipment. The contents of the cabinet are listed on the inside of the door and the First Aid instruction chart is displayed on the wall. Only those contents listed on the inside of the door should be kept in the cabinet.

  - No more than 10 Paracetamol tablets should be kept in the cabinet. Additional supplies of the tablets must be kept in the Medical Cabinet under lock and key or in another suitable locked container.

  - Zoff must only be used for removing plaster and must be kept in the original container.

The Staff Manageress must check the contents of the First Aid cabinet regularly and replenish supplies when necessary.

- *Medical Cabinet*

  This cabinet is for the storage of medical supplies. It is kept locked at all times and the Staff Manageress holds the key.

# GENERAL INDUSTRIAL ROOFING
## AND CONSTRUCTION GROUP OF COMPANIES:
### SAFETY AND WELFARE POLICY
#### (Procedures and Responsibilities)

## HEALTH AND SAFETY POLICY

Bearing in mind the inherently dangerous nature of our work as roofing contractors, and also the processes and procedures used in carrying out this work, which by its very nature does not lend itself readily to safety precautions giving an absolute certainty of Safety; it is essential that the absolute maximum of attention be paid to the consideration of safety at all times by all personnel and in all stages of our work.

Furthermore, as our employees must, of necessity, in general, work on their own and unsupervised, they must themselves be expected to take extra care for their own safety and the safety of others by both carrying out the safety procedures laid down and using safety equipment provided for them, and use their own intelligence and experience in order to ensure the best safety methods possible in the prevailing circumstances.

In addition as all our work is carried out on buildings or structures owned by others, which are often in a dilapidated condition and where we have no opportunity to obtain factual knowledge of the inherent structural soundness or otherwise of the building or structure on which we work, special care must be exercised by our employees not only for their own safety, but also for that of others, and close liaison must be kept with our Clients with a view to obtaining the maximum of assistance and information concerning Safety matters and bringing to their notice as far as practicable their responsibility under Sections 3 and 4 of the Act.

In the light of the above, our Safety Policy is based on the following major considerations:

1   *The employment of personnel with the maximum experience possible,* who will be expected to exercise special care not only for their own safety, but that of less experienced personnel working with them.
2   *Careful assessment of Safety requirements:*
    a   in relation to our own employees
    b   third parties, equipment and plant.
3   *Instruction and persuasion of operatives*
    Instruction and persuasion of operatives in safety matters and

methods of work to obtain their full co-operation and where reasonably practicable, site supervision to ensure as far as possible the carrying out of the procedures and the use of equipment.

4    *Proper documentation*
Proper documentation to ensure as far as practicable compliance with and control over safety matters.

5    *Close co-operation with our Clients*
Close co-operation with our Clients' Safety Departments, Factory Inspectors, CITB and others to ensure the maximum efficiency of our procedures and all possible assistance in accordance with our Clients' responsibility under Section 3 of the Act.

6    *Safety Officer*
The Act gives us the opportunity to re-emphasize the high level of safety awareness required at all levels throughout our organisation. As it is not practical to have an effective Safety Officer appointed to cover all sites, the responsibility for safety rests on each and every employee at all times in the areas of his work and particularly on heads of Departments to ensure as far as practicable the carrying out of the necessary procedures.

7    *Safety Committee*
As it is not practicable, due to the widespread nature of our work locality and otherwise, to have an overall area Safety Committee, our policy is to include on the agenda of all meetings at all levels and particularly executive meetings, a period of discussion and where necessary consultation on all matters arising from and in connection with Safety at Work.

8    *Alteration to Company Safety Policy*
Alteration to Safety Policy shall only be made by the Directors. All employees will be informed of any alteration.

## PROCEDURES AND RESPONSIBILITIES

In accordance with our declared policy our procedures must be such as to ensure a constant flow of information on safety matters and to define responsibility throughout the organisation and the following will be established:

### Directors

The Directors will ensure that sufficient funds are made available to implement the Company's safety policy.

The Directors shall delegate responsibility for the implementation of the Company's policies to the Executive Directors or Managers of each Company.

## Executive Directors and Managers

Executive Directors and Managers will be fully responsible to the Board of Directors for all matters concerning safety and the implementation and provisions of the Health and Safety at Work Act 1974. However, they will delegate as far as is reasonable and practicable the detailed responsibilities to the heads of Departments i.e. Sales Manager and Contracts Manager.

## Contracts Manager

The Contracts Manager will be responsible for the total safety on all sites and the observance of the regulations. In particular he will:

1    Regularly visit the sites to ensure that safety procedures and methods of work comply with the Act.
2    Advise senior management on all matters concerning safety in conjunction with the Executive Director or the Manager.
3    Be responsible for the training of operatives.
4    Provide all necessary safety equipment and aids to safety on site.
5    Establish and enforce safe methods of work.
6    Ensure that all plant sent on site is safe and complies with all relevant legislation.
7    Check that all plant and equipment is periodically inspected and maintained.
8    Check that all hire plant carries correct and up-to-date Test Certificates and is being properly used.
9    The Contracts Manager will ensure that sub-Contractors are properly instructed as to their responsibility in accordance with the Section headed Sub-Contractors hereunder.
10   He will be responsible for ensuring that all scaffolding structures are inspected weekly and signed for as to their safety and will be responsible for a special book providing a record of the inspection.
11   He will be responsible for ensuring that alterations to existing scaffolding must only be carried out by skilled scaffolders.
12   An inspection of general plant, i.e. electrical machines, wheels, ropes, ladders, staging, etc. will be carried out at not less than

monthly intervals, signed for and recorded in the relevant job file.

13   On receiving an order to carry out work, he will ensure that the necessary scaffolding and safety equipment as specified in the original survey is properly ordered, is of the right type in the light of conditions existing at the time of receipt of the order and should any alterations be required these should be brought to the attention of the management immediately and we will then consult with the clients regarding increased costs of alternative methods of work to be arranged.

14   Before the commencement of any work it is essential that the Contracts Manager ensures that all material required for safety is on site, in useable condition and that he obtains a certificate signed by the personnel concerned and this is to be placed on the appropriate file.

15   He will be responsible that when the men are put on site that the safety equipment is brought to the notice of the foreman, leading hand and operatives and is further checked for soundness. Its use and method of work will be discussed and agreed with the operatives.

16   He will be responsible for seeing that the clients' Safety Officer is approached and advised of the commencement of our work on his premises and his approval sought for our method of work and safety arrangements.

17   He will be responsible for obtaining statements in the event of an accident and for appropriate and satisfactory completion of entry of details in the Accident Report Book, and other relevant statutory requirements.

18   He will be responsible that new operatives applying for work are experienced in the work, used to working on roofs and at a height.

19   It is also essential that he ensures as far as is practicable that new operatives are in good health, and that our medical form and other documentation is fully and properly filled in.

### Contracts supervisor and leading hands

1   Should be familiar with safety requirements.
2   Restrain men from taking any unnecessary and avoidable risks.
3   Ensure appropriate use of safety equipment.
4   Discourage horseplay.
5   Ensure that all employees take necessary safety precautions.
6   Report to management defects of plant or equipment.
7   Report any breach of safety regulations or failure to use safety

equipment provided.

8    A signature for the safety equipment will be obtained from the leading hand and put on file and failure to do this will be considered as gross negligence and dealt with accordingly.

9    The leading hand will be personally responsible for the care of safety equipment, the correct use of the equipment by himself and all operatives on site, and to ensure that no breach of the regulations occurs on the site under his control.

10   The leading hand will consider it a matter of primary importance to ensure the safety of persons and equipment in the vicinity of the work which he is carrying out.

## Operatives

The attention of all operatives will be drawn to the provisions of the Act and they will be responsible for:

1    Their own safety and that of others.
2    To warn new men of known hazards.
3    To use all tools and equipment correctly.
4    Keep all tools and equipment in good order.
5    Work in a safety conscious manner.
6    Comply with the provisions of Codes of Practice in force particularly 6(a), (b) and (d).
7    All operatives will be responsible for reading and applying the Recommendations and Codes of Practice with which they are issued.

## Sales Manager

The Sales Manager will be responsible for ensuring that the Representatives/Surveyors are fully aware of the dangers involved in their work and fully realise their full and total responsibility for their own safety. In particular, attention must be drawn to the dangers of:

1    Asbestos roofs.
2    Slated roofs.
3    Glazing.
4    Defective ladders and walkways found on clients' premises.

**Representatives/Surveyors**

1   By the very nature of their work they will be alone and entirely responsible for their own safety. They are expected to take extra care and use their own experience and judgment for their own safety and that of others.

2   They must take no unnecessary risks and must request the client to provide all necessary equipment and help which is reasonably practicable to enable them to carry out their survey in an efficient and safe manner to themselves and others.

3   Surveyors will be responsible for making a careful assessment of the dangers and safety requirements at the time of the original survey or inspection which must be made in consultation with the client and taking due note of the recommendations of the client's Safety Officer or other nominated person. These requirements to be included in our quotation and specification as a separate item of cost and as a separate specification which must be handed to the leading hand and explained to all the operatives at the commencement of the work.

**Sub-contractors**

At the estimating stage and further at the commencement of every stage of the sub-contract, all sub-contractors shall be made aware of their responsibility regarding their employees in relation to all aspects of safety in accordance with the Act. They will be required in particular to produce:

1   Exemption Certificate or its equivalent.

2   Policy of Insurance valid and affording adequate cover to their own employees, to our clients, and to ourselves.

3   They will also be responsible for ensuring the provision by us of the necessary equipment required to comply with the requirements of the Act, as arranged at the tendering stage, and will be fully responsible for its use and maintenance.

4   The sub-contractors will be informed by the Contracts Manager that they are fully responsible for their own safety and that we cannot accept any responsibility whatsoever for the men under their control and that they undertake to employ only men skilled and experienced in the work to be performed.

## DOCUMENTATION

### 1   Executive Directors and Managers in Charge of Offices

Executive Directors and Managers in Charge of Offices will render to the London Office a signed statement on Form CERT/1 each month stating that to the best of their knowledge and belief all relevant measures have been taken to comply with the requirements of the Health and Safety at Work Act 1974, and with our Policy and Procedures. They will be responsible also for checking and initialling reports from the following.

### 2   Contracts Managers/Sales Managers

Contracts Managers/Sales Managers will render monthly on Form CERT/2 to the Executive Director or Manager in Charge of each Office a similar report stating that they have taken all reasonable and practical steps to ensure compliance with the Act and that personnel under their control are supplied with and are using the safety equipment provided. A file will be kept containing these monthly reports to be available for inspection at all times.

### 3   Contracts Managers

Contracts Managers, in addition to the above, will

a   be responsible for providing a special book in which they will certify that all scaffolding structures have been inspected weekly and that, to the best of the inspector's knowledge and ability, are safe and in good order. This book to be produced for initialling by the Manager weekly.

b   be responsible for a weekly inspection of all electrically operated machines, i.e. drills, etc., gin wheels, ropes, ladders, Youngman Boards and other safety equipment provided, and provide a certificate on Form CERT/3 to this effect. This certificate will be placed in and clipped separately in the relevant job file after initialling by the Manager.

## 4   On site visits

Every time a site is visited a report will be given on Form CERT/4 by the person visiting the site to the Contracts Manager, to be initialled by the Manager, before being filed on the Job File.


## 5   Foremen or Leading Hands

Foremen or Leading Hands will sign on Form CERT/5, for all safety equipment provided and also an acknowledgement that they are employing a safe method of work and that they are using correctly and understand the use of the safety equipment provided.

These documents will be filed and clipped to the Job File, counter-signed by the Contracts Manager and initialled by the Executive Director or Manager in Charge of each Office before filing.


## 6   Operatives

Operatives will sign for safety equipment received for personal use on Form CERT/6.

A clause will be inserted on all Time Sheets stating that:

'I certify that I have worked the above hours and that the ladders, scaffolding and safety equipment provided are sound, in good order, and used as required and instructed',

and signed weekly by all operatives and filed.


## 7   New Employees

New employees will sign a receipt for the Contract of Employment, the Statement of Employment, and that they are in good health, experienced in roofing works and working on high structures and any other relevant documentation provided, on Form CERT/7, and will complete and sign the Company's Medical Sheet.

# Disciplinary procedures

The Employment Protection Act provides that written particulars of terms of service must either set out disciplinary procedures or state where they are easily accessible to the employee. Brief samples appear in the appropriate places in the book.

Disciplinary procedures themselves are under review thanks to the Disciplinary Code which — as we go to press — is in consultative form. This Code (produced, as usual, by the Advisory, Conciliation and Arbitration Service) gives guidance which it is wise to follow — failure to do so may be used in evidence in any proceeding to which it is relevant.

In its final form, the Code is unlikely to differ greatly from the final draft — which is set out in full in this appendix, along with two good, representative samples of disciplinary procedures currently in use. My thanks to those who kindly supplied these.

**Example 1**

In the case of a misdemeanour or unsatisfactory behaviour on the part of an employee a verbal warning may be given by the employee's immediate supervisor or above and it will be recorded on his/her personal file on the recommendation of his/her Departmental Executive.

If there is no improvement in the behaviour which necessitated the first verbal warning the employee will be interviewed by his/her Departmental Executive who, in conjunction with the Personnel Manager or Deputy, will hear the complaint and issue a second warning as necessary.

Should there still be no improvement in the employee's performance or behaviour a final written warning will be issued by the Departmental Executive and the Personnel Manager.

If at any stage the employee considers that he/she has been unfairly or unjustly disciplined he/she should as soon as possible after the incident approach the person who administered the discipline and request a meeting to discuss the matter with his/her Departmental Executive or the Personnel Manager.

If the employee's behaviour continues to be unsatisfactory no further warning need be given to effect dismissal should this be considered necessary by the Departmental Executive.

If an employee feels he/she has been unfairly or unjustly dismissed he/she may appeal in writing to the Personnel Manager within one week of receiving notice.

The Personnel Manager will arrange an interview within one week to determine the matter finally.

The following are Departmental Executives: . . . .

**Example 2**

THERE CAN BE NO PRECISE RULES AS TO THE APPROACH FOR DISCIPLINARY PROCEDURE.

Normally, a verbal reprimand between a Manager and an individual, is adequate. However, a persistent offender will be aware that he will be called to task officially at some time. There may be occasions where a member of staff, who does not normally err, finds himself in the position of an official warning due to the degree of his misdemeanour.

*Stages of Disciplinary Procedure*
In essence there are three stages:
1   Verbal warning (1a — verbal warning and letter).
2   Final warning in writing.
3   Letter of dismissal.

*Stage 1: verbal warning*   A reprimand for misconduct will be administered to the offender in the presence of his Chapel Officer and a Management Representative. In the event of no Manager being available from own department as a witness, a Manager will be requested from Central Production or another Production Department.

A detailed report must be made to the Production Manager; copied to Personnel Department and departmental files. The offender must be informed that the facts of the incident will be noted in his personnel record.

It may be felt necessary that at Stage 1 the offender is issued with a letter confirming that any further problems will result in a final warning letter. This is a useful device when the offender is taken to task on a matter not quite so obvious, such as performance at his work. It may also serve a useful purpose when there are some special circumstances surrounding an incident.

*Stage 2: final warning*   In the event of an individual, previously dealt with above, again being disciplined for misconduct he will be advised verbally that a letter, from his Department Manager, will be sent to him concerning this reprimand and advising him that any further serious misconduct will result in dismissal.

The interview will again take place before the individual, his Chapel Official and a Management Representative.

The Department Manager will write the letter, copies of which will be sent to the Production Manager, Chapel Official and Personnel Department. He will also advise the individual that the letter of warning will be included in his personnel record.

Furthermore, a detailed report of the incident which necessitated the letter will be made to the Production Manager, copied to Personnel Department and departmental files.

*Deputy Managers*   If the Deputy Manager is unacquainted with the previous record of the offender and does not at the time have access to the written information on the offender, he may, before committing the Company, advise the individual that the incident will be fully reported to the Department Manager.

*Stage 3: letter of dismissal*   Any further misconduct will result in confrontation as before; dismissal verbally, followed by dismissal letter from Department Manager, copied to Production Manager, Chapel Official, Branch Secretary and Personnel Department.

As previously a detailed report will be prepared.

It is imperative that the man dismissed is advised that he has the right of appeal, to the Production Manager, and may be accompanied by a Chapel Official if he wishes. Time must be allowed for him to properly prepare his case. At least three working days is recommended.

*Deputy Managers*   Procedure as far as the Deputy Manager is concerned must vary. The Deputy Manager could carry out the verbal dismissal, before the witnesses previously mentioned, and instruct the dismissed that a letter confirming the dismissal will be sent by the Department Manager. There could be a situation whereby the offender is sent home by the Deputy Manager and told to report to the Department Manager the following day. Again this action would take place before the normal witnesses.

The Deputy Manager, if not fully acquainted with the previous history of the offender, should call Central Production for advice.

Having quoted the broad lines of Disciplinary Procedure to be followed in three stages, it must be borne in mind that the action to be taken will at all times depend on the circumstances and nature of the misconduct.

Full documentation is essential in order to establish the basis of a dismissal at all times. Deputy Managers must be able to have access to all relevant information.

*Note:* a further point concerning proof of delivery of Final Warnings and Letter of Dismissal is to post such correspondence by Recorded Delivery.

### *Federated Chapel*

It should be noted that the Federated House Chapel have made representations to the Company that letters of warning should have a specific life and that disciplinary measures should not be based on a historical misdemeanour of long standing.

The Company has replied to the Federated House Chapel that although no formal arrangement will be made for automatic destruction of warning letters after a given period of time, the Company has no wish to be unreasonable and will obviously take into account the age of previous warnings issued to a member of staff. If the employee has for example worked well and normally over the last three years then it is possible that the previous warnings will be ignored by the Departmental Manager.

*DISMISSAL:*                              *Date . . .*

Dear Mr. . .

Last night you were (circumstances — witnesses etc.).

You were previously reprimanded verbally in the presence of etc., etc., for your conduct on (date) and my subsequent letter to you dated . . . is quite explicit as to the Company's attitude.

You have clearly chosen to ignore the verbal and written warnings previously given and I therefore have to advise you that you are dismissed from the Company as from the date of this letter.

As stated to you in the presence of your Chapel Official, you are entitled to make representations concerning my decision to the Production Manager within three working days, when you may, if you wish, be accompanied by a Chapel Official.

Your appropriate documents and holiday entitlement, less any deduction due by you to the Company, will be forwarded immediately. You will also be advised of your pension entitlement within the next few weeks.

Yours sincerely

**Example 3**

Should it be necessary for the Company to take disciplinary action against any employee, the normal procedure will be:

Recorded verbal warnings.

Final warning in writing.

Dismissal.

This procedure will not apply where an employee is guilty of breach of contract or gross misconduct.

Employees who are members of a trade union or staff organisation recognised by the Company may be accompanied by a representative of that body whenever a disciplinary interview is taking place.

At the request of the employee, the Company will provide a written statement of the reason for the dismissal.

Any dismissed employee who wishes to appeal against dismissal, may do so within two working days, by applying to his Manager. The appeal will be considered by the Managing Director of the Operating Company concerned, unless he has been involved in the decision to dismiss. In this case the appeal will be considered by the Chairman of the Operating Company.

# Index

Absence from work, 9-10, 14
Accident, 12
  allegation regarding, 261
  employee, caused by, 222-7
  liability for, 224
  *See also* Health and safety
Accommodation, provision of, 6
Accounts of employee, 6
Advisory, Conciliation and Arbitration Service, 135, 138, 157-71
  adviser, as, 158-62
  application for reference of a recognition issue to, 350-51
  appreciation of, 165-6
  arbitrator, as, 159-60, 164-5
  codes of practice of, 93, 160, 163, 178, 202, 337, 341
  conciliator, as, 159-61, 163-4
  disputes, dealing with, 167-71, 189
  field of operation of, 158-60
  functions of, 342
  guarantee payments, dealing with, 197
Agent, letter of appointment of, 15-16
Alkali and Works Regulations, 236
Application for reference of a recognition issue to ACAS, 350-51
Application to the Secretary of State for Employment for a payment under *The Redundancy Payments Act, 1965,* 356-7
Apprentice
  redundancy of, 40-41
  re-employment of, 39
Apprenticeship
  offer of, 37
  termination of, 36
Aptitude, dismissal for lack of, 75-6
Arbitrator
  acceptance of decisions of, 165
  request for, 164
Arrest
  apology following, 302

entitlelement to, 293-4, 298, 306
  procedure on, 299-301
ASLEF, 165

Borrowing
  company rules on, 306-8
  motor vehicle, of, 307-8
Breach of confidence, 95
Bribery, 309-11
British Rail, 165
Buyer, liability of, 261-4
Business, small, dismissal from, 89

Capability
  definition of, 74
  dismissal for lack of, 73-5
Central Arbitration Committee, 160, 168, 179, 341
Certification Officer, 172, 175-6
Chairman, friendship with, 114-15
Child
  -birth
    intention to return after, 141-8
    reinstatement of mother after, 131, 139, 141-8
  danger to, 252-5
  protection of, 241-2
  visitor, 252-5
Christmas, gist, 309-11
Closed shop, 172
  denial of right to remain outside, 173
  religious objection to, 174
Clothing, protective, 275-6
  provision of, 275
Code of Industrial Practice, 223
Codes of Conduct, 376-7
Code of Industrial Relations Practice, 51, 63, 66-7, 160, 337
Collective bargaining, 160
  information disclosure for, 178-82
  recognition of trade union for, 167-9
Commission, basis for, 309-10
Commission for Racial Equality, 150-51